Royal
Horticultural
Society

THE ROYAL HORTICULTURAL SOCIETY

Allotment

THE EXPERT GUIDE FOR EVERY
FRUIT AND VEG GROWER

Handbook

Royal
Horticultural
Society

THE ROYAL HORTICULTURAL SOCIETY

Allotment

THE EXPERT GUIDE FOR EVERY
FRUIT AND VEG GROWER
Handbook

MITCHELL BEAZLEY

RHS Allotment Handbook

First published in Great Britain in 2010 by Mitchell Beazley,
an imprint of Octopus Publishing Group Ltd,
in association with The Royal Horticultural Society.
Endeavour House, 189 Shaftesbury Avenue, London, WC2H 8JY.
www.octopusbooks.co.uk

An Hachette UK Company
www.hachette.co.uk

Reprinted 2010.

ISBN: 978 1 84533 539 7

A CIP record for this book is available from the British Library.

Set in Interstate and Granjon Vietnamese.
Printed and bound in China.

Authors (in alpha order) Simon Akeroyd, Guy Barter,
  Sara Draycott, Geoff Hodge
RHS Publisher Susannah Charlton
RHS Commissioning Editor Rae Spencer-Jones
Commissioning Editor Helen Griffin
Senior Editor Leanne Bryan
Copy-editor Candida Frith-Macdonald
Proofreader Susan McLeish
Indexer Helen Snaith
Art Director Pene Parker
Senior Art Editor Juliette Norsworthy
Designer Victoria Easton
Design Co-ordinator Gary Almond
Picture Research Manager Giulia Hetherington
Picture Library Manager Jennifer Veall
Production Controller Susan Meldrum

Note The Royal Horticultural Society's
Award of Garden Merit (AGM) helps
gardeners to make informed choices
about plants. This award indicates that
the plant is recommended by the RHS.
Awards are usually given after a period
of trial at an RHS garden, often Wisley.
Plants are judged by one of the RHS
plant committees.

Of the 'tried and tested RHS varieties'
featured in this book, those that have
been awarded the Award of Garden Merit
are followed by the letters 'AGM'.

A full list of AGM plants may be found
on the RHS website at:
www.rhs.org.uk/plants/award_plants.asp.

Contents

Foreword 6

GO FOR AN ALLOTMENT 8
The healthy option 10
The best of the good life 12
The traditional escape 16
Family allotments 18

WHERE TO START 20
First impressions 22
The next step 24
Basic groundwork 26
Choosing your crops 30
Identifying your style 34

PLANNING YOUR ALLOTMENT 40
Things to consider 42
Sheds and furniture 48
Managing expectations 50

ROOT CROPS 54
Basic techniques 56
Potatoes 58
Carrots 60
Beetroots 62
Parsnips 64
Swedes 65
Turnips 66
Jerusalem artichokes 67
Radishes 68

VEGETABLE FRUITS 70
Basic techniques 72
Tomatoes 74
Cucumbers 76
Melons 77
Courgettes, marrows, and summer squashes 78
Pumpkins and winter squashes 80
Aubergines 82
Sweetcorn 83
Peppers 84
Chilli peppers 85

THE ONION FAMILY 86
Basic techniques 88
Onions 90
Garlic 92
Shallots 93
Leeks 94

STEM AND PERENNIAL VEG 96
Asparagus 98
Celery 99
Celeriac 100
Chard and leaf beets 101

PEAS AND BEANS 102
Basic techniques 104
Peas 106
Broad beans 108
Runner beans 110
French beans 112

BRASSICAS 114
Basic techniques 116
Cabbages 118
Cauliflowers 120
Broccoli 121
Brussels sprouts 122
Kale 123

SALADS AND LEAVES 124
Basic techniques 126
Lettuce 128
Spinach 130
Chicory 131
Edible flowers 132
Salad leaves and Oriental vegetables 134
Rocket 139

HERBS 140
Basil 142
Bay 143
Borage 144
Chives 145
Coriander 146
Dill 147
Fennel 148
Marjoram 149
Mint 150
Parsley 151
Rosemary 152

Sage 153
Tarragon 154
Thyme 155

TREE FRUIT 156
Basic techniques 158
Pollination 162
Apples 164
Pears 168
Plums 170
Cherries 171
Figs 172
Peaches 173

SOFT FRUIT 174
Basic techniques 176
Blackcurrants 178
Redcurrants 179
Gooseberries 180
Blueberries 181
Raspberries 182
Blackberries 183
Strawberries 184

VINE FRUIT AND STEMS 186
Grapes 188
Kiwi fruit 190
Rhubarb 191

ALLOTMENT FLOWERS 192
Basic techniques 194
Spring flowers 196
Summer flowers 198
Autumn and winter flowers 202

KEEPING LIVESTOCK 204
Beekeeping 206
Chickens, hens, and bantams 208

REFERENCE 210
Crop planner 210
Weeds 214
Pests 216
Diseases 218
Useful contacts 220
Index 222
Acknowledgements 224

Foreword

The last time that keeping an allotment was as popular as it is now was in the mid 1970s when the public's imagination was captured by the cult television programme 'The Good Life'. Interest waned in the late 1980s and the early 1990s, but with the current challenges presented by a straitened economy, pressures on the environment, and a desire by the public to embrace the momentum behind growing their own fruit and vegetables, allotmenteering is on the up. Surveys have shown that as many as 100,000 people countrywide are on waiting lists for plots that they could take up to 10 years to obtain.

With this rise in enthusiasm for growing our own fruit and vegetables comes a new generation of allotment-holders who are not only seeking the knowledge and skills to grow a wider range of crops than the traditional, but also branching out into keeping livestock on their plots and managing their allotments with both the environment and their families in mind. This is reflected in the growing number of questions and comments about allotments received by the RHS at our shows, in our gardens, and through the RHS Advisory service.

This new book aims to arm allotment-holders, new and experienced, with the knowledge to ask the right questions. It is arranged in three main sections. The first covers getting started with your allotment, from all-important allotment etiquette to allotmenteering with children, and choosing what to grow from the enormous range of fruit and vegetable crops available. The main body of the book will guide you through cultivating fruit and vegetables successfully, as well as growing cut flowers and the basics of managing livestock on your plot. Finally, a reference section ties up all the other strands of allotment keeping, with easily accessible pages on planning, yields, and problems – particularly pests, diseases, and weeds – as well as a host of useful organisations. There is something for all levels of allotment-holders, from simply getting seeds and plants to grow, using the principles of crop rotation, and how to store produce, to tips for more ambitious growers on how to win prizes at local shows.

Garden and science staff at the RHS have combined their experience and knowledge to present a book that endeavours to demystify the art and science of managing an allotment, while providing readers with the wherewithal to avoid the pitfalls that await the uninformed when taking on an allotment.

The authors who contributed to this book are not only trained professionals, but also keen allotment-holders in their spare time. They are confident that the wisdom they have captured in this book will enthuse readers into enjoying their allotments as much as they do and will fuel the pleasure and satisfaction that comes with growing your own.

Giles Coode-Adams
President
Royal Horticultural Society

Go for an allotment

The healthy option

Anyone can, for the price of a modest fee and sticking to a few simple and not very onerous rules, gain access to a little land on which to garden. How they go about it can vary with their skills, resources, and lifestyle choices, but that doesn't matter. On an allotment there are no bosses to please, no deadlines, and no pressure - you pretty much please yourself. It's a simple pastime with straightforward rewards and joys.

Some people like company and gossip (watch out for these if you want to get anything done), others are quite happy on their own, and luckily there are usually a few who want to organise and run things. They will be very useful to you, so befriend them and help them out from time to time - they'll look out for you in return. Finally, beware friends bearing gifts. These tend to be plants that will run amok, crops of which you too have a glut, or plants bearing pests or diseases that they may have overlooked, but you would be unwise to. But be careful, as before long people will be tactfully declining your gifts too.

Food provenance

Provenance is where food is grown and how it has been produced. The reasons for concern are many and complex - the welfare of workers and consumers; the environmental cost of production, transport, and packaging; or freshness and nutrient levels, for example. These are not always easy issues, but one that is often mentioned by allotment-holders is food safety. People are confused, and not without reason, by the conflicting, confusing, often-changing advice and information on what food and food production method is 'best', or at least has most benefits for the consumer or does least damage to the environment. High-profile cases of food problems such as BSE in meat have undermined confidence in experts and authorities, and packaged and processed foods have become distrusted.

But there is no doubting what your own produce contains or how it has been handled. The simplicity and lack of ambiguity in growing your own herbs, fruit, and vegetables is very attractive. If you grow things yourself you know where they come from and how they were grown. That is not to say that supermarket produce is substandard, let alone potentially harmful, just that there is nothing quite like knowing that, for example, the sweetcorn on your barbecue was growing in plot two hours previously and there is no possibility that it was produced with any method that you would be uneasy about.

Other aspects of growing your own food might be called craft, story, and heritage. What people are and where they belong is tied up with their food. There is a strong feeling that modern crop varieties are international, lack distinctive flavour, and represent turning your back on the past. Heritage varieties may not always give the best yields, but they have become very popular, and having a story attached to your crops and food is very satisfying.

Even allotment-holders unconcerned about provenance might still welcome the other benefits of allotments.

Good for mind and body

Allotments are not all about exercise, although they do provide physical activity; some cultivation regimes demand quite a lot of exertion. Potato growing will give you more aerobic exercise than the more sedentary fruit growing, but gardeners should only do as much of either as they are comfortable with. Plan your cropping to take into account the labour needed so you don't over-stretch yourself. When jobs are rushed the enjoyment leaks away, and this is when accidents can happen.

During a visit to the allotment every muscle is used, and you can cover quite a lot of ground by just walking about. Go easy on heavy tasks you're not used to, and alternate heavy and light tasks.

But mere movement is only part of the benefits of allotments to health. An absorbing activity in the open air takes you out of yourself. You literally forget your worries. Gardening is a deeply absorbing hobby to those bitten by the bug, and absorbing and rewarding pastimes are held to promote mental well-being. Just being different from most people's daily work is part of gardening's therapeutic effect.

Disability and allotment growing

Gardening is a wonderful hobby enjoyed by people of every age, nationality, and ability. Lack of mobility, weak grip, heart disease, or sight loss do not preclude the enjoyment of having an allotment, and it can be incredibly beneficial for general and emotional well-being. An increasing number of sites have raised beds at wheelchair height, narrow enough to allow a seated person to reach the middle, and helpful facilities such as accessible toilets, ramps, and textured paths. Some even offer reduced rents for people who are registered as disabled.

There are ever-more products on the market to make gardening with a disability easier, with special tools and equipment that are designed specifically for those who garden from a chair, or which are lighter and easier to grip. Simple things like seed tapes, with seed evenly spaced along a biodegradable tape to be rolled out in a drill, make sowing much less fiddly.

Thrive, the charity that uses gardening to help improve people's lives, has a wealth of information, including a 'buddy' system to help gardeners with similar disabilities to make contact and help and inspire each other. See www.carryongardening.org.uk for details.

Opposite *Allotments are not only about fresh wholesome produce; outdoor living and the joy of growing things come into it too.*

The best of the good life

Land can be extraordinarily productive; the 250 sq m (300 sq y) or so of an allotment has the potential of generating an enormous amount of produce, depending on the intensity with which it is cultivated. Although it is true that the more labour and cash poured into an allotment the greater the output, even a modest outlay can be highly rewarding. Your aim on your allotment is to get the best return for your investment of not just money, but time and toil.

Choosing the best varieties

Choosing varieties, officially called cultivars, is one of the most important and exciting parts of growing crops. Important because no matter how good a gardener you are, your crops can never be better than their genetic potential, and exciting because there is so much choice, with seed suppliers struggling to outdo each other in offering the best and the newest.

As ever in gardening, allotment holders are bombarded with information, and not unreasonably can get confused. Naturally you want a productive cultivar that rewards you with plenty of produce that you work to grow. On the other hand, plenty of something not to your taste soon palls. Then again, crops that you like and which yield heavily are not all they seem if they have to be heavily fertilised, watered, or sprayed with pesticides. Fortunately allotment holders have a special advantage – they are surrounded by experts with unrivalled local knowledge. Some are more expert than others, but a glance at their plots will help you judge the opinions on offer.

Don't deprive yourself of the pleasure of scanning web sites and catalogues, but temper your enthusiasm by growing at least some local recommendations. With luck you may get the opportunity

to taste before you buy seeds and plants. You may even be offered seeds and plants, but remember that plants are a common source of unwanted pests and diseases. One of the great pleasures of allotment gardening is that you can give, receive, and swap material. Giving is better than receiving here; an open hand will reap rewards in time on an allotment.

There are few comparative trials, but magazines and gardening organisations do test fruit and vegetable cultivars. The RHS has its own trials programme and awards its AGM (Award of Garden Merit) to the best plants in these. However, the sheer costs of running trials means that they are often based on relatively few plants in a year or two of trials, so they

don't make local recommendation and individual trial and error redundant.

The riskiest plants to grow are the 'heirloom' varieties preserved from the varieties of yesterday. Although fun and fascinating, their yields and resistance to problems are lower than those of modern varieties, and new gardeners should be wary of putting too many of their eggs in this basket. Having said that the tastes and textures of these varieties may be more to individual preferences, and it would be a loss to disregard them. You really do reap what you sow, and it is worth spending a high proportion of even the most limited budget on good quality seeds from leading seed companies.

Clear weedy plots without strain by taking small 'bites' with a long-handled spade.

Allotment-grown French beans have a freshness and flavour unlike any supermarket beans.

Choosing the best crops

The traditional allotment grew all the vegetables needed by a family of four with the exception of potatoes; this is a rather humdrum objective to many modern allotment holders with access to better materials and plants. Those were the days when the more humble but enormously productive vegetables were highly thought of; beetroot, leeks, cabbages, carrots, parsnips, runner beans, and swedes for example.

Nowadays different tastes prevail and calabrese, courgettes, French beans, tomatoes, salad leaves, squash, and sweetcorn hold a higher place in our priorities. Some, including calabrese, courgettes, French beans, and salad leaves, are very high yielding, but others, such as squash and sweetcorn, are rather unproductive for the space they demand. New varieties are often much heavier yielding than old ones: second early potatoes such as 'Cosmos' are not only more disease resistant and higher yielding than old-fashioned maincrops, but they leave the ground clear for another crop by midsummer. On balance, choosing the best of old and new favourites makes it possible to generate at least as much produce on modern allotments as on old.

Fruit has traditionally been second to vegetables on allotments, but now that more vegetables are produced from a smaller area there is potential to greatly increase the area devoted to fruit. Raspberries and hybrid berries such as cultivated blackberries are especially rewarding. Gooseberries and currants are also very productive and at least a few bushes are well worth growing. Strawberries are less prolific, but well-chosen modern varieties have transformed the potential of this crop.

Checking other people's plots reveals a wide range of potential yields. Some plots are very productive, but others do not repay the effort put in. Many are run at a loss: more is put in than is gathered. Taking the best practice from other plots is the quickest way to get the best out of an allotment. Otherwise, you may end up with more ground than you can manage and without the return to justify it. It is a good idea to relinquish land that is a drain on energy and resources, but even better to avoid the problem.

Why you need a shed

A shed can be the heart and hub of an allotment plot. Inside, it's a personal space, somewhere to shelter from wind, rain, or sun, and a place for inspiration to strike and grand ideas to develop. You sit in a shed to reflect on your plans for the season, or on successes or failures so far. It's a place to store your forks, hoes, rakes and spades, a rack to hold trowels, lines, and secateurs. It might be the perfect place to chit seed potatoes at the start of the year, and store the harvest in potato sacks later. From a peg on the wall, you can string up your onions, and neatly filed in an old tin box is your season's seed collection. You need a shed to store all sorts of vital equipment, few more vital than your old garden chairs and thermos of coffee for when it's time for a break.

Your shed is a useful water collecting surface, if you configure some guttering to divert rainwater into butts. It can even blend in to the surroundings by being topped with a well-constructed green roof planted with sedums and attracting bees.

Not all allotment sites allow sheds, or there may be restrictions on the size or number of constructions (allowing a shed or a greenhouse, but not both) so check your tenancy agreement.

Maximizing the benefits

Allotments produce a lot of food, and to get through this abundance, diets at certain times of year are very rich in vegetables; yet studies indicate that the annual output is worth a few hundred pounds – worthwhile, but hardly life changing. By concentrating on high-yielding crops that are expensive in the shops, and avoiding low cost carrots, onions, and maincrop potatoes, the value of output can be boosted. Organic produce is especially costly to buy, and the financial reward of growing it is greater than of conventional produce.

Asparagus and soft fruits are very expensive, but easy to grow and high yielding, so these modest luxuries that you might think twice over in the shops become affordable when home grown.

Other crops are expensive to grow (tomatoes may need costly spraying against blight, for example), and thrifty gardeners limit their numbers. Failed crops greatly reduce the benefit of an allotment. It is also questionable how much is saved when produce is frozen: running a deep freeze has a monetary as well as environmental cost.

It is easy to get carried away planning and buying desirable but ultimately impractical things for your plot. Elegant but costly glass cloches, for example, are not durable in an allotment environment, and although it would be nice to have several packets of salad seed, one economy size mixed pack is more cost effective – and seeds are much cheaper than transplants. Allotment trading huts are a good source of low-cost materials and also a hot-bed of news, knowledge, and gossip.

Sudden, unplanned gluts are common even for the best gardeners. Giving away surpluses and later accepting others' over-supply in times of shortage is all part of getting the most from a plot.

Get to know your allotment neighbours; you'll be amazed how much you can learn from them.

Community spirit and action

The social centre of allotments is the trading hut, which often opens for a short period, typically Sunday morning. This is not only where gardening materials are sold, but also where people catch up on what is going on. Allotment officials are usually on hand to raise any questions and discuss any problems, and it is an opportunity to offer to help with the many duties and chores associated with running an allotment site, from helping clean out dip tanks to a little in the way of making plumbing repairs or mending fences. Notices can be left, especially to buy and sell, or more often to exchange, and particularly for those staples of the allotment economy, wooden pallets and corrugated iron. If you want to know where to buy manure or get pea or bean sticks, or indeed for any need you might have, you only have to put the word about and help soon flows in.

Many allotment sites have barbecues in summer or advertise their site by taking stands in fêtes and fairs – offers to participate in these are always gratefully received by officials.

Volunteer working parties to mend fences, cut hedges, repair paths, replace pipes, and dig ditches are often called for, and joining these is a good way to do your bit for the site and meet fellow allotment-holders.

Sharing stories, plants, and even plots

The ways that people use their plots – the way the plot is laid out, what sheds and other facilities are built, and what plants are grown – are amazingly diverse. Books often set out the same ways of growing crops, so it all seems uniform to the beginner, but on the ground things are less clear cut. People have brainwaves, happy accidents occur, and experienced gardeners have an innate feeling for soil and plants that helps them to fine-tune their methods. Gardeners, although usually modest, are seldom secretive about their achievements. Ideas are shared and cross-fertilise other people's thoughts, and the result is one of the endless rewards of allotment gardening.

People of many cultures and areas of the world hold allotments in Britain, and they bring their traditional methods

and crops (climate permitting) to their plot. They are usually only too pleased to find their birthright is of interest to others, and are very willing to share knowledge, seeds, cuttings, and culinary advice. Different approaches to common problems are a fascinating part of allotment holding. For example, the spade may be traditional in Britain, but in hotter countries the mattock is preferred, being less hard work.

Treat crops for storing, like these marrows, gently. Any damage lets in rots.

More and more people are now sharing allotments; families and friends get together to share the cost and effort, and this is a great way to undertake the often daunting task of clearing and stocking a new plot. Also, a full plot can generate a huge amount of produce, and a half or a third of a plot is enough for many people. Plot ownership can be very fluid, but it is good manners to keep officials informed on who holds a key and is responsible for upkeep and rent.

Allotment holders often share and exchange seeds and plants, a practice

that saves money and allows everyone to grow a more interesting range of crops at low cost. In fact, it is a good policy to raise some surplus plants for exactly this purpose, but be choosy about who you accept plants with soil on their roots from. The same applies in reverse, of course: your name will be tarnished for years if you distribute pests and diseases across the site together with your spare plants.

To avoid inadvertently eating next year's crops, mark pods and plants selected for seed.

Getting the best value from your plot

Grow crops that are expensive in shops - leeks or asparagus for example.

Use crops fresh, when the home-grown benefits are greatest.

Stored or frozen crops seldom save much money over shop-bought when you count the cost of freezing.

Unless you have luxurious amounts of time and space, rely on shops for low-cost winter carrots and potatoes.

Swap and share plants and seeds to get a good range of crops without buying lots of seeds.

Expensive and elaborate equipment is seldom cost-effective.

The traditional escape

How long the current enthusiasm for allotments will last is anyone's guess, but old allotment-holders will be only too pleased to tell you they've seen it all before ... and it's true.

A potted allotment history

Allotments as we know them began in the 19th century, when the rural poor were provided with small areas of land to raise food. Formerly they had access to common land, but with the enclosures of commons in the early 19th century this was lost. Early allotments were four to eight times larger than they are now and were used to grow wheat and keep livestock. The dire poverty that led to the establishment of allotments is no longer an issue and allotments are now more of a lifestyle and leisure choice.

This came about gradually. With the rise of industrial towns more allotments were provided, sometimes to allow the poorest to grow food, sometimes to give the better-off an opportunity to garden in their leisure time. This went on in a haphazard but large-scale way until these various systems were consolidated

Wigwams of beans provide height, colour, and allow heavy crops in a small space.

by the Smallholdings and Allotments Act of 1908. This law obliged local authorities to provide allotments for the poor in both town and countryside. This led to an increase in urban allotments that received a major boost in the First World War, when German submarine blockades seriously reduced food supplies. From something like 500,000 allotments in 1913, there were over 1.3 million by 1918. There was a campaign to grow more food in gardens, and local authorities were given powers to take over vacant land for allotments. Allotments were now recognised by officialdom.

However, it was necessary to protect the rights of plot-holders with more legislation in the 1920s. Despite this, allotment numbers dwindled through the 1930s, although never back to the levels of pre-1914. A familiar story begins in the 1930s: long periods of neglect when allotments fall prey to developers and languish for lack of demand.

In the Second World War, allotments had another moment of glory. Although some accounts suggest their apparent success was more propaganda than fact, over 1.5 million plots were in use and large numbers of people were introduced to allotment gardening.

By the 1950s and 1960s interest waned again, and allotments were seen as wasted land used for outdated purposes by obstinate people who stood in the way of progress. But a great renaissance occurred in the 1970s when the 'good life' and self-sufficiency became highly fashionable. Boom was inevitably followed by decline as the nation embraced iceberg lettuce and bagged salads – but only for allotments to rise again to their current popularity.

Alternative approaches

Allotments of the utilitarian British sort are found elsewhere in northern Europe (Holland and France, for example) and arose in a similar way and for much the same reasons. In Germany and Austria another sort of allotment or leisure garden has often been held up as the model to arrest the periodic declines in popularity of British allotments. Here they are pleasure gardens, often with little pavilions, not so much to grow food but to allow citizens, especially children, access to space, exercise, and fresh air. People will actually live on their plot for long periods in summer.

Further east, in Russia for example, residents of high-rise cities with no gardens have plots in the countryside, complete with summer houses where they live for weekends or longer in the summer, growing and preserving food for the long continental winters.

So far, the British allotment-holder has sturdily resisted the temptations of pleasure gardens (probably aided by planning laws and building regulations), but maybe things are changing, as people now grow flowers on allotments and bring barbecues in the summer.

Opposite, clockwise from top Mixing fruit, flowers, and vegetables not only looks good but can help fox pests too; with the use of both push and push-pull hoes, weeds will be well controlled here; 'pre-owned' tools are usually good enough, but good quality new secateurs are a sound investment.

The tools you will need to make life easier

Theoretically an allotment can be worked with only a spade, but it would be difficult without a fork, rake, hoe, trowel, garden line, and bucket too. A couple of watering cans, a good sprayer and a wheelbarrow are almost as essential. Then there are less vital but handy tools: an armoury of push, draw, and short-handled onion hoes take the drudgery out of weed control, a mattock is a useful alternative to the spade, and a three pronged cultivator to the fork. A crow bar and sledgehammer save time and effort. Loppers, secateurs, and a pruning saw are essential for fruit growers. And the importance of always having string, a plastic bag, and a knife in your pocket cannot be overstated.

Family allotments

Allotments are no longer the preserve of the over 60s. These days they buzz with the sound of children's laughter. Having a family work together on a plot gives a sense of community, and learning where food comes from, seeing something come to fruition and be served for tea, brings to youngsters its own sense of wonderment at the magic of growing.

A family allotment should be managed just as any other, but with special thought in a few areas. Firstly, consider what time you'll have to work on the plot once the freedom to come and go at leisure has been replaced by the needs of the children. Young children have a short attention span, so visits to the plot are best kept to frequent short-and-sweet trips to maintain their interest. Or take the opposite approach: make longer visits and have lunch down there, maybe with a camping stove so that you can cook produce immediately. There's nothing to beat freshly barbecued sweetcorn for keeping up interest. Ensure you all know what you want to do each visit, so that you're raring to go on arrival.

Exercise caution and be safe. Make sure that potentially dangerous chemicals are out of reach, be vigilant about physical dangers (such as tools left on paths as a tripping hazard, or within easy reach in the shed), ensure all stakes and canes are topped off to save eyes, be aware of water containers that could present a drowning danger, and take care if there are vehicles moving around on site. Likewise some crops might need a little careful explanation to the uninitiated: gooseberries can be very thorny and sharp, rhubarb leaves can't be eaten even though they look similar to chard, and just because we eat the mangetout peas, it doesn't mean you can eat the pods of sweet peas.

What to grow with a family

Choose crops that tick at least one of these boxes: quick results (like radishes or rocket); minimal work (like rhubarb); popular with the children (strawberries); exciting to harvest (like potatoes); easy to harvest (try peas); likely to succeed (courgettes) as failure is discouraging; and something to inspire young minds. Pumpkins and sunflowers are firm favourites on the last count and give an incentive to get down to the plot regularly to see how big they've become.

Harvesting strawberries is instantly gratifying – as long as you have grown enough!

Let the children help choose what to grow, even if this means sometimes selecting cultivars for their name rather than other qualities. Give a patch of ground over to each child, so they get to choose what to do with it. They may choose flowers, fruits, vegetables, or herbs, or a lucky dip of spare seeds. Show them how to sow in rows, patterns, or letters to spell their name. Remember, it's their space, but make sure that they feel connected to and are involved with the whole plot.

Think about the quantities of harvests and size of appetites you're dealing with. Enthusiasm for a crop is great, but too much of a good thing can become a turn-off. Some things crop over a period of time, but others ripen all at once. If your family loves blackberries, then during the summer holidays you might enlist the help of the children to pick them (try a thornless cultivar). Long evenings might mean the preparation for eating and storing the produce becomes a shared job too.

Opportunities to tend and care for plants initiate children into the joy of gardening.

Keeping children occupied

Apart from sowing and harvesting there are other ways to engage your children with useful tasks around the plot. For example, most youngsters love getting their hands dirty and will want to play with the soil. If you ask them to clear a defined (and small) patch of ground of all weeds with a trowel, it'll give them a sense of achievement and the chance to get dirty. Then load up a small plastic wheelbarrow with weeds and ask them to empty it. Keep them entertained by giving them a spray pump full of water, though it may not be just the plants that get wet! Let them make a bird scarer out of old CDs strung up, or a parade of cans on sticks where smaller plants are put in. As well as keeping the pigeons off, it gives the little ones something to do, and can be used as target practice with small clods of earth or hard peas.

Sometimes, children will relish the challenges that we might retreat from. Task a youngster with the responsibility for finding, removing, and disposing of all the cabbage white caterpillars from the brassicas – it's a necessary job and keeps them busy. Or, armed with gloves and a bucket, get them collecting slugs and snails. Some allotment sites are so geared up for families that they have a dedicated play area, so there is a safe environment to have some fun whilst the grown-ups get on with serious work.

For families, the allotment is a place to have fun and exercise in the fresh air, learn about plants and insects, possibly spot the odd mammal or friendly birds, and meet friends to play with. Just keep to a few basic rules so that it is clear where and where not to tread, what and what not to pick, and so on, and family life on the allotment really can be a pleasure for everyone.

Top *The allotment is a place for children to learn about life, including where eggs come from.*
Right *Allotments give children the opportunity to get close to soil, plants, and insects.*

Where to start

First impressions

Just by looking around many allotment plots you can see that you don't need to be a particularly skilled or conscientious gardener to hold an allotment. Although this is sometimes a source of irritation to other plot-holders, it should be a source of comfort to any prospective allotment-holders - it surely can't be very difficult to do better than that!

With this in mind, you need not be intimidated or overawed. While you find your particular style, just copy the best practice that you see around you. But don't be too judgemental - the owners of those unkempt plots often have their own problems. Most starters want their plot to stand out, and be productive and a source of pride. So learn from the sorry state of some people's plots; what makes a plot look good and what makes it look bad? Where are you going to be most challenged? What can you do about it? How much time and effort can you truly put in? By getting these things right from the outset, you can achieve the plot of your dreams. (One tip: neat paths and edges are immediately effective. Many allotment sites own strimmers and mowers, so use them and look good.)

Applying for a plot

If you cannot see an allotment site in your area, local libraries and council offices can put you in touch with allotment authorities. Many council websites hold information too, but you may need to dig for it. Approach the chair, secretary, or other officials and, if necessary, get on a waiting list.

There are also private allotment sites that are not owned by local authorities, so it is well worth sniffing about - ask at garden centres and gardening clubs, for example - to get wind of what may be small and elusive opportunities. Taking another tack, Google Earth or mapping websites that use aerial photography can be a useful aid to reconnaissance. Some ingenious people approach

landowners to ask if there is a spare patch they can use, and there are also 'landshare' schemes that act as match-makers between prospective gardeners and people with surplus land for letting, often for a share of the produce.

Remember that many people apply for plots at several sites, even across different council areas, so a long waiting list is not always what it seems. Often it's deceptive, because people on it have changed their minds, found plots on other sites, or left the district.

If a wait is necessary, gently remind site officials from time to time that you're keen. Rents are due in late winter on many sites, so it's worth jogging the memories of site officials in the new

year. This is when plot-holders whose circumstances have changed so that they do not want to keep up their allotment habit tend to relinquish their plots, gathering the last of their winter produce. People who have not kept their plots to the required standard often get their notice to quit in early autumn, so again be sure to have your details on file at this time too. Those running allotments are much more inclined to be firm with miscreants if there is a healthy waiting list of keen people.

Be frank with the allotment officials; bragging and bravado tend to indicate people who will fail as gardeners, and such people tend to be allocated plots where poor gardening will not be too

Ruthlessly discard and destroy inherited spent crops along with their pests and diseases.

Pace out your new allotment plot to get an idea of the dimensions.

Use a garden line to cut neat edges and avoid damaging paths.

detrimental to the allotment site as a whole. These sites are far from being the best available. Tell them your skills, wishes and aims honestly, and they will do their best to find you a site that will allow you to achieve these.

What size of plot?

A full plot is about 250 square metres (300 square yards). A skilled gardener can easily use this to full advantage, but depending on what you choose to grow this usually means at least eight hours work per week – every week, for much of the year. In fact, it is not difficult to lavish 16 hours if you are not a fast worker and have the time to spare.

This is a lot of time, so now most new allotment-holders start on a half plot – in fact even just a third of a plot can be enough. Once people have proved themselves, developed the necessary skills, and feel the extra land would be useful and manageable, allotment officials are usually happy to find them a full plot – good, conscientious plot-holders are not that common. It works the other way too. People who start families, develop health problems, or simply age often downsize to half plots.

In past periods when allotments were not in great demand, it was not unusual for people to take on two or more plots. Then, this was perfectly justified to keep the land in cultivation, to deter builders, and keep the rents coming in to sustain the site. In times when allotment plots are in short supply, it is hard to justify having more than one. Although people who have invested years of work in building up fertility have a case for enjoying their investment, the trend is to use smaller plots more intensively, using clever cropping plans and higher levels of irrigation and manuring, and extending the season with fleece and cloches. The last question is how much produce do you need? This depends on how many of you there are and what you grow. The output from a well-run full plot can actually be hard for a small household to consume. If winter veg such as leeks, swedes, and cabbages are not part of your preferred diet, or if you wish to leave growing these to farmers who are paid to wade through mud and prise roots out of frozen soil, then a full plot might be overkill.

Check-list of things to think about before you commit

How much spare time will you have?

Will you have to be away for long periods in the growing season?

Can you cope with any heavy labour?

Will you be able to grow the things that you really like?

How much produce do you need?

Will your family help? (Be absolutely honest with yourself on this one.)

Are you comfortable with things like worms, spiders, and manure? (Don't laugh – quite a lot of people aren't.)

The next step

So, you know you want a plot, you know what size of plot you want, you're sure of the effort you can put in, and you're on a waiting list – or maybe more than one. The next step is what happens when a plot finally becomes available.

Meeting new neighbours

It's old but true: good fences really do make good neighbours, so agree the boundaries. If necessary, insist that they are clearly marked on your behalf to avoid disputes later. Some facilities like sheds, dip tanks, and composting areas might be shared: find out the rules on these and be ready to chip in with path mowing and other shared chores.

Remember that long-standing plot-holders might have invested years of work in their plots and won't thank you if you move in and erect a large shed that shades their best land. Find out and respect the feelings of other plot-holders if only for self-interest, as they might well be the source of plants and advice and may even look after your plot while you are on holiday. A little expression of appreciation for their beloved plot right from the start is very effective at winning them over.

Viewing potential sites

The best sites are well known to long-standing plot-holders and tend to get snapped up as soon as they fall free, so new allotment-holders are often offered the second tier of plots, while gardeners who have lapses in standards are often eventually shuffled off to out-of-the-way plots where they can garden in peace. Once you're in, you can prove yourself and upgrade your plot later, if need be.

Nonetheless allotment officials have a conscience. They will see that you get a fair deal for your rent and will answer all your questions truthfully. In fact they love talking about gardening, so try open questions such as 'what's good about this plot?' and you will soon know all that you need – often, rather more.

Evaluating an inherited site

Weeds are, oddly enough, a good sign – the more weeds the less the recent cropping and the lower the level of soil-borne pests and diseases. In fact, a plot with neither weeds nor crops should be regarded with deep suspicion. Old fruit bushes are often so riddled with disease as to be worthless, but if they are dug up, burned, and cultivated back in they leave a rich soil that has had a long rest from vegetable growing and will yield good crops. Try to avoid plots that are shaded by nearby trees, although some shade can be used to erect sheds and compost bins.

Proximity to water tanks and a paved road or parking area is very valuable. Out-of-the-way plots, remote from roads, water, and other plot-holders can at first seem attractive to uncertain newcomers who are anxious to hide their inexperience, but in the end these plots can be unsatisfying and their inconvenience very irksome.

Remember that allotment sites tend to be on ground that no one else wants, so are often subject to flooding: check for ditches and drains and avoid very low-lying plots. Low-lying plots that have higher ground nearby tend to be 'frost pockets', where late frosts limit early crops and autumn arrives early.

Check the soil for broken glass and wire, which are a particular menace for children. Try to avoid being next to ramshackle plots, which are fruitful sources of pests, diseases, and weed seeds from their neglected crops. If delinquency persists, it is worth asking officials to intervene.

Clockwise from top *With every inch cropped and wide access paths, this allotment is very well run; flowers may seem an indulgence but provide aviation fuel for hoverflies that hunt down greenfly; good sites with fertile, well-drained soil will get snapped up when they become vacant; these very wide, well-mulched paths permit all weather access, but waste cropping space.*

Good allotment etiquette

Allotments are a community in their own right, and good etiquette is essential for their smooth and friendly operation. There are some straightforward do's and don'ts to remember.

DO

- Share surplus seeds, seedlings, and harvests, especially if you and your neighbours grow different things.
- Keep your plot neat and tidy, and clear of weeds and rubbish.
- Show consideration when sharing the communal water supply.
- Account for wind drift if applying chemicals of any kind.
- Make sure children have enough to keep them entertained when on site.
- Talk to fellow allotment-holders, and ask their advice.
- Think about the shade that might be cast over a neighbour's plot by a tree, shed, climbing plants, or anything else.
- Label spare seeds or plants and donate to the allotment shop, if you have one.
- Support local growers and suppliers, and your allotment shop.
- Take part in allotment life, be it social occasions or the running of the site. Allotments survive by the dedication of the committees that look after them.
- Enjoy yourself!

DON'T

- Take anything from another plot without the owner's express permission.
- Let your plants or possessions stray over pathways or neighbouring plots.
- Allow weeds to get out of hand and spread seeds to neighbouring plots.
- Let children or pets run wild.
- Have bonfires or barbecues (if allowed) that might cause a nuisance or danger to other people on site or neighbours outside the boundary. (For more detail on bonfires, *see* page 39).

Basic groundwork

Departing tenants seldom leave their plots in good condition, but committees are usually happy to help you clear junk, perhaps hiring a skip on your behalf. Then roll up your sleeves and begin.

Clearing the ground

Ground clearing can look daunting, but even a full plot is only 250 square metres (300 square yards) and if you clear just five of those each week, the job will be done in a year. Covering the land awaiting your attention with a black plastic sheet for a growing season or treating with a glyphosate-based weedkiller will bring the ground into a much more readily workable condition.

Heavy nettle and bramble infestations can be treated with hormone weedkillers, but these remain active in the soil so there is a period of delay before new sowing and planting can begin.

Some allotment-holders and societies are uneasy about weedkillers (although those available to gardeners nowadays are essentially benign), so act with sensitivity if this is the case. After clearing, destroy all vegetation by burning (again, be sensitive and follow the rules) or, better still, by composting.

Next, dig over the soil bit by bit, getting rid of any weed roots as you go, working to the depth of a spade or fork. Deeper digging is not essential.

If there are no perennial weed roots, or if you have killed them with weedkiller, you can hire a rotavator to break the soil up quickly. But beware, a rotavator chops weed roots into fine pieces making any remaining problem even worse, and if used in the wet it can ruin the soil structure for several years.

Check the soil structure

A very simple but necessary test at the outset is to dig a pit with straight sides

Lightly weed-infested soil can be forked over rather than deeply dug, and quickly made productive.

1) *Use the spade to bury annual weeds, organic matter and debris, leaving a level surface.*
2) *Use a cultivator and rake to level and crumble the soil ready to sow and plant.*
3) *Soft, fluffy soil needs firming by treading, but only if the top spade's depth is dry.*

about 60cm (24in) deep. You should see about 25cm (10in) depth of dark topsoil, without hard, compressed zones that plant roots cannot penetrate. To check that the underlying subsoil is not rock hard but will allow water to drain, fill the pit with water, cover to keep out rain, and leave overnight. If the water is gone by morning all is well; if not, drainage may be a problem. If topsoil or good subsoil are lacking, serious soil improvement will be required, but this is unlikely on established allotment sites. Drainage is often best addressed by raised beds, which can be invaluable for clay and other heavy, poorly drained soils, but are not a necessity elsewhere.

Soil testing

Plants need nutrients to grow, especially nitrogen, phosphorus, potassium, and magnesium. Although generous use of organic manure evens everything out in time, a laboratory soil test is well worth

investing in. It will tell you not just whether a soil is acid or alkaline, but how much phosphorus, potassium, and magnesium it contains. This allows you to choose a fertiliser regime to meet any deficiencies, and can save much expense on unnecessary fertiliser – for example, allotment soils are often rich in phosphorus. Soil changes very slowly, so a test is only needed every four or five years. Don't bother with DIY kits for nutrients, as they are often misleading.

Nitrogen is hard to test for and levels fluctuate widely in a season. Normal manuring and fertilising generally add enough, but if growth is not what you expect, remedy any water shortage and give high-nitrogen feed until it improves.

If the soil is acid it will need lime to 'sweeten' it. Fruit likes acid soil, so aim for pH6–6.5 here, but for vegetables alkaline conditions will reduce diseases, especially club root, so aim for pH6.5–7 for these. In fact, pH7–7.5 is wise where cabbage-family plants succumb to club root (common on allotments), but you will then have to choose potatoes that resist common scab disease, which is seen more in alkaline soils. Use a cheap pH test kit each season (meters are less reliable) and lime the soil as required.

What is lime?

Lime, or limes, can be confusing. Garden lime is calcium carbonate and is simply ground up limestone. Sellers sometimes offer ground chalk, which is virtually the same. Hydrated lime and quicklime are more concentrated but less safe to handle (they can burn) and best avoided. Calcified seaweed is an expensive form of lime that includes some minor nutrients.

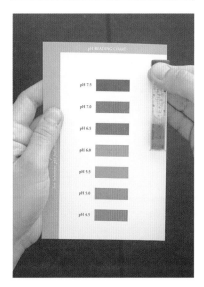

Carpet mulches and more attractive options

A mulch is any blanket of material used on soil to suppress weed growth, protect the surface from the elements (including drying winds and heavy rain), and if the mulch is of organic matter, to increase fertility and texture. For a really attractive mulch, there's nothing to beat a green manure or a thick layer of organic matter, but other options have other benefits.

The allotment holder often tries to re-use rather than buy, and carpet is an old favourite for suppressing weeds. It may not look great, but it does make allotment care easier in theory. There's a catch, though: many sites now discourage or ban the use of carpet on their plots. The main reason is the fear of chemicals leaching into the soil. Even carpets of natural fibres are now often treated with fire retardants, possibly insecticides, and who knows what else.

Luckily there are other options. Thick cardboard is cheap, but black plastic, weed-control fabrics, and permeable mulch matting are the most common. If you have an allotment shop, it probably sells them. Black mulches absorb heat and 'cook' weeds and seeds beneath, and the lack of light weakens anything that survives. Some fabrics can be moved around the plot as crops or weeds are cleared, and permeable types allow good air and moisture circulation.

Perennial weeds

Years of haphazard gardening may have left a residue of weed seeds and roots in the soil of a plot. Dealing with these in an efficient and low-labour way is one of the skills of running an allotment, and one that is not difficult to master.

Perennial weeds – bindweed, couch grass, and ground elder for example – are the worst. It's essential to eliminate these before you plant any permanent crops, such as fruit trees and asparagus, as once they get a grip they can spoil the planting, and the only option is replacing the crop on a new weed-free site. Reduce them to a low level in your preliminary clearance, and after that every time one appears dig it out with a fork or trowel.

Perennial weeds cannot stand digging. In fact, the main point of digging is to control weeds, and autumn digging can get you on top of even the worst perennial weed problem. Spot-treating with glyphosate-based weedkiller is also very effective, but no weedkiller must touch valuable plants, and unfortunately crop plants are far more susceptible to it than weeds. Where possible it is very good practice to cover alleys between

Neglected plots are soon colonised by weeds, storing up trouble for future plot-holders.

fruit crops with porous, opaque weed-control membrane. Although not cheap, it greatly reduces the weeding burden. Old carpets are nowadays frowned on, as synthetic ones pollute the soil and even natural fibres use synthetic glues that can't be assumed to be safe.

In spring, patrol your plot for docks and dandelions; their seeds lie dormant for years, but can be readily winkled out with a fork at this time of year.

Horsetail is almost impossible to remove. It thrives in the ill-drained soils

common on allotments. However, it cannot cope with shade and is vulnerable to hoeing. If growing fruit bushes, cover the alleys with black plastic membrane to force horsetail to grow in the shade of the fruit canes and bushes, where its weakened growth can be hand-weeded. Well-fed vegetable crops, especially beetroot, beans, potatoes, and pumpkins, will smother it, and straight, easily hoed rows keep it down. In raised beds, it can creep in along boards and paths where only hand weeding can get at it.

Annual weeds

Although perennial weeds are most damaging to fruit and other permanent crops, it is annual weeds that trouble vegetable crops. Weed seeds remain viable for years in the soil, and many weeds can set hundreds or even thousands of seeds if allowed to mature. No weed should ever be allowed to set seed on an allotment. Unfortunately in most allotment soils there is already a 'seed bank', and a large number will germinate when the soil is disturbed.

Weed seeds sense their environment, and fluctuating temperatures or light levels signal to the weed that it is near the surface and can germinate. You can use this to your advantage by creating 'stale seedbeds'. Break the soil down to the fine crumbly 'tilth' that's needed to sow seeds at an even shallow depth or set out transplants – but do it a few weeks before it's time to sow or plant. The weeds will emerge, and once you've polished them off with shallow hoeing or contact weedkiller few more will emerge that year,

With no room for weeds to grow there are no recruits to the weed 'seed bank'.

allowing the crop to be relatively weed-free. This is ideal for carrots and onions, whose slender foliage provides no competition for weeds. Onions in particular can be grown through an opaque ground-cover membrane, and this is a method you can also use on other crops when you need to keep weeding to a minimum.

Invasive weeds and reportable weeds

The Weed Act of 1959 aimed to compel farmers to keep down ragwort, spear thistle, creeping or field thistle, broad-leaved dock, and curled dock. These weeds are not of great significance to allotment-holders. More important are Japanese knotweed and giant hogweed, officially called invasive non-native species. Although seldom found on plots, they occur around ditches and on waste land. You are not obliged to report them, but it is an offence to dispose of their remains except in licensed landfill, as they are what is called controlled waste. It is best to destroy on site the small amounts usually found on allotments.

1) *Bindweed can be treated with glyphosate-based weedkillers, which will kill both top and roots.*
2) *Horsetail is hard to eradicate, but is readily weakened by hoeing or thick, smothering crops.*
3) *Groundsel, an annual weed, can set thousands of seeds per plant if it is allowed to flower.*

1

2

3

Choosing your crops

Obviously it makes sense to grow what you like on your plot, but this has to be tempered both by what is possible and by what lifestyle choices you want to make with respect to your allotment.

If your allotment is intended to provide a significant proportion of your food, then you may be swapping those imported Kenyan beans for cabbage in winter, and have to cultivate a taste for Jerusalem artichokes.

On the other hand, you may prefer your allotment to provide an abundance of summer flowers, fruit, and tasty Mediterranean vegetables, and be happy to rely on the shops or a box scheme for the rest of the year. Some foods taste better the fresher they are, and these are mostly herbs, salads, legumes, and fruit; others, such as roots and winter vegetables, do not show such a pronounced difference. Concentrating on the former gives your taste buds more return on your labour.

With more experience the cropping of a plot tends to get more ambitious, as you start to make use of techniques such as successional sowing and inter- and catch-cropping. Truly there is no end to planning what to grow and how.

Growing nearly all your own

Where a degree of self-sufficiency is the aim, you might decide to go with the heaviest yielding crops. Brassicas and root vegetables are very productive, but peas, broad beans, and French beans less so. Leafy salads and greens will yield far more useful material than an equivalent area of plants that need to 'head' before you can cut them, like lettuces or cauliflower. Crops that only have a brief, late-summer season, such as peppers and cucumbers, may be tasty, but can be the least productive of all.

When trying to achieve all-year-round supplies, there is a tricky period from early to mid-spring when few crops are available, and planning overwintered and early-spring-sown crops for this time will

be a major preoccupation. There is a good case for buying imported or greenhouse-grown food at this difficult time. A diet of only spring cabbages, spring onions, turnip greens, spinach, and spinach beet (and in mild regions, cauliflowers) can be monotonous until the early-summer salads, peas, broad beans, and new potatoes arrive.

Grow something special

Some crops that are commercially grown and harvested, like carrots, onions, or potatoes, are very cheap to buy. You may prefer to get these from the supermarket, especially in late winter when home-grown supplies may not be as good as professionally stored material. But if you hanker after black potatoes, purple or white carrots, or torpedo-shaped Italian onions (all delicious, by the way), or the much underrated scorzonera and winter radish, you might have to search far and wide to buy them.

There is also produce that requires hand labour: asparagus, leeks, spring onions, leafy salads, 'Little Gem' lettuce, and soft fruits. These are costly to buy, but very easy to grow yourself.

If your plot is some way from home, storable produce such as squash, pumpkins, root vegetables, and storing cabbages are valuable. Winter vegetables such as leeks and cabbages can be temporarily replanted in the garden or even in a large pot for convenience, a process officially known as 'heeling in'. On the other hand, herbs that are needed as fresh as possible and in small quantities might be best grown at home.

Other users (and uses) need to be considered too: cabbages and parsnips usually fail to excite children, but peas, sunflowers, and fruit may well do. Flower arrangers will want to bring home blooms and foliage, winemakers will relish new ingredients for their brews, and barbecue enthusiasts will want plenty of sweetcorn – and some growers

just won't be happy unless they can grow some chrysanthemums or dahlias for the local flower show.

Know your limits

After thinking about what you want to grow, think realistically about what you can grow. Less physically able gardeners may not relish weeding carrots and onions or the heavy lifting associated with potatoes, but find fruit and climbing beans more to their liking.

Soil also plays a part. Sandy soils are brilliant for early crops, and in mild areas even for over-wintered crops, but they are so prone to drought stress that main and late crops are hard work to keep watered and often of second-rate quality. Clay soils, in contrast, grow abundant yields of late and main crops of excellent quality but are so slow to warm up in spring that early crops are out of the question.

It makes sense to play to your soil's strengths where you can, rather than fight nature. For example, celery will do well on rich, moist soils, but celeriac is more tolerant of drier ones. Clay soils are relished by slugs, so quick-maturing crops of second-early potatoes are ideal for getting out of the ground and safely in store before they can be tunnelled by slugs. Root crops are more vulnerable than taller plants such as cauliflowers and Brussels sprouts. Crops that can be planted as large pot-grown transplants, including brassicas and broad beans, stand a better chance of getting away from slugs than the small, vulnerable seedlings of salads and carrots.

Allotments that have long been under cultivation accumulate a legacy of soil-borne pests and diseases; three of the more serious examples are clubroot of cabbage family crops, white

Neatly defined plots and beds make it easier to plan and manage growing a wide range of crops to achieve heavy yields and a succession of harvests.

rot of the onion tribe, and potato cyst nematodes which also attack tomatoes.

In some cases resistant varieties are available, but growing crop groups that are not susceptible to these problems can side-step a lot of disappointment. Sweet potatoes, sweetcorn, squashes, and French beans are crops that appeal very much to modern tastes and have no significant soil-borne tribulations.

Soil-dwelling enemies can also be starved out by planting long-term crops such as asparagus and soft fruit. You do have to be in for the long haul, but after five to ten years under these, the spore and cyst populations in the soil show a marked decline.

Growing fruit and flowers

Fruit has historically been neglected on the allotment - there is a limit to how much jam you can eat and how much bottling and freezing you want to do. But modern cultivars such as autumn-fruiting raspberries and perpetual strawberries greatly extend the season, and new techniques of growing small apple and pear trees can allow these crops to be grown in the limited space of allotments (local site rules permitting). Soft fruit is a good way of cropping shady areas, as they can yield useful amounts in shade that would make vegetable yields disappointing.

Very shady areas are best left to sheds and compost bins, but where the shade is caused by trees that lose their leaves in winter, daffodils can be planted for cut flowers. Cut flowers might be frowned on by traditionalists, but even one wigwam of sweet peas or a small patch of cosmos, sunflowers, and zinnias can produce a large number of cut stems.

Opposite, clockwise from top left Peppers need a hot summer, but a fleece covering can greatly increase chances of success; runner beans crop continuously for at least six weeks and are an especially valuable allotment crop; leeks yield heavily and can be planted after early potatoes, making good use of space; pumpkins store well from autumn onwards, and can be grown in any part of the rotation.

Cheap and easy to grow but relatively expensive to buy

- Beetroot
- Broad beans
- Brussels sprouts
- Calabrese
- Celeriac
- Courgettes
- French beans
- Herbs of all sorts
- Leeks
- Lettuces
- Mangetout peas
- Mixed salad leaves
- Purple and white sprouting broccoli
- Radishes
- Runner beans
- Salad onions
- Shallots
- Spinach
- Spinach beet and chard
- Turnips and kohlrabi
- Soft fruit of all sorts
- Rhubarb

Cheap to buy, have a short season, or take up much space (possibly not worth growing)

- Cabbages
- Carrots
- Celery
- Garlic
- Onions
- Outdoor tomatoes
- Melons
- Parsnips
- Peas
- Potatoes (except early potatoes)
- Pumpkins
- Squash
- Cauliflowers
- Swedes
- Sweet potatoes

Money can't buy – grow your own or go without

CROP	COMMENT
Beetroot leaves	Earthy, spinach substitute
Chinese artichokes	Hard to harvest commercially, but easily grown at home
Courgette flowers	Too frail to travel easily. Great to eat
Hop shoots	Used like asparagus in spring - Kent delicacy
Japanese wineberry	Small fruits, costly to pick
Oriental flowering kales	Flowers deteriorate quickly after picking
Pea tendrils	Costly to harvest and pack
Radish seedpods	Good for snacks and stir-fries
Romanesco broccoli	Easily bruised in transit
Sorrel	Low growing salad that is costly to pick
Tomatillo	Mexican cuisine, good for chutney, does not get blight
Unripe wheat berries	Used in some Continental and Middle Eastern recipes

---

Allotment eccentricities

You find people from every walk of life on an allotment plot, of every age and every nationality: every one of them ready to sell the virtues of their pastime to the uninitiated. Characters abound: people passionate about a particular plant; fanatical about flowers; mad about chickens or bees; obsessed with order on their plot. There are those who take control, making themselves the boss and everything their business, others who insist on giving every newcomer some special advice or plant offsets to get them going. Some old souls have a twinkle in their eye, and some enthuse about growing enormous dahlias or prize-winning leeks. Individuality comes to the fore with the more artistic, with beautifully painted sheds, clever designs for bed layout, or the ingenious use of strange structures to support plants.

You may meet someone like the woman obsessed with pumpkins on one site. She and her husband shared a plot, but she needed more space to grow her treasured, space-hungry plants, so took on her own entire plot dedicated to them. Every day she went and talked to them, caressed them, and then measured them. It wasn't just her own pumpkins either - she'd wander around the whole site of 120 plots, talking and measuring the competition too.

Identifying your style

There is no set style of allotment gardening and, despite the magisterial tone in older books, there probably never was. Allotment-holders are individualists who want to express their needs and desires in their own way. They will borrow any method that suits and seems good, and find their own solutions if none exist. Nevertheless, there are some broad themes to which gardeners often adhere.

Each style always has its enthusiasts, but there is no evidence that any are of such great merit, with such outstanding health, flavour, or environmental benefits, that they should supplant all others and are the only possible way to get good results. Most gardeners take what they like or need from each theme to make their own style.

Organic gardening

Organic gardening is a system that avoids using synthetic chemicals, such as pesticides or fertilisers, and instead relies on crop rotation, composting, animal manures, legumes, green manures, and biological controls to keep the soil fertile in the long term and to manage pest, disease, and weed problems.

The underlying principle is that soil is a living system, and that gardeners work with it rather than attempt to dominate by intervention with powerful fertilisers and pesticides. Aspects of this approach include maintaining genetic diversity of crops by growing a wide range of varieties, encouraging the presence of wildlife in and around the plot, avoiding waste and pollution, recycling organic materials, and using renewable resources whenever possible.

When it comes to pest problems, organic gardeners will use mechanical methods (such as mesh and fleece to exclude insects) rather than pesticides, although organic pesticides can be used if all other options are exhausted. They subscribe to the use of companion planting (*see* page 44), will tolerate a certain level of damage, and believe that the food produced by organic methods is superior to that produced by other means. Even gardeners who do not subscribe to every aspect of organic gardening have been heavily influenced by its sound basic tenets (netting against carrot fly is now the norm), and broadly support its aims.

Hardcore organic gardeners believe that organic gardening is an all-or-nothing commitment – that the garden is an indivisible system, and all the relationships between different aspects are inseparable – you cannot pick and choose which bits you follow. Other gardeners who loosely call themselves organic take a more relaxed view.

There is no compulsion here, and allotment gardeners must make up their own minds. However, be aware that your neighbouring plot-holders may have strong views on these matters, and try to act in a considerate way that takes their feelings into account. On some sites feelings have run high enough for the allotment authorities to divide the whole site into organic and non-organic areas.

Whichever system or methods you choose in the end, the principles of using the lowest possible inputs and making the fertility of the soil of over-riding importance are sound. They will enhance your results whether you are strictly organic or not.

Fabric barriers for weeds and (background) carrots are effective and, if reused, have limited environmental impact.

Double digging

Gardeners of old would often delve deep, going down not one spade's depth but two (double-digging) or even three (trenching). The horticultural merit of this technique is now considered questionable. Nevertheless, double digging has its uses in getting ground ready for future no-dig regimes, for raised beds, or to counter problems with drainage or soil so compacted that roots cannot penetrate deeply.

In double digging, a trench is taken out, 60cm (18in) wide and a spade's depth deep. The excavated soil is barrowed to the far end of the area to be dug. The base of the trench is then forked or dug over, ideally adding one or two bucketfuls of manure or other organic matter per square metre or yard. The organic matter stabilises the loosened soil, prolonging the benefits of digging for some years (as long as the soil is not trampled or worked when wet). Another trench next to the original is then taken out and the soil, fortified with organic matter, is shifted into the first trench. The base of this trench is dug over in turn, and so on until the end of the plot. Here the original soil from the first trench is used to fill the last.

Double digging in trenches will increase the depth of the topsoil and produce better crops.

No-dig alternatives

Digging is mainly needed to control weeds and occasionally to incorporate lime, phosphorus, and potassium. These often penetrate soil slowly and in cases of deficiency need help. Digging is also needed to restore the structure lost when wet soil is trampled. Good soil dries to little crumbs and if damaged when wet these are lost, but they can be restored by digging and manuring.

To avoid trampling, 'no-dig' usually involves growing crops in beds that can be reached from narrow (45cm/18in) paths each side and are never trodden on. These beds may be raised or on the flat. On the flat is better where the soil is sandy and in low-rainfall areas: sandy soil has little inherent structure and is least suited to no-dig regimes. Raised beds are especially valuable in wet districts, on poorly drained soils, and if it is important to avoid back strain.

In a no-dig regime, weeds are controlled by shallow hoeing, hand weeding, contact weedkillers, and mulching. Debris is gathered up rather than dug in. Mulches are taken into the soil by soil organisms and fertilisers are washed in by rain. Mulches also take the place of earthing-up for potatoes, and seeds are sown shallowly and transplants eased in with minimal disturbance.

Because there is little disturbance of the soil, no weed seeds are brought up, and once those near the surface have germinated, weed problems decline. The absence of the clods produced by digging reduces cover for slugs. No-dig gardening is well worth trying, and it is often essential for less fit gardeners, or those with heavy, intractable soils.

Raised beds suit 'no-dig' – there is room in these for the essential mulch of organic matter.

Using raised beds

Raising soil by 15–50cm (6–20in) can improve drainage, ease the management of plants, and reduce the amount of back bending needed. Busy gardeners and those who have clay soils, a wet climate, or health or strength problems all find raised beds especially helpful. Working from the pathways means that the beds are not trampled, and digging can often be omitted (*see* page 35). Limited supplies of manure can be concentrated on the area of the beds. In wet seasons the soil will be workable more often than soil that has not been raised.

There are many ways to raise a bed. Boards are commonly used, and are ideal for the allotment. Pressure-treated timber lasts longest, and modern wood treatments do not contain arsenic or chromium. As old carpets are best avoided (*see* page 28), wood chips, often donated by council tree surgeons, are used to floor paths between beds.

Enhanced drainage means the soil warms up and becomes workable earlier in the year, allowing earlier sowing and planting. At the end of the season, winter waterlogging is less likely to harm mature plants. Both slugs and root diseases are much less problematic in the well-drained conditions of raised beds, but in droughts the beds may need more watering. To some extent preparing raised beds by double digging first will increase potential rooting depth and help plants cope with drought, as indeed will generous mulching of plants.

Juggling sizes and layout makes for interesting plots, customised to meet their owners' needs.

Using chemicals

Pesticides for amateur gardeners must be extremely safe so they can be used without protection and any misuse isn't harmful. As a result only a limited range is available. Even with this safety margin, the law requires that gardeners follow the instructions on the labels of pesticides exactly – and given the mild nature of the products, this is essential to get the effect. Organic remedies may also cause harm if misused.

The limited range and effectiveness of what's available mean other methods are the first line of defence, and using chemicals is a last resort. In fact, for many problems no effective controls are offered. This may sound depressing, but measures such as pest-excluding mesh and using watering and crop hygiene to control diseases can produce better results than chemicals. Potatoes and tomatoes are a special case: blight will devastate crops in wet conditions without a fungicide regime.

If gardeners embrace the concept of promoting soil fertility by using organic matter, the usefulness of fertilisers is limited. An exception is potassium: natural sources are limited, and you may need a bottle to correct deficiency.

It is wasteful and potentially harmful to scatter slug pellets too thickly, as seen here.

Biodynamic theories

Unlike organic gardening, the tenets of biodynamic gardening appear to lack a genuine scientific basis. Like organic gardening, it promotes use of and reuse of organic materials and manures and excludes the use of synthetic fertilisers and pesticides. It treats the garden, or plot, as an indivisible whole, and includes the use of cover crops, green manures, and crop rotation.

But biodynamic systems go beyond organic gardening in promoting the use of certain mineral materials and products of fermentation as special additives to be sprayed on to crops and added to composts. Examples of these include 'horn manure' which is a preparation of cow manure that has been buried and fermented in a horn, to be applied in the evening in a coarse spray to the soil to encourage healthy root growth. Another is 'horn silica' which is finely ground quartz meal 'energised' through spending the summer in the soil inside a cow horn. It is applied to plants as a fine spray at certain stages of growth. Both preparations are claimed to possess certain special properties that have elements of the occult: the method specifies exactly how you stir them into the water when diluting them.

Other aspects of the biodynamic method include practices such as planting and sowing according to phases of the moon, and reference to astrological calendars that are drawn up afresh for each year.

The absence of any recognisable scientific basis to these methods is not of concern to their practitioners, as biodynamic gardening is part of a unique belief system. It makes perfect sense to those who subscribe to this system, even if it might perplex other gardeners. The methods are harmless to practitioners and consumers of the produce alike.

Vegetables only

Vegetables are mostly easy to grow, and give a quick return on your investment of time and labour. The downside is that they do take a lot of time and labour, and need constant attention for good results. They are also expensive to produce: seed, manures, and fertiliser all add up. An allotment can produce an awful lot of vegetables, although if you eat many potatoes this won't be such a concern as these will be plentiful.

Most allotment-holders start off with a veg-only plot as they clear the ground and eliminate weed or fertility problems. Once they have gained confidence or are sure they intend staying for a while, they are ready to invest in long-term crops such as asparagus and fruit.

Monoculture crops

Enthusiasts often use an allotment for their hobby; there are plenty of plots given over to blooms for showing, with perhaps a little breeding activity as well. Others might plant up fruit collections, or a vineyard for amateur winemakers. Although not in the class of growing food, this allows people to experience the joys of gardening even though they might not own a garden. In truth, other allotment-holders are rather proud of these specialists, especially if, as is often the case, their hardworking owners have won renown far and wide for their perfect blooms and produce.

Crop choice is a matter of personal taste – a leek monoculture is perfectly acceptable.

Veg plus fruit

Adding permanent plantings to a plot alters the workflow and creates different peaks and troughs of labour. Fruit needs far less work than vegetables, which helps reduce the labour involved in running the plot. Fruit bushes or trees may yield lower volumes of produce than vegetables, but these are crops of higher value. Something has to give however, and large areas of fruit means that the least rewarding vegetables are dropped from the cropping scheme.

There is a drop in production while fruit bushes are establishing and before they reach full production, and for this reason fruit is generally added gradually to a plot. But excluding birds is essential for fruit growing, so it is probably better to build a fruit cage and plant fruit all at once, just cropping between the fruit for a while until the bushes get going.

Stepover apples are a classy and spacesaving, way to add fruit to an allotment.

A fruit cage

Fruit cages are tall, netted enclosures where fruit bushes and small trees can grow to full height and allow the gardener to stand. The net is usually of small-gauge mesh, 15-20mm (½–¾in), to exclude even the smallest birds. Ideally the top should be removable to give pollinators access at flowering time and avoid damage from winter snowfall. Fruit cages won't keep out squirrels, but might deter the casual pilfering that is occasionally encountered on allotments.

Most allotment fruit cages are of recycled material and not always things of beauty. Indeed proper fruit cages are quite costly. However, functional and tidy structures can be built using poles and wires at reasonable cost.

Recent mild winters and changes in agricultural practice have led to high populations of wood pigeons and deer. The damage these can cause to both fruit and vegetables has led to a major increase in the use of cages on allotments. To prevent sites becoming ugly, some allotments restrict what you can build. Removal of derelict cages after plot-holders leave, often at significant cost to the allotment, is also common.

Feathered and furred pests won't like this smart cage, but the allotment management will!

Room for herbs and flowers

Although at one time this was often discouraged, many allotment-holders make their allotment a haven from home. If home is a small flat or a shared house, a plot with beds of flowers, well-kept paths, a seating area and even a pond becomes a welcome retreat. Few would begrudge this, and in fact you'll find that even the most traditional plot-holder will have some flowers around their shed door and a patch of herbs in a sunny spot (but where they won't get in the way of their 'proper gardening').

Any horticultural goods can be produced on allotments, and it is not uncommon to see a little nursery bed of flowers to be transplanted into the garden: sweet Williams, hollyhocks, and wallflowers for example. Some gardeners cannot bear to throw plants away, so excess from their garden ends up on their allotment. The practice is unwise. Golden rod is a prime example – it can soon become a weed. It's better to regard these as fertiliser for the allotment and add them to your compost bin.

Allotment herbs are inconveniently far from the kitchen, but it's worth growing some for drying or making dishes such as pesto or tabbouleh (which rely on massive amounts of basil or parsley respectively). Invasive mint and horseradish should be kept in check on the allotment by the aid of a spade.

Sedum and sage – good to look at and good for the kitchen and wildlife.

Growing under cover

Greenhouses and polytunnels can be very valuable additions to allotments, but raise problems. They can be scruffy if home-made from scrap materials, and may be left derelict when, as often happens, their owner moves. With time, glass gets broken and plastic degrades and is dispersed by the wind. Because of this, many allotments ban structures over 1m (3ft) high, or require plans to be submitted for approval. On a practical note, in summer, crops under cover need attention almost every day and without taps and electricity it is hard to tend them properly.

One way round this is to have shared polytunnels or greenhouses, where the allotment society buys and maintains a tunnel, letting space within it to tenants.

Bonfires

Rules about bonfires vary from site to site, so check the rules that apply to your site first. Some sites have an incinerator that you can borrow to burn diseased material. When councils ban bonfires it is usually due to the nuisance caused to neighbours. Bear this in mind if bonfires are allowed: permission may be rescinded if there are complaints. If you are permitted to burn, there are some simple rules to follow:

- Burn only dry material on a small, hot fire, to minimise smoke.

- Never use an accelerant such as petrol.

- Burn only diseased, non-compostable allotment waste.

- Avoid burning when the weather conditions are unsuitable.

- Never leave a fire unattended. Douse with soil or water when you leave.

- Check for animals in the waste before lighting the fire.

Under highways and environmental laws it is an offence to let smoke drift across a road or cause a statutory nuisance – and penalties can include four-figure fines.

Planning your allotment

Things to consider

It is unusual to take over a pristine plot; many are in very bad shape, covered in weeds, debris, and rubbish. If you take over in winter you have more scope for planning; in spring and summer, you just get what you can from the plot in what is left of the growing season. Planning can save you work and time for years to come. The first step is looking at the plot as whole and identifying what will give most pleasure and productivity.

A pleasant plot

On allotments form follows function. If looks come first, a plot will be laborious and output may suffer: low, clipped hedges, for example, are troublesome, and narrow paved paths are awkward, inflexible, and need a lot of weeding. But function need not be just functional: beans on wigwams and plantings of mixed foliage types are both practical and pretty, and useful objects can be chosen with an eye for attractive shapes.

New sheds and other items are not obligatory. Using reclaimed materials is part of allotment culture, but be selective rather than use your plot to be rid of old baths and fence panels. Sheds can be festooned with spring-flowering clematis, lockers for unsightly junk can be made alongside the shed, storage racks for stakes and canes look very smart, and raised beds with defined edges make it much easier to keep the plot looking neat. Compost bins are not things of beauty, but can be positioned in the least-valued part of your plot and disguised with ornamental plants.

Ponds, wildflower areas, and other ornamental features can be added without compromising the productivity of your allotment. Trees look nice, but even if they are allowed on your plot, they won't be loved if they shade your neighbours. Perhaps they might be squeezed in at the end of the plot, where they will shade a roadway?

Inexpensive treated gravel boards can be sawn and pegged to make pleasing planting schemes.

Practical constraints

It can be tricky to fit allotments in with work and family commitments. The peak of allotment work and harvest coincides with summer holidays, for example, so consider planting crops that mature before or after this time to ease the pressure. In the summer when the days are long and the weather good, it may be easier to find time to tend your plants. However, the wise plot-holder does as much as possible in winter to ease the summer workload.

If changes in family, health, or work circumstances affect your time, it might be wise to downsize to a smaller plot for a while. Perhaps take a year's fallow, covering the soil with a thick mulch or a weed-suppressing membrane. Conditions often stipulate that at least two thirds of a plot must be under cultivation, so you need to agree this in advance. The opposite also applies; people change jobs or retire, or children leave home, leaving more time to tend an allotment, and 'upscaling' might be an option for some.

Look at what you've got

Plots may seem to be blank canvasses of earth, but no two are quite alike. Areas near trees are hard to crop but are ideal for compost bins and sheds. Boughs can be pruned (with permission)

Daring allotment designs

Once upon a time (it feels that long ago) we all knew what an allotment or a veg plot in the garden looked like. Long rows of crops marched across it in perfect step with soil between them. But straight lines, square beds, and bare soil are not rules or a magic formula. Allotment plots can have squiggly paths (but do road-test them with a wheelbarrow), ponds, and circular beds. Fruit and long-term crops, such as asparagus, jostle with patches of salads and veg. These might be harder to plan or tend – but they might be worth it.

for stakes, and their leaves composted. Terracing can be used on slopes to make easy-to-work raised beds.

Wet patches are problematic, but are perfect if you hanker after a pond. Most sites have areas of neglect, such as banks, hedges, and ditches, that offer potential sources of pea sticks, leaves for leaf mould, vegetation for compost, and extra soil. Exploiting these will keep them in better repair, but do agree any activities with the site management first.

Build a compost bin

Do this right at the start: a compost bin will swallow all the weeds from clearing your plot. Plots generate huge amounts of waste vegetation, but it rots down to surprisingly little: other organic matter will still have to be imported.

Old wooden pallets are traditional bin material and, with a bit of skill and care, can be quite attractive. Bins of less than a cubic metre/yard seldom rot really well, but exceeding 2m (6ft) either way results in an airless interior and poor rotting. Realistically, because the bin fills bit by bit it seldom gets really warm, so compost is never quite as good as council stuff made in bulk, and weeds and spores survive, but you can still get fine, usable compost (*see* box).

Paths and boundaries

Good access to all parts, with paths to tend and gather your crops, is crucial. Most sites have grass paths around the plot and it's a plot-holder's responsibility to keep these in good repair. Many sites have their own mower for this. Paths within the plot use cropping space and are best avoided, but are essential for working beds.

Permanent paths between raised beds can be kept weed-free with a membrane or chipped wood. Council tree contractors often supply allotment sites with chipped timber. Temporary paths can be left as bare soil.

Beautiful compost

It smells of damp woods, is full of worms, and is called black gold. Beautiful compost is a joyous thing that every allotment holder has the ability (and responsibility) to make. All you need is a little space and a little patience. Add shredded woody prunings and softer material in equal layers. Leave for six weeks, turn to get some air in, leave for a few months, and hey presto – you've recycled the waste from your plot and can put it back to improve the soil. You'll know when it's ready: it will smell sweet, look dark and crumbly, and feel friable in your hand. You'll feel the soil would want to be blanketed with it. If you turn your heap regularly (far easier if you have more than one bin) it should be like this all the way through. If not, just leave the less-rotted bits a few more months. A heap that is ready in early summer but won't be spread until autumn can even support a courgette plant or two. The roots will help aerate the compost, and when the plant dies off, let it rot in place and then return the whole heap to the soil. Keep diseased material, weed seeds, and parts of perennial weeds that can regenerate out of the compost heap. But virtually all other organic waste can go in.

Edges and boundaries are crucial to a well-kept plot. Boards reduce the labour of trimming, often at the busiest time of the growing season. At a pinch, a narrow jet of a contact weedkiller along the edge can prevent incursion of grass and weeds. As you are expected to leave the plot as you find it, installing old, broken slabs and other construction debris is frowned upon. Use recyclable materials such as bark or wood chips instead.

Water wisely

Dip tanks filled from the mains are the commonest watering arrangement on allotments. One tank about every four plots is ideal, so you don't have to lug water too far – but a bit of lugging ensures that you think about how much you're using. Sprinklers, standpipes, and hoses are rare, and push rents up.

Much water used on plots is wasted. To be useful, it has to soak in. This can mean as much as two watering cans a square metre/yard. Water plants thoroughly in rotation, rather than distributing water widely and thinly. On average a crop needs 2.5cm (1in) every 10–14 days, so a good soak every two weeks is effective and achievable without great labour or using excessive water.

The cost of water is included in the rent and you are expected to use it responsibly. Do not wash anything in the tanks or fill pesticide sprayers directly. Draw off a bucket or a can of water for washing or filling.

Plan a rotation scheme

Never growing crops in the same place twice in a row thwarts soil-borne pests and diseases. It sadly has no effect on airborne diseases or flying pests, such as potato blight and carrot fly. For the crops a typical plot-holder grows, a four course rotation is best. Each bed should grow, in order: potatoes and tomatoes in year one; root vegetables (including onions) in year two; peas and broad beans in year three; and brassicas in year four. Pumpkins, squash, courgettes, French and runner beans, sweetcorn, and sweet potatoes have few pests or diseases and can be slotted in where convenient. Rotation also allows you to plan where to manure (before potatoes) and add lime (after potatoes).

Vary rotations to suit the plot. In a very small area you might even try potatoes and tomatoes in year one, and everything else in year two.

Mix up your crops

According to the theory of companion planting, mixing plants together confuses insects, especially if you mix a strongly scented plant like French marigolds with vulnerable crops like runner beans. There is little hard evidence that this works, but the only cost is the loss of some cropping space. Research does suggest that insects find plants on bare soil easily, so a mat of green foliage like clover under a widely spaced crop like Brussels sprouts will hinder pests. The difficulty is finding a balance between camouflage and cultivating weeds.

When intercropping, however, a quick crop is sown and harvested between a widely spaced, slow-growing crop before its leaves meet across rows. Widely spaced Brussels sprouts, for example, allow lettuce to be sown in early spring and crop before the sprouts, planted in late spring, grow too large. This shades into 'catch cropping'. With skill (and good weather) you can fit in a quick-growing crop before or after the main crop is finished: early peas allow for a quick crop of autumn turnips, for example.

Paths and edges

1) *Birch logs will quickly rot but in the process support insect life including stag beetles.*
2) *Narrow (45cm/18in) paths are easy to work from and maximise cropping space.*
3) *Woodchips, ideally over weed control membrane, reduce path maintenance.*
4) *Weedkillers keep block paths weedfree effortlessly, but if growing organically lay over weed control membrane.*

Accommodating wildlife

Allotments are full of wild creatures. Some – from rabbits and pigeons down to aphids – are the natural enemy of the gardener, but other creatures will keep a check on these. Robins need no invitation: they are constant companions to many allotment gardeners. As you dig up invertebrates, they hop around and gobble them up – rest your back a moment and observe.

Cultivation is obviously your intended land use, but at the boundaries an area of dense undergrowth will encourage birds, hedgehogs, toads, and frogs to move in and feast upon aphids and insect pests, slugs and snails. Large stones or low, spreading plants create cool, dark environments to provide shelter for newts and ground beetles that will devour soil pests. A small pond, as long as it is not a hazard, can attract toads and frogs. Bird feeders will bring in birds, but watch out for squirrels, or mice feeding on debris on the ground below.

Flowers don't just make a plot attractive to us, they also lure in pollinating and pest-eating insects. Create nesting opportunities: some solitary bees will use hollow stems 10–30cm (4–12in) long with holes 2–8mm (1/16–3/8in) across. Bundle the stems together or pack them into a topped-and-tailed plastic bottle, and hang horizontally in a sunny place at about head height.

Successional sowing at intervals spreads a crop out: you might sow peas in early spring and then again each time the last sowing is 5cm (2in) high so they mature in turn without gluts.

Crop protection

Protection from the weather will boost growth and exclude pests. Fleece is cheap and gives a two week 'advance' in spring-sown crops by providing extra warmth and shelter from wind; plastic cloches do slightly better. Both are vulnerable to wind and other damage, and often need netting over them. Glass cloches are liable to break, and broken glass is a tiresome soil contaminant. Old windows are traditional allotment coldframes, but are also easily broken. Proprietary frames are expensive and you might think twice before leaving them on the plot, but a well-made frame can advance crops by up to a month, so it's worth exercising your creative skills.

1) *Netting, strung on twine stretched between stakes, gives cheap, flexible protection.*
2) *After the beans have cropped, the turnip seedlings will fill the available space.*
3) *Large compost bins (over a cubic metre/ yard) give plenty of excellent soil improver.*
4) *Marigolds may or may not deter pests, but they certainly add to the plot's charm.*

What to do when taking on a new allotment

- Clear and compost or burn vegetation.
- Remove any fruit bushes that are not in good condition.
- Clear and dig widely spaced strips of soil and crop these first, working from undug areas between them. Go back to finish the undug strips later.
- Control growth in uncropped areas with weed-suppressing sheeting or glyphosate weedkiller.
- Eliminate perennial weeds before planting long term asparagus or fruit.
- Remember it's a marathon, not a sprint.

Scarecrows and bird scarers

You are never alone on an allotment, especially if you have a scarecrow. They're fun to make, especially with children, and can be useful in deterring a few unwanted visitors. Simply gather together some old clothes, some straw or other suitable stuffing material, and a secure frame, then put it all together to resemble a human body, and the job's done.

In practice, most traditional scarecrows are pretty ineffective at actually scaring birds. Instead there are a number of other methods for keeping winged visitors off your allotment crops. Old CDs, strips of foil, or upturned empty drinks cans on sticks can be placed around susceptible plants. Anything that flaps around in the wind, reflecting light and making noise, will help to keep feathered friends at bay. Keep it safe, and make sure no one else is disturbed by noisy birdscarers. For when there is no wind, a bird of prey decoy may do the trick, or a 'humming line' that vibrates to create a noise and ward off animal pests. It helps to rotate all these regularly: birds (and mammals) quickly learn that an alarming new sight isn't really a threat, so move scarers about or retire them and bring out different ones throughout the growing season for maximum effect.

Physical barriers, such as netting over brassicas or a cage for your fruit, are the ultimate and best defence against birds who want to share your bountiful feast, but it's still charming company to have a real scarecrow around.

From top to bottom *If wit and ingenuity deters birds this plot will be free of damage; it is unclear if avian courage will be tested by this delightful ornamental plant support; flashing CDs are a traditional deterrent, but birds soon lose their fear of them; moles too are said to be detered by windmills, but as with birds the evidence is contradictory.*

Sheds and furniture

Allotment holders like to express their personalities through their sheds, subject to the usual allotment practice of using whatever materials come to hand, from old road workers' huts to car panels.

Sheds are usually placed to the north edge of a plot, ideally where cropping is tricky, such as under trees. They are often grouped away from plots along the sides of the site, to avoid disputes over shade and to keep the site tidy. Some sites even have communal sheds with lockers instead. Even if sheds are allowed, permission may well be required for each new one.

Allotments are insecure places, and arson, theft of tools and produce, and vandalism are common. It is unwise to keep valuable equipment and materials in sheds. Tools stolen from sheds can be used in burglary of nearby homes; if this is common gardeners might choose to take their kit home with them.

This is a pity, because a shed is often a home-from-home: a quiet refuge, a place to drink your tea (or home-made wines and beer) and, especially for flat dwellers, an indoor-outdoor living area. Patio furniture, barbecues, and other homely objects are used to make a private eating and recreational space, often with sheltering shrubs, trees, and trellis. Guttering leading from the roof to water butts gives convenient access to your own water even when the dip tanks are turned off for winter.

Sheds tend to proliferate over the years. Small 'service areas' develop, and things that 'might be useful one day' accumulate. Avoiding this tendency will make your site management committee happier and ease the day when you have to pass the plot on.

Your allotment plot can be both a place for hard work and for relaxation.

Opposite, clockwise from top left
Tongued and grooved boards make this shed fully weather proof; sheds set against trees or hedges at the edge of the plot cast no damaging shade; charming artwork turns this utilitarian shed into a feature in its own right; an old roadmen's hut will never rot and will be a serviceable shelter from cloudbursts.

Great shed stories

Perhaps it is the often anarchic defiance of a neat, orderly, planned society that makes allotment sheds so appealing. Behind these facades, which range from unkempt to artistic, in these unassuming shelters ostensibly for rain and storage, hide tea-making facilities, home-brewing and wine-making equipment, and many other aspects of domesticity. Although rather less believable, romantic rumours of trysts and hiding out from the law in allotment sheds are also not uncommon.

Managing expectations

Allotments can use up a lot of time, so require some planning. Go for a plot size suited to your needs – half a plot is adequate for most people and ideal for beginners. This might need eight hours' work a week for inexperienced gardeners, half that for experienced ones. This means you will need to find the equivalent of up to a day each week to tend your plot in summer (but much less each winter). As you will often have more produce than you can consume in summer, invite friends to help with the work and share the spoils. Sharing a plot is often very successful, providing cover for holidays and emergencies.

Keep down the weeds
Weeds are the main burden of work for plot-holders and most allotments need continual hoeing and weeding. Planning allotments to limit weeding is a good first step. Pumpkins, squash, courgettes, and potatoes smother weeds, so plant them in the weediest areas. Carrots, peas, and onions cast little shade and weeds can quickly smother them. Onions are easily grown through black membrane, carrots can be grown in beds with paths to allow access for the repeated weedings required, and peas can be pulled and gathered early in the crop's life to be rid of the weeds before they set seed, although at the cost of some loss of crop. Late-sown or planted crops such as tomatoes and French beans allow time for stale seedbeds (*see* page 29) to knock back weeds.

Perennial crops such as asparagus and fruit need no cultivation or sowing, but must be planted in areas that are clear of all perennial weeds. Mulching between fruit bushes with organic matter or a weed-suppressing membrane reduces weeding in these areas. But no matter how you try to minimise weeding, it's worth investing in a push hoe, a draw hoe, and a short-handled onion hoe to be fully equipped to deal with any weed problems.

Stocking your plot
Sowing and raising plants soaks up the hours. To save time, consider buying in transplants. Nurseries offer a wide range of plants in cell trays, and as most plants are only needed in numbers of less than a dozen it makes sense to buy some in rather than raising a few plants from a packet of many seeds.

This is especially the case with tender plants that need heated conditions to thrive. The nursery's greenhouse is far superior to the sunniest windowsill. Sharing plant raising and exchanging plants with friends and neighbours makes sense and is likely to be cheaper.

Keep an eye on costs
Allotments, like any enterprise, need working capital. Not much, just enough for a few tools and some seeds, but some careful, modest investment will yield better crops and reward your effort. In order of priority, tools come first (*see* page 17). Next come the best seeds and plants you can afford. Then fertiliser, worthwhile because the benefit is much higher than the cost, especially if you buy large bags of a balanced fertiliser. Manure and other organic matter is nearly as cost-effective and comes next in priority. Allotment societies often bulk buy these things, so start there. Having

invested in good plants and fed them well, it makes sense to protect them with nets, insect-proof mesh, and fleece, all relatively cheap. Cloches, frames, tunnels, and greenhouses are costly, and the return is fairly low. Well-grown crops escape most pests and diseases, but a minimum pesticide input can make a lot of difference. Hire power tools such as rotavators.

To work out the annual cost of your allotment, tot up the rent for the plot, your outlay on seeds, plants, fertiliser, manure, pesticides, wear and tear on tools and equipment, and the cost of stakes, canes, string, and other sundries. Against this set the value of the output from your plot. Naturally these costs and outputs can vary enormously with yields, crops chosen, and the ingenuity of the gardener for money-saving ideas.

Allotments are the home of ingenuity. Posts, canes, and stakes are made from old pipes, steel reinforcing bars from building work, timber, or pallets. Nets left over from construction sites are used to protect crops, string from hay bales at stables is saved, old floorboards and scaffold boards make new edging.

Coping with wet conditions
Weather can limit allotment activity. Soils, especially clay ones, are often impossible to work in wet periods and are damaged if you try. The heavier the soil, the fewer days of the year it can be worked, and in wet seasons waterlogged soils can limit what can be grown.

Raised beds enhance drainage and greatly extend the time when sticky soils are workable. Failing these, try digging the soil while it is dry in autumn, perhaps making ridges as you go by throwing the soil from three spade widths into a ridge down the middle of each three-spade-wide section. The use of transplants can help overcome a shorter season.

Seeds are easily spoilt by damp; a sturdy tin with a good seal helps maintain their viability.

When planning your allotment year consider how much you will be limited if the season turns wet. Choose maincrop cultivars of peas, potatoes, and carrots that give heavy yields even if sown late. Where slugs are a problem, they will be at their most damaging in wet seasons and second-early potatoes gathered before the soil gets too soggy and slugs too numerous are a sound choice.

Coping with dry conditions

Sandy soils are workable most of the year, but dryness in summer, most often a problem in southern and eastern areas, can limit their productivity.

To some extent dry seasons can be overcome by watering, but do plan for the possibility of periods without rain, especially if your plot has sandy soil. Avoid growing too much of crops such as celery, leafy salads, and runner beans, which suffer on dry soils. Root crops are much less susceptible, squash, pumpkin, and sweetcorn are very resilient, and there are drought-resistant potato cultivars. Overwintered and early-sown crops do their growing while the soil is still moist from winter rains.

Make every effort in dry areas to conserve the winter rain in your soil by finishing all digging by mid-spring.

A good mix of well-fed crops, spaced carefully fully uses available space.

Exposing soil after this results in much loss of moisture. Adding ample organic matter to the soil in winter also helps: one application of two bucketfuls of manure every square metre or yard will hold the equivalent of 5cm (2in) of rain. Crops consume soil water at the rate of about 2.5cm (1in) in 14 days, so this can really extend time between waterings.

In droughts there may be restrictions on water use; hosepipes and sprinklers are usually prohibited early in a drought but few allotment sites allow these.

The next stage is a drought order, when severe water shortage is forecast. Rules may vary – usually allotments may still be watered – but the spirit of a drought order is to stop all but essential watering. An average water butt holds enough to water at most just 14 square metres (17 square yards) once, so storing water won't do much unless you have several. Neither will carting washing up water and other waste water from home – in any case much waste water from homes is not wholesome enough for crops. With an eye to the future under a changing climate, allotment sites are beginning to invest in boreholes.

Although allotment holders complain about the weather non-stop, good growers are experts at making the weather work for them. But what weather do gardeners really need?

The average British year

In late winter, rains should have restored the soil to full moisture levels, but not

left it soggy, battered, and emptied of nutrients. In practice, most British winters do just that, and putting matters right requires a warm, windy, dry spring.

British springs, however, are often cold and wet, or (nearly as bad) very dry, windy, and cold. Skill with water, seedbeds, seeds, and fleece can still get crops off to a good start, although on difficult clay soils transplants raised indoors might be necessary.

Getting plants going well before late spring is essential. Crops grow best during the long, warm days and high light levels of late spring to late summer, and for this they need plenty of leaves. Wet, but not too wet, summers are much better for allotments than hot, dry ones; crops need water to grow.

By autumn, growth is tailing off in lower light levels, so little rain is needed; warm, dry weather is better for ripening produce now. Wet weather leads to rots, unripe produce that won't store well, and wet soil that cannot be dug before winter rains arrive.

By early winter, the weather is of no consequence. The allotment gardener's work is done for the year and they can relax in front of the fire and dream of a better spring.

Security and burglar alarms

Some sites suffer many break-ins from thieves or vandals. The saddest crime we suffer is when crops are simply wrecked by intruders. Events like this are an unfortunate fact of life on many sites, but the incidence and severity does vary. Secure entrances and fences or thorny hedges will go a long way to keep the site safe. Motion-sensing lights and in extreme cases security cameras may be a solution. It's worth joining your local 'Allotment Watch' scheme and getting to know your community police. Most vandalism is the work of bored locals, so there might be a way to include them and reduce crime. In some areas where theft is a problem, the plot holders have swapped sheds for greenhouses, so that inquisitive intruders are more easily spotted. Forcible entry can cause damage, so if the would-be thieves can see in, they will see there's nothing worth taking. But you may find that too much glass is impractical if it attracts vandals. Elsewhere (and for insurance reasons) it might be necessary to use a strong padlock on a shed door along with other sensible precautions: make sure hinges can't be easily removed and windows are secure, mark equipment with postcodes and make it obvious that they belong to someone, and install a battery-powered alarm. You may simply need to store anything valuable off-site.

Below, left to right *Stand pipes and hoses are a boon to busy gardeners but are seldom found on allotments; up to four watering cans per square metre/yard are needed to soak the root zone; mulching crops will suppress moisture-robbing weeds, feed crops, and slightly reduce evaporation losses; water butts are especially valuable in winter, for washing tools and produce, when the mains are off.*

Opposite *The owner of this plot will be well-rewarded for his well-chosen, weed-free crops.*

Root crops

Basic techniques

Root vegetable plants are perennial or biennial, growing in their first year, flowering and setting seed in their second year. They store food reserves to keep them going in their roots or tubers, and it is these food storage organs that we eat. Celeriac (see page 102) is used like a root vegetable, but in fact develops a swollen stem base.

Swedes and turnips are brassicas, or members of the cabbage family (see pages 116–23), and should be included with these crops if you practice rotation, because they are subject to the same soil pests and diseases.

Soil preparation

All root crops like a deep, well-dug, moisture-retentive soil that has had some well-rotted organic matter added. This can be anything from home-made compost, manure, or leafmould to spent mushroom compost. The emphasis is on well rotted, since manure and other strong soil improvers can cause the roots to fork if added fresh. Whatever you add, it is best applied in the autumn or, better still, for a previous crop, to give it time to rot down. The one exception is potatoes, which don't mind too much if the organic matter is added at the same time as planting.

Two weeks before sowing or planting, you can rake in a general granular fertiliser at the rate of 50g/sq m (2oz/sq yd).

Generally, root crops do less well in light soils. These can dry out too quickly in summer, leading to poor cropping, bolting (going to seed prematurely), woody growth, poor flavour, or cracking. Stony soils can cause the roots to fork, so try to remove as many stones as possible. On very heavy soils, stick to stump- or round-rooted varieties as the roots don't go down so far and are more likely to produce a better yield.

Where the soil is poor, and if you're growing crops like beetroots, parsnips or carrots, take a tip from exhibition

growers. They use oil drums filled with sand and sieved soil to ensure long, clean roots. Try making deep holes with a metal pole or crowbar and filling these with compost or a mixture of compost and fine soil. Then sow a few seeds on top of each filled hole and cover them with more sieved soil.

Growing

To get the best results, you will probably have to water root crops regularly during extended dry periods. Irregular watering – when the soil goes from

bone dry to soaking wet – can lead to cracked roots and reduced flavour and succulence. The organic matter should help even out fluctuations.

Raising from seed

None of the seed-raised root crops like to be transplanted or disturbed once growing, so it is usually better to sow seed thinly to do away with thinning out. Alternatively, sow a couple of seeds at 'stations' – at the recommended final spacing – and then carefully remove the weakest seedlings to leave just one.

1) *Thinly sprinkle root crop seeds in rows (drills) made in well-prepared soil.*
2) *For an earlier crop, seeds can be sown under cover in cell or module trays.*
3) *Seed potatoes can be planted in containers – even heavy-duty plastic sacks.*
4) *Traditionally, seed potatoes are planted 'eyes up' in shallow trenches.*
5) *Potatoes should be earthed up early in their growth – mounding soil over the developing stems.*

after hardening off for 10-14 days, gradually acclimatising them to the outdoor conditions.

Even at more favourable times of the year, starting seeds indoors in cell trays - sowing two or three seeds per cell and then carefully thinning out to the strongest seedling - can give better results than direct sowing outdoors. This is especially true on allotment sites that are in exposed areas or where slugs and other pests, such as flea beetle, are a problem.

Crops to grow

The commonest root crops grown on allotments are potatoes, carrots, beetroots, turnips, swedes, and radishes. But Jerusalem artichokes are gaining in popularity, and you may also consider growing Florence fennel and kohlrabi.

Florence fennel is grown for its swollen, bulb-like base, which has a distinctive taste of aniseed; the feathery foliage can be used as a substitute for fennel herb. It is not an easy crop to grow, needing a warm summer to do well and running to seed quickly if there is a check in growth. It should be sown in mid-spring and plants thinned to 30cm (1ft) apart in rows 45cm (18in) apart. Water when dry and earth up the bulbs during the growing period.

Kohlrabi produces an edible stem base. It too needs a warm summer, and will succeed in conditions that turnips often fail in. Sow seed thinly between early spring and midsummer and thin out the seedlings to 15cm (6in) apart.

If you've sown too thickly in rows, make sure that you thin out the young seedlings at the earliest opportunity. If the seedlings are too cramped for too long, it can severely affect their growth and prevent them from producing good-sized roots.

When sowing seeds in rows (drills) in dry soil in summer, water the bottom of the drill thoroughly before sowing the seeds, then cover with dry soil. Making the drill slightly deeper and lining it with moist compost before sowing will give even better results.

Early sowing when soil and weather conditions are not at their best not only leads to poorly developed crops, it can also cause the young plants to bolt. To avoid this, delay sowing until conditions improve: these later sowings will usually overtake earlier ones made in poor conditions anyway. Alternatively, warm the soil for a couple of weeks before sowing by covering it with polythene sheets or cloches and grow on your seedlings under cloches or fleece. You can also sow indoors in cell trays or modules and plant out young seedlings

Potatoes

Potatoes come in a wide range of sizes, shapes, and colours, but there are three main types – first earlies, second earlies, and maincrops – which are named for when they are planted and harvested.

The earlies are planted and harvested first and include thin-skinned 'new' potatoes, but can be stored if needed. Maincrops are the long-term storing potatoes; in the right conditions, they can be kept for several months over winter. Grow a selection of all three for the longest cropping period.

Very early potatoes can be obtained by warming the soil under plastic sheeting for two to three weeks before planting, and then planting first earlies from late winter, growing them on under fleece. Or, better still, try growing them in containers under glass. You can even plant specially prepared potatoes in summer for a winter crop.

Potatoes need a sunny site away from frost pockets as newly emerging foliage is susceptible to frost damage. Prevent this by earthing up the soil around the shoots or covering them with fleece.

Grown well, potatoes will produce a bumper crop and can be stored for future use.

Add plenty of well-rotted organic matter in the autumn or winter before planting. You can just line the trench with the material before planting or use grass clippings.

Heavy, clay soils that are well prepared tend to give the best crops. Light, free-draining soils may produce a small crop unless plenty of organic matter is added. Scab disease can often be worse in these soils too. Always aim to rotate potato crops, leaving a gap of three years before growing again in the same area, otherwise soil pests and diseases can build up.

It's important to keep light away from the developing new tubers. Light turns them green, and green potatoes are poisonous. Growing under black polythene or earthing up the rows as the plants develop are two methods of preventing this problem.

Planting

Choose certified 'seed' potatoes; these have been produced specifically for the job and are guaranteed virus free.

Seed tubers should be planted in early spring for first earlies, early to mid-spring for second earlies, and mid-spring for maincrops.

If you want to 'chit' or sprout your seed potatoes, buy them in late winter and stand them in a light, cool but frost-free place. Place them with the rose end, the end with the most eyes, facing up; egg boxes are perfect to keep them in position. The tubers are ready to plant when the short green shoots are about 2.5cm (1in) long. Make sure you give them plenty of light, otherwise the shoots will be tall and thin, and plant them carefully so as not to damage the shoots.

Growing

There are numerous ways of growing potatoes. Whichever you choose, add a general balanced fertiliser to the soil and rake in just before planting.

The traditional way is to dig a narrow trench 13–15cm (5–6in) deep. The seed tubers are spaced 30cm (12in) apart for earlies and 38cm (15in) for maincrop varieties in rows 24in (60cm) apart for earlies and 75cm (30in) apart for maincrops. Sprinkle slug pellets or other slug deterrents between the tubers, as keel slugs can be a problem. When the shoots are about 23cm (9in) high, start earthing up by drawing soil up to the stems and covering to produce a flat-topped ridge about 15cm (6in) high. This can be done little and often or in one go.

The other method is to grow under black polythene, planting the tubers through slits in the sheet. With this method there is no need to earth up, and the potatoes form just below soil level, so there's no digging at harvest.

You can also grow potatoes in large containers, or even compost bags, that are at least 30cm (12in) deep. Fill the

bottom 15cm (6in) of the container with potting or good garden compost and plant the seed tuber just below this. As the new stems start growing, keep adding compost until the container is full. Plenty of people are experimenting with this method, and some recommend filling the container completely and then planting the tubers 15cm (6in) deep.

Keep crops well watered in dry weather; the vital times are early in the growth cycle and once tubers start to form. A liquid feed of a general fertiliser every fortnight can help increase yields.

Harvesting

The approximate time between planting and harvesting is 13 weeks for earlies and 22 weeks for maincrops. This means first earlies should be ready in early to midsummer, second earlies in mid- to late summer and maincrops from late summer to mid-autumn. The longer

Carefully lift potatoes with a garden fork, taking care not to spear or damage them.

they are in the ground, the greater the risk of slug damage.

With earlies, wait until the flowers open or the buds drop; carefully scrape away a little soil to check they are big enough. With maincrops for storage, wait until the foliage turns yellow, then cut it down and leave for ten days before harvesting.

Carefully dig up the plants with a garden fork to avoid damaging the tubers. Leave maincrops to dry on the ground for a few hours before storing.

Yield: **Earlies:** 5.5kg from a 3m row (12lb from a 10ft row).
Maincrop: 9kg from a 3m row (20lb from a 10ft row).

'Pink Fir Apple' is a superb maincrop variety and is delicious hot or cold.

Carrots

Carrots can be grouped by cropping periods, with early and maincrop varieties, but there are also two main shapes: long-rooted and stump-rooted or round. Round carrots are best where the soil is stony, shallow, or heavy clay. If this is your soil but you still want long-rooted varieties, grow them in deep containers of potting compost or a mix of good soil and garden compost.

Sowing

Sow 1.5cm (0.5in) deep in rows 15cm (6in) apart. Sow thinly to avoid the need to thin out later, or thin to 5-7.5cm (2-3in) apart when the seedlings are large enough to handle. You can use the thinnings as baby carrots.

A minimum soil temperature of 7°C (45°F) is needed for germination. Early varieties can be sown in late winter or early spring in soil that is pre-warmed, but the main sowing season is from late spring to midsummer. For a regular supply of young roots, sow every three to four weeks.

Growing

Keep the soil evenly moist to prevent the roots splitting. Weed rigorously, as weeds can easily swamp carrots.

Carrot root fly is the major pest that attacks carrot. The females lay eggs in the soil and the developing maggots burrow into the roots. Affected carrots start to rot and cannot be stored.

There are several ways of combating carrot root fly. The most effective is to cover the soil and plants with fleece, which acts as a barrier to prevent the female from getting at her goal. Bury the edges of the fleece in the soil to ensure that there are no access points.

The females are attracted to the carrots by their smell; limit this by disturbing the crop as little as possible, because bruising the foliage or roots releases the smell that attracts carrot root fly. Sow thinly to avoid thinning, or be careful when thinning out, and when

Covering carrot crops with fleece will protect them from attack by carrot root fly.

weeding. Interplanting rows of carrots with onions or similar strongly scented crops may also help to confuse the female carrot flies.

Grow varieties that are less attractive to the flies, such as 'Flyaway'. Sow maincrop varieties in early summer to avoid the main egg-laying period in late spring; there may be a second laying season in autumn.

Harvesting

The approximate time between sowing and harvesting is 10-12 weeks for early varieties and up to 16 weeks for maincrop varieties.

Harvest carrots as soon as they are large enough to use; if you aim to grow the largest roots, you will sacrifice flavour and also increase the risk of carrot fly damage.

Young and stump-rooted carrots may be pulled carefully by hand, whereas larger ones intended for storage should be lifted carefully using a fork.

Yield: Long carrots (less from stump-rooted types) **Earlies:** 3.5kg from a 3m row (8lb from a 10ft row).
Maincrop: 4.5kg from a 3m row (10lb from a 10ft row).

Pulling carrots when they're young will ensure they are at their best and full of flavour.

Beetroots

Once regarded as something to pickle and eat with a salad, beetroots are more popular than ever and are delicious eaten raw and used in soups and stews. Baking them whole helps to keep their unique, earthy flavour.

The seed of beetroot, called a cluster, is actually the dried seedhead, which may contain as many as four true seeds. Monogerm varieties are bred to produce just one seed per cluster.

There are varieties suitable for sowing early in the year and others that are best suited to late spring sowing. Most beetroots produce round or globe-shaped roots, but there are some that produce long, cylindrical roots, as well as stump-rooted types. The latter are best for heavy soils. As well as the familiar purple-red beetroot, there are yellow- and white-rooted types.

Sowing

Sow two seeds at 10cm (4in) intervals or 'stations', 2.5cm (1in) deep in rows 30cm (12in) apart. When the seedlings are about 2.5cm (1in) high, thin out to leave one seedling per station.

Beetroot seeds need a minimum soil temperature of 7°C (45°F) to germinate.

Carefully lift beetroot with a hand fork to ensure you don't damage or bruise the skin.

Lift beetroot before they get too big as they can become woody and lose their flavour.

Early varieties can be sown in early spring in soil that has been pre-warmed under cloches or similar protection. Or, better still, sow in cell or module trays indoors and plant out the young seedlings when they are large enough, after hardening off for 10–14 days first.

Sow at fortnightly intervals from mid-spring to midsummer for a succession of tender, tasty roots; those sown from early summer onwards can be used for storing in winter.

Growing

Dry soils lead to woody roots, whereas a fluctuating water supply causes splitting, so make sure the soil is kept evenly moist by watering every 10–14 days during dry spells. Help to preserve soil moisture by adding a mulch.

Harvesting

The approximate time between sowing and harvesting beetroot is 10–15 weeks, depending on the variety.

Harvest the roots when they're young and tender. Early spring sowings should be ready to lift in early to midsummer, later sowings through the summer until mid-autumn.

Pull up alternate plants once they are golf ball size for a tasty treat, then harvest the others when they reach maturity (no more than cricket ball size).

Yield: Globes: 4.5kg from a 3m row (10lb from a 10ft row).
Long varieties: 7kg from a 3m row (16lb from a 10ft row).

Opposite Beetroot is available in a number of different shapes and sizes, but they all taste excellent, whether they're boiled, steamed or roasted and eaten hot or cold.

AT A GLANCE

Beetroot is a fairly easy crop to grow well. The roots are best picked when young and tender and cooked fresh; when young they can even be eaten raw. Pickling is another option. If roots are stored in winter, you can have beetroot almost all year round. The young leaves can also be used raw in salads.

ALLOTMENT ADVICE:
what I wish I'd known

Young beet plants are sensitive to cold weather, and early sowings outdoors can run to seed prematurely if the temperature is too cold or they receive any other check in growth. Bolt-resistant varieties, such as 'Bikores' and 'Boltardy', should be your first choice for early sowing.

TRIED AND TESTED
RHS VARIETIES

Globes: 'Bikores' (AGM), 'Boltardy' (AGM), 'Bonel' (AGM), 'Burpees Golden', 'Detroit 2 Crimson Globe', 'Kestrel', 'Pablo' (AGM), 'Pronto' (AGM), 'Red Ace' (AGM), 'Solo' (AGM), 'Wodan' (AGM)
Long varieties: 'Cylindra', 'Cheltenham Green Top' (AGM), 'Forono' (AGM).

Parsnips

Parsnips like a well-prepared, moisture-retentive soil, but dislike those that are too heavy, cold, and wet in early spring and winter. Their seed is notoriously slow to germinate. Early sowings in poor conditions are less likely to germinate and are also more prone to parsnip canker disease.

Sowing

Sow three seeds 1.5cm (0.5in) deep at 15cm (6in) intervals or stations, in rows 30cm (12in) apart.

Although seed only needs a minimum soil temperature of 2°C (36°F) to germinate and sowing in late winter is sometimes recommended, this can lead to failure. Sowings made in early to mid-spring and even late spring will do much better. You can also warm the soil before sowing with cloches or similar; leave in place until the seedlings have developed two true leaves. Parsnip seed won't germinate when the soil temperature is above 17°C (63°F).

Because germination is slow, intersow radish as row markers to help mark out the rows of parsnips. When the parsnip seedlings are about 2.5cm (1in) high, thin out to leave the strongest seedling at each 15cm (6in) station.

Ensure that parsnips grow well without a check to their growth – keep weeds down wherever possible.

Growing

Keep the soil evenly moist to avoid splitting and tough roots. Water every 10–14 days if necessary during dry spells and to aid germination of later sowings.

Harvesting

The approximate time between sowing and harvesting is 32-35 weeks.

The roots are ready to lift when the foliage starts to die down in autumn; use a fork to carefully lift them. Lightly frosted roots tend to produce the best

Parsnips can be left in the ground until you're ready to use them in the kitchen.

flavour, and they can be left in the soil and lifted as required, but they may be vulnerable to attack by carrot root fly (*see* page 60). Lifting a few extra in early winter will ensure that you still have parsnips to eat even if the soil is frozen hard.

Yield: 3.5kg from a 3m row (8lb from a 10ft row).

AT A GLANCE

Although fairly disappointing when boiled, roasted or baked parsnips are a joy to eat - and parsnips are gorgeous in stews.

They are easy to grow, once the seed has germinated, need little maintenance, and can be left in the soil until ready to use.

ALLOTMENT ADVICE:
what I wish I'd known

If your soil is heavy or particularly stony, try growing 'Avonresister', which tolerates poor soils and produces shorter roots. Or, make a deep hole with a metal pole or crowbar and fill this with compost or a mixture of compost and fine soil.

TRIED AND TESTED
RHS VARIETIES

'Albion', 'Avonresistor', 'Countess' (AGM), 'Gladiator' (AGM), 'Javelin' (AGM), 'Tender and True' (AGM), 'White Gem', 'White Spear' (AGM)

Swedes

Swedes are brassicas (*see* pages 116–23) and so are normally grown alongside other members of the cabbage family as they have similar requirements. As brassicas, they are prone to clubroot, so prefer an alkaline soil; check the pH and if your soil is acidic add a dressing of lime before sowing.

The soil should be moisture retentive, but should not become waterlogged or the roots will rot over winter. Make sure the soil contains plenty of organic matter, preferably added for a previous crop or in the autumn. Add a light dressing of a general fertiliser containing trace elements a couple of weeks before sowing.

Sowing

Sow seeds 1.5cm (0.5in) deep in rows 38–45cm (15–18in) apart from early spring until early summer. Earlier sowings will provide a late summer harvest and are better suited to cold regions; later sowings are better in warmer regions.

Thin out the seedlings in stages when large enough to handle, leaving plants 23cm (9in) apart.

Growing

Weed regularly to minimise competition for water and nutrients. Water weekly

Rather than pulling swedes when ready, carefully lift them with a trowel or hand fork.

A well-grown swede is something to be proud of. Weed regularly to reduce water competition.

during dry periods, and try to keep the soil evenly moist to prevent cracking and corky growth. Dryness at the roots can also lead to a bitter taste.

Cabbage root fly (*see* page 117) and flea beetles can affect swedes; covering the plants with fleece or fine-mesh netting will help keep these pests at bay.

Harvesting

The approximate time between sowing and harvesting is 21–25 weeks.

Start lifting the roots once they are large enough to use; this may be as early as late summer. The roots can be left to grow, often reaching a good size, about 10–15cm (4–6in) across.

Swedes are hardy and can be kept in the ground over winter if the soil is well drained and not waterlogged. Some varieties do become woody, however, when left beyond early winter.

Yield: 11–13.5kg from a 3m row (24–30lb from a 10ft row).

AT A GLANCE

Swedes are generally an easy crop to grow, maturing over the winter months. The green- or purple-skinned roots have a yellow flesh that tastes mild and sweet. Mashed swede with butter and black pepper is a simple dish – but absolutely delicious. The name is a contraction of Swedish turnips, and swedes are still sometimes known as turnips or 'neeps' in Scotland, and called 'rutabaga' in North America.

ALLOTMENT ADVICE:
what I wish I'd known

If you have had problems with clubroot in the past, grow clubroot-resistant varieties, such as 'Marian'; this variety is also resistant to mildew.

TRIED AND TESTED RHS VARIETIES

'Angela', 'Brora' (AGM), 'Invitation', 'Magres' (AGM), 'Marian', 'Ruby' (AGM)

Turnips

Turnips tend to do best in cool climates or certainly in cooler summers. They prefer soils that are not overly rich and hold plenty of moisture, otherwise they can become tough and fibrous.

They are best sown little and often to have a continuous supply of roots. Early and maincrop varieties are available.

Sowing

Sow seeds 1.5cm (0.5in) deep. Early turnip varieties 'Atlantic' or 'Milan Purple Top' can be sown under cloches in late winter and other varieties from early spring to early summer, in rows 23cm (9in) apart. Sow maincrop turnips from mid- to late summer in rows 30cm (12in) apart. To harvest turnip tops as spring greens, sow in late summer or early autumn in rows 7.5cm (3in) apart.

Thin out turnips grown for their roots in stages until they are eventually

Thin out young plants to achieve the required spacing; use the thinnings for turnip tops.

10-15cm (4-6in) apart for early crops, or 20-23cm (8-9in) apart for maincrops.

Growing

Protect early sowings with fleece if frost is forecast. Hot, dry weather inhibits seed germination; later sowings are also best covered with fleece to keep them cool.

Water weekly during dry weather or the roots will be small and woody. Keep the soil evenly moist or the roots will split.

Harvesting

The approximate time between sowing and harvesting is 6-12 weeks.

Pull early turnips from late spring to early autumn when the size of a golf ball for eating raw or the size of a tennis ball for cooking. Lift maincrop turnips from mid-autumn onwards when the size of a golf ball. Turnips are not winter hardy, so need lifting before cold weather.

Cut turnip tops in mid- to late spring. Leave the plants to re-sprout, as several cuts can be obtained.

Yield: Earlies: 3kg from a 3m row (7lb from a 10ft row); **Maincrop:** 5.5kg from a 3m row (12lb from a 10ft row).

Harvesting turnips when they're young ensures they have the best texture and flavour.

AT A GLANCE

Turnips are a very versatile vegetable - they can be harvested when mature or younger, and cooked or eaten raw. The young tops have a peppery taste and can be added to salads or steamed and used like spring greens. Plants are quick to mature and easy to grow.

ALLOTMENT ADVICE: what I wish I'd known

Flea beetle can be a problem, and will certainly make turnip tops inedible, so cover with fleece or fine-mesh netting if this pest troubles you.

TRIED AND TESTED RHS VARIETIES

'Atlantic' (AGM), 'Golden Ball', 'Market Express' (AGM), 'Milan Purple Top', 'Snowball', 'Tokyo Cross' (AGM)

Jerusalem artichokes

Jerusalem artichokes grow in even the poorest of soil, and even in shade. Some allotment holders grow them in the same position permanently, leaving the tubers in the ground from year to year, lifting them as and when they are needed. They are a useful crop on a new plot, as the roots will help break up the soil.

Planting

Plant small tubers in early to mid-spring in well-dug, well-fertilised soil. Plant in rows 15cm (6in) deep and 45–60cm (18–24in) apart with rows 90cm (36in) apart. Large tubers can be cut into sections, providing each one has two or three buds.

Tubers can also be grown in large tubs filled with good garden soil or compost, or a mix of both.

Growing

There is no need to feed the plants; they need very little care and attention during the growing season and are rarely troubled by pests and diseases.

Lift the tubers in autumn and winter; save the small ones for replanting in spring.

Jerusalem artichokes grow into tall plants that can even be used as a windbreak on exposed sites.

Weeding should not be necessary either, as they make a dense canopy of foliage.

On exposed sites, pile up earth around the stems once they reach 30cm (12in) high, to make the plants more stable.

Since Jerusalem artichokes grow tall (up to 3m/10ft) they can be used as an effective screen, but may need some support on exposed and windy sites.

Harvesting

The approximate time between planting and harvesting is 40–50 weeks.

Harvest as needed from early to late winter, lifting in the same way as potatoes (*see* page 59). The tubers will survive all but the harshest winters in the ground, although slugs, snails, and waterlogging can be a problem; either mulch to protect from cold or lift and store them if necessary.

To use in the kitchen, scrub and then boil or steam until tender, then peel.

Yield: 1.5–2.5kg (3–5lb) per plant.

AT A GLANCE

The knobbly roots of Jerusalem artichokes are a great winter treat – although they are an acquired taste for some people, and some cannot digest their carbohydrate well. Plants are easy to grow, producing huge yields even in poor soils. The roots store well, providing a valuable food source throughout winter. Try them roasted, fried into chips, or in a soup. Jerusalem artichokes are unrelated to globe artichokes; let the plants flower, and it becomes obvious how close they are to sunflowers.

ALLOTMENT ADVICE:
what I wish I'd known

If you would rather not cope with cleaning and peeling knobbly roots, grow 'Fuseau' - this is a larger, smooth-skinned variety that is easy to peel.

TRIED AND TESTED RHS VARIETIES

Common, 'Fuseau', 'Gerrard'

Radishes

The most familiar radish is the red summer radish, which is either round or cylindrical and should be picked when it is small. Because summer radishes are quick to mature they can be used as a 'catch crop', sown between rows of slower-growing vegetables, such as peas and parsnips, and lifted before these other crops need the space.

They can even be used as row markers of slow-germinating crops, such as parsnips and onions. Sown with the main crop seed, the radishes germinate quickly, marking out the row where the other crop has been sown, and can be pulled before they compete.

Sow the seed thinly into shallow drills made in well-prepared, stone-free soil.

There are also winter and Oriental (mooli) radishes, larger and in various colours, that can be used raw or cooked.

For something different, try 'München Bier', a variety grown for its 7.5cm (3in) green, stringless seed pods. With a spicy flavour, these are ideal for stir-fry or in salads. The white root can also be used from late summer into autumn.

Sowing

Sow thinly 1.5cm (0.5in) deep in rows 15cm (6in) apart for summer types or 23-25cm (9-10in) apart for winter ones.

Summer varieties are sown from early spring to late summer; for an early crop sow in late winter in pre-warmed soil and protect with cloches. Winter and Oriental varieties are sown from early to late summer.

By sowing seed thinly (approximately 2.5cm/1in apart), you should avoid the need to thin summer varieties, but any thinning that is needed should be done as soon as possible. Winter varieties should be thinned to 10-25 (4-10in) apart, depending on the variety.

Growing

Keep the soil moist to ensure rapid growth, and to keep the roots fleshy and tasty, and prevent splitting. Sowings made in mid- to late summer can be a problem due to the hotter, drier conditions, so make sure these are well looked after and even protect them by covering the rows with fleece.

Thin out radish seedlings as soon as they're large enough to handle for the best crops.

Harvesting

The approximate time between sowing and harvesting is three to six weeks for the summer varieties and up to 12 weeks for winter varieties. Pull summer radishes as required, but don't let them mature and become woody. Winter varieties can be left in the ground and dug up as required, or lifted in early winter and stored; frost improves the flavour.

Yield: **Summer varieties:** 1.5-2kg from a 3m row (3-4lb from a 10ft row). **Winter varieties:** 4.5kg from a 3m row (10lb from a 10ft row).

Opposite *A couple of short rows of radishes can produce a bumper crop; sow regularly to extend the cropping period.*

AT A GLANCE

The humble summer radish is either loved or loathed. When grown well, it is juicy with a lovely spicy flavour. When grown badly, it is dry and pithy. Fast-growing and taking up little room, they are always worth including on the plot for their red, pink, or white roots. Whether they are round, cylindrical or pointed, they all add crunch and bite to summer salads.

ALLOTMENT ADVICE:
what I wish I'd known

Summer radishes need to be grown steadily, without a check in growth, and harvested young to ensure that they remain succulent, otherwise they can become woody and inedible. They grow quickly, so keep an eye on them to avoid this, and sow every couple of weeks.

TRIED AND TESTED
RHS VARIETIES

Summer: 'Amethyst', 'April Cross' (mooli), 'Cherry Belle' (AGM), 'Flamboyant Sabina' (AGM), 'French Breakfast', 'Mirabeau' (AGM), 'Rudi' (AGM), 'Scarlet Globe' (AGM), 'Short Top Forcing' (AGM), 'Sparkler' (AGM) **Oriental:** 'Mantanghong', 'Minowase' **Winter:** 'Black Spanish Round', 'China Rose'

Vegetable fruits

Basic techniques

Vegetable fruits are all cold and frost sensitive: even one night of cold temperatures when they are young or establishing outside can severely set them back or even kill them.

They can be grown outdoors, but aubergines, peppers, and some varieties of cucumbers and tomatoes will crop much better when grown to maturity in a greenhouse, polytunnel, or frame. Some allotment holders construct individual full-height 'cloches' around each plant from bamboo canes and clear polythene, in order to protect them from cold and frost.

Raising from seed

Some of these crops can be sown directly outside in mid- to late spring (sweetcorn and courgettes being good examples), but most will perform much better if sown indoors in small pots with heat. This ensures a reliable supply of plants, reduces the effects of cold weather, and ensures plants get off to a flying start in spring and continue strong into summer which is essential for some to crop well.

Because of their cold sensitivity, sowing and planting-out times need to be adjusted to your local conditions. Although you don't want to plant them out too early, leaving them to get overgrown in their small pots indoors can also affect their growth and reduce their yields. Try to work backwards from your proposed planting-out time to calculate the optimum sowing time.

Thorough hardening off before planting outside is essential to prevent the plants suffering a check to their growth. Gradually acclimatise them to the cooler outdoor temperatures over 10–14 days. The process has several stages. Start by putting them out in a warm, sheltered spot during the day covered with fleece and bringing them in at night. Then put them out without fleece during the day, then start to leave them out overnight with fleece, until

finally they can tolerate being outside permanently without protection.

Garden centres stock young plants from a wide range of fruiting crops in spring, and these are a good bet where you can't raise them from seed yourself. Make sure you check over the plants carefully and choose those that are vigorous and healthy, with good colour in their leaves. These plants will have been given warmth and protection, so will need some hardening off before planting outside after the fear of frosts has passed.

Growing outdoors

Most allotment holders will have to grow at least some of these crops outdoors. All will need a warm, sunny, protected position. The soil should be fertile and well drained but able to hold adequate moisture, as they need a steady water supply. Paying careful attention to soil preparation, and even growing in planting 'pockets', will ensure bigger crops and healthier plants.

Covering the soil with black polythene before planting will warm it up and keep it warm. Do anything you can to protect

1) *For an earlier crop or in exposed areas, sow sweetcorn in cell or module trays indoors and plant out when the young plants have established.*

2) *Protect young plants outside with cloches but check often for signs of overheating and damage caused by slugs.*

3) *Give young plants a thorough watering after planting them out.*

4) *Peppers need to be tied in at regular intervals to bamboo canes or other supports using soft string.*

5) *Courgette plants produce a profusion of fruits in summer – always pick them when they are young and tender.*

6) *Pinching out the tips of trailing squashes will produce sideshoots and so increase the number of fruits produced.*

7) *When sweetcorn is ready to harvest, carefully pull the ripened cobs away from the main stem.*

8) *The fruits of marrows and squashes should be kept off the damp soil on a dry surface such as a tile or a piece of wood, to prevent them from rotting.*

crops. Two to three weeks before sowing outside or planting out young plants, dig holes 30cm (12in) square and deep and fill with a mixture of compost or well-rotted manure and soil. Leave a low mound at the top of the planting medium and sprinkle a general fertiliser over the soil.

Feeding & watering

To ensure that fruits reach their full size and potential, regular watering is vital. Any check in growth can reduce overall yield and quality and cause the skins to harden. When the next watering occurs after the check, the sudden uptake of water causes the fruits to swell and the dry skin may crack.

It is essential that plants also have plenty of potash – sunshine in a bottle – which promotes good flower production, flower set and fruiting. While in growth, water plants every seven to ten days with a high potash liquid fertiliser, such as a tomato feed at the recommended strength, or use a half strength diluted feed twice a week for fast-growing crops such as tomatoes.

the young plants while they're getting established outside – including covering them with cloches, glass jars or even cut-down lemonade bottles.

Nearly all these crops (apart from the mammoth pumpkins, squashes and marrows) can be planted and grown in containers; these can either be growing bags or 23–25cm (9–10in) pots filled with good potting compost. When using the former, take extra care over feeding and watering, because the small volume of compost they contain quickly dries out, leading to poor crops, disease and

cultural problems, such as blossom end rot on tomatoes (*see* page 75). Put growing rings or large bottomless pots on top of the bag and fill with compost to increase the growing volume and give better results.

Planting pockets

Crops that produce large fruits (such as pumpkins, squashes, marrows, cucumbers and courgettes) will give better results if they are grown in planting pockets. These will hold lots of moisture and ensure large, regular

Tomatoes

Cherry tomatoes will produce a bumper crop of small, bite-sized fruit over several weeks.

There are numerous tomato varieties – just over 500 are listed – including all sorts of colours and types. They range from the small-fruited cherry types through plum tomatoes to the monster beefsteaks; from the standard red to yellow, orange, green, purple, and striped; from the tall cordon varieties to bush and even hanging-basket types. In fact, the choice can be overwhelming when deciding which ones to grow each year. The large seed companies stock a wide range of varieties, but because tomato growing is so popular, there are now several smaller companies offering an even wider range of older or heritage or heirloom varieties too.

On the allotment, unless you have a greenhouse or polytunnel, you'll be restricted to growing outdoor varieties. But if you do have the warmth these structures provide, then your choice will be even wider. Beefsteak tomatoes, for instance, are only reliable if grown indoors. You'll also benefit from earlier, longer, and bigger harvests.

Pot up young plants into small pots once two true leaves have fully formed.

Standard tall varieties (sometimes referred to as indeterminate) are grown as cordons and need to have their sideshoots removed and be tied to a support. The shorter bush varieties (also called determinate) are allowed to get on with it and need little or no support.

F1 varieties produce the most reliable crops, and many have been bred to be resistant to a range of diseases. An increasing range of grafted tomatoes, with one variety grafted on to another rootstock, is also available. These have been shown to be even more reliable, especially in an indifferent summer, and resistant to a number of diseases.

Blight

A range of pests and diseases can attack tomatoes, but there is one that all tomato growers fear: blight. This turns first the leaves, then the stems and fruit brown, and renders the fruit mushy and inedible. Ultimately, the plants die. Early control is essential: remove affected parts and spray with a copper or mancozeb fungicide. Blight needs specific conditions of warmth and humidity in summer to strike: these can be anticipated and blight alerts are given on farming radio programmes and the internet.

Sowing

Sow at 18°C (64°F) in either seed trays or small pots. Transplant individually

Remove the sideshoots from cordon-grown tomato plants as soon as they're large enough to handle.

into 7–9cm (3–3½in) pots when two true leaves have formed. Grow on the young plants at a minimum of 10°C (50°F).

For greenhouse cultivation, this means you can sow from mid- to late winter to grow on in a heated greenhouse, or from late winter to early spring for an unheated greenhouse.

For outdoor cultivation, sow in early to mid-spring, or eight weeks before the last frosts are expected locally. Harden plants off for 10–14 days before planting outside, after the last heavy frost is thought to have passed.

Growing

Choose your warmest, sunniest position for outdoor tomatoes. Tomatoes are not frost hardy, so don't plant outside until all fear of frosts has passed. Even if they survive a frost, you could be better off starting again with new plants.

Plant in growing bags or 23cm (9in) pots, or plant 45–60cm (18–24in) apart when the flowers of the first truss are beginning to open.

Although growing bags are a favourite choice for tomatoes, the plants in them need a lot more care than those growing in pots or in the ground. There is so little compost in the bags that it soon dries out and the plants suffer as a result. Regular watering, even two or three times a day, is essential to keep the compost moist.

Outside, ensure the soil has been enriched with plenty of well-rotted organic matter and add a general fertiliser just before planting out.

Upright cordon varieties will need supporting. The commonest method is to tie the main stem to a sturdy vertical 1.8m (6ft) bamboo cane with 30cm (1ft) inserted into the ground. Remove the sideshoots from leaf axils regularly once they are about 2.5cm (1in) long.

Water all tomatoes regularly to keep the soil or compost evenly moist. Feed every 10–14 days with a balanced liquid fertiliser, changing to a high-potash feed and more frequent application once the

Beefsteak tomatoes produce irregularly shaped fruit, but they have a fantastic flavour.

first fruits start to set. Remove the growing point of the main stem at two leaves above the top truss once outdoor cordon-grown plants have set four trusses. Do the same to indoor tomatoes when they have seven trusses or once they reach the top of the greenhouse or polytunnel. This will stop further fruiting and allow those that have set to ripen.

Always aim to keep plants evenly moist to avoid fruits cracking. Irregular watering together with a lack of calcium in the soil also leads to blossom end rot, which causes the bottom of the fruit to turn black and become sunken.

Harvesting

The approximate time between sowing and harvesting is 16–20 weeks. Start picking as soon as the fruits are ripe and fully coloured. Don't leave mature fruits on the plant to soften and split. At the end of the season lift plants with unripe fruit and lay them on straw under cloches or hang them in a cool

Tomatoes come in a wide range of shapes, sizes and colours. Try to grow a good selection.

shed to ripen. Alternatively, pick the green fruits and store them with a ripe apple or banana.

Yield: Up to 4.5kg (10lb) per plant.

AT A GLANCE

Tomatoes are among our most popular vegetables, and that's not surprising since their taste fresh from the vine is unbeatable. With good conditions and a bit of care you can be picking tomatoes for several weeks into autumn. Even green, unripened tomatoes at the end of the year are worth picking for green tomato chutney or the American classic, fried green tomatoes.

ALLOTMENT ADVICE:
what I wish I'd known

Flavour is an important factor when choosing varieties, and most gardeners have favourites. But bear in mind that how you grow also has a major influence on flavour. Keep the soil or compost evenly moist throughout the growing period and feed regularly with a high-potash fertiliser

to enhance the flavour. Good warmth and sunshine are also needed.

TRIED AND TESTED
RHS VARIETIES

Standard: 'Ailsa Craig', 'Alicante' (AGM), 'Ferline', 'Moneymaker', 'Outdoor Girl' (AGM), 'Shirley' (AGM)
Beefsteak: 'Beefsteak' (AGM), 'Costoluto Fiorentino' (AGM), 'Marmande' (AGM)
Cherry: 'Gardener's Delight' (AGM), 'Golden Sweet' (AGM), 'Sakura' (AGM), 'Sun Baby' (AGM), 'Suncherry Premium' (AGM), 'Sungold' (AGM), 'Sunset' (AGM)
Plum: 'Floridity' (AGM), 'Ildi' (AGM), 'Olivade' F1 (AGM), 'Roma', 'Summer Sweet' (AGM), 'Sweet Olive' (AGM)
Bush: 'Red Alert', 'Tornado' (AGM), 'Totem'
Hanging basket: 'Tumbler', 'Tumbling Tom Red', 'Tumbling Tom Yellow'

Cucumbers

Under glass, cucumber crops are more reliable, and the plants start producing earlier and for longer. But outdoor or 'ridge' cucumbers have a better taste.

Sowing

Cucumbers are usually sown indoors in small pots at 24-27°C (75-80°F). After germination and when growing on, maintain a temperature of 18-21°C (65-70°F). Be careful not to overwater and when the first true leaves have expanded, transfer to 10cm (4in) pots. For greenhouse cultivation, sow from late winter to early spring in a heated greenhouse, or mid-spring in an unheated greenhouse. For outdoor cultivation, sow indoors in late spring.

Alternatively, you can sow outdoor varieties directly outside in late spring or early summer, in pre-warmed soil. Cover the seeds with a cloche or a glass jar after sowing.

Sow the seeds on their side, 1cm (½in) deep in pots indoors, or 2.5cm (1in) deep when sowing direct outside.

Growing

Cucumbers need plenty of warmth and sunlight, plus regular supplies of water. Transfer young plants to 25cm (10in)

Carefully tie developing plants to their supports using soft string tied in a figure-of-eight.

pots of good compost in early spring in a heated greenhouse, late spring in an unheated greenhouse, or early summer outdoors. Keep the compost evenly moist: little and often is best. Plants can also be grown in growing bags, but will need careful watering. For outdoor growing, dig planting pockets (*see* page 73) 45cm (18in) apart two weeks before sowing or planting out.

Feed plants every 10-14 days once planted out with a balanced liquid fertiliser, changing to a high-potash one when the first fruits start to set.

Indoors

Keep the humidity around the plants high by watering the floor. Train the main stem up a wire or cane. Pinch out the growing point when it reaches the roof, and the tips of sideshoots two leaves beyond a female flower. Pinch out the tips of flowerless sideshoots once they reach 60cm (2ft) long.

Outdoors

Covering the soil around the plants with black polythene will warm the soil, helping growth and improving yields. Pinch out the growing tip when the

Greenhouse cucumber plants need plenty of water to ensure they produce lots of tasty fruit.

plants have developed seven leaves. The developing sideshoots can be either left to trail over the ground or trained up stout netting. Pinch out the tips of flowerless sideshoots when they have seven leaves. Keep the soil moist by watering around the plants, not on them.

Harvesting

The approximate time between sowing and harvesting is 12-14 weeks. Cut the fruit using a sharp knife when it reaches a good size (small fruits can be bitter) with a rounded end and parallel sides.

Yield: 6-10 cucumbers per plant.

AT A GLANCE

Growing cucumbers outdoors used to be frowned on by those with greenhouses. But indoor cucumbers need a fair bit of care and attention, which makes outdoor growing much easier.

ALLOTMENT ADVICE: what I wish I'd known

Different varieties are needed for indoor or outside culture. For indoors, select F1 all-female varieties as these do not, under good growing conditions, produce male flowers. If male flowers are produced, remove them, otherwise the flowers will be pollinated and the fruit will taste bitter. Do not remove male flowers from outdoor cucumbers, as pollination is necessary for these types to fruit.

TRIED AND TESTED RHS VARIETIES

Outdoor: 'Bush Champion' (AGM), 'Marketmore' (AGM), 'Masterpiece' (AGM), 'Tokyo Slicer' (AGM)
Indoor: 'Femdan' (AGM), 'Femspot', 'Pepinex 69', 'Telegraph Improved'

Melons

There are three main groups of melons. Cantaloupes have ribbed, rough fruit and orange flesh, and are most likely to succeed in cool climates. Honeydews have firm yellow flesh and keep well, while musk have yellow- or green-netted skin and green to orange flesh, and are only worth growing under glass.

Sowing

Sow in early spring for growing on under glass, and mid-spring for outdoor crops. Sow seeds individually in a 9cm (3½in) pot and germinate at 20-25°C (68-77°F) in a propagator in good light.

After germination, keep the compost moist but not saturated. Once three or four leaves have formed, remove the plants from the propagator and grow at 18-20°C (64-68°F). Harden off plants over 10-14 days if planting outdoors.

Growing

Outdoor melons must have a warm, sunny, sheltered, and preferably humid position. They need humus-rich, well-drained, light soil that warms up quickly in spring, deeply cultivated to allow roots to grow down for moisture. They can also be grown in 30cm (12in) pots.

For best results, grow in a greenhouse or cold frame, against a very warm wall,

Melons produce separate male (left) and female (right) flowers. The female flower has a swelling underneath the petals that, once fertilised, becomes the fruit.

or under cloches, covering the soil with black plastic to increase temperatures.

In early summer, plant out in the final cropping position, spaced 60cm (2ft) apart and with the top of the rootball just below soil level. Keep plants well watered at all times and feed weekly with a high-potash feed.

Pinch out the growing tips to encourage sideshoots, which will bear the flowers. When plenty of flowers have formed, ensure there is good access for pollinating insects. Pinch out the sideshoots at one or two leaves past the pollinated flowers. Once the fruits have reached golf-ball size, thin out to leave two to four per plant on outdoor melons; greenhouse melons can ripen up to six before the end of the season.

As the fruit swells, it may need supporting in a net, as it can get quite heavy. Fruit ripening on the soil is best lifted off the ground, on a piece of wood or tile, to prevent rotting. Late varieties may need protecting with fleece during the first cool nights of autumn.

Harvesting

The approximate time between sowing and harvesting is 13-16 weeks. Ripe melons will emit a strong scent and start to soften around the stalk.

Yield: Up to 6 fruit per plant.

Fruits of climbing plants should be supported in a net to prevent damaging the plant.

Keep the fruit of trailing melon plants off the soil by placing it on a tile.

AT A GLANCE

Sweet melons are a tender annual with climbing or scrambling growth. They need plenty of warmth and sunlight to grow and fruit well. Not strictly reliable on allotments, they are one of those crops that you want to succeed with if only to be able to tell everyone else you've actually grown one.

ALLOTMENT ADVICE:
what I wish I'd known

Water the compost the day before transplanting melons into their final containers, and leave it in the sun to warm up. This helps to avoid any transplanting problems.

TRIED AND TESTED RHS VARIETIES

Cantaloupe: 'Charentais' , 'Edonis' (AGM), 'Ogen' (AGM), 'Sweetheart' (AGM)
Musk: 'Blenheim Orange', 'Early Dawn' (AGM)

Courgettes, marrows, and summer squashes

Marrows grown to a reasonable (rather than prize-winning) size are a useful crop for keeping over winter. Courgettes are best picked while still quite young, which means the plants will go on cropping for months, but if unchecked they are notorious for producing unmanageable crops. Unless the summer is miserable, two to three plants are all you will need to feed even the biggest family and have plenty left over for freezing. Summer squashes are similar to courgettes in their culinary uses, but come in a much wider range of shapes, sizes, and colours.

Courgettes are usually bushy plants, whereas marrows and summer squashes can be bushy or trailing.

Sowing

Sow two or three seeds 2.5cm (1in) deep outdoors in late spring or early summer, and cover them with cloches, jars, or plastic bottles. Leave in place for two weeks, or as long as possible, after germination. Thin the seedlings to the strongest one. For earlier crops or in cold regions, sow indoors from mid-

You'll get the best results if you sow seeds under cover in pots of good compost.

spring. Sow seeds individually and on their sides, 1cm (½in) deep in 7–9cm (3in) pots of compost. Place the pots in a propagator or other warm place at 18–21°C (64–70°F). Harden off before planting outside in late spring or early summer, after fear of frosts has passed.

Growing

These plants need a sunny position out of cold winds and a fertile, moisture-

Marrows are heavy croppers and most families will only need a couple of plants.

retentive soil. Covering the soil with black polythene will help growth and improve yields, keep down weeds, and keep the fruit off the soil.

Prepare the soil in advance by digging in plenty of well-rotted organic matter. Alternatively, one of the best ways of growing these crops is to make planting

How to cope with a glut

With some crops, a bit of careful planning and cultivar selection will help spread the harvest. There are those like lettuce, that can be successfully sown little and often. For others, such as Brussels sprouts, sow different cultivars at the same time that will then mature in turn. You could take 'baby veg' of beetroot, carrots, or Florence fennel, as well as the main crop.

Some fruit and vegetables will simply be ready when they're ready, so enjoy the asparagus in late spring and courgettes in the summer, because seasonal eating is one of the pleasures of growing your own. And if there's more than you can possibly eat? Once you've filled the freezer, try your friends (there will be plenty who don't grow their own), or local good causes, who will be happy to relieve you of a bowl of tomatoes or bag of beans. Pickles, preserves, jams, and chutneys all make a virtue of a necessity. Making them takes a little time, but it can be social and fun, which is one of the differences between gardening at home and gardening in the community setting of allotments. You could even make an event out of a bountiful harvest by having a festival at the allotments, complete with tastings.

pockets (*see* page 73). Dig these 60cm (2ft) apart for bush varieties and up to 1.2m (4ft) apart for trailers. Put one plant or two to three seeds into the top of the mound and water in thoroughly; if sowing direct, thin to the strongest seedling shortly after germination.

Pinch out the tips of the main shoots of trailing varieties when they are 60cm (2ft) long. In early spring, especially when temperatures and light levels are on the low side, the plants may only produce male flowers. This is normal and nothing to worry about – although obviously it will mean the plants start cropping later – and there's certainly nothing you can do to prevent it.

Keep the soil constantly moist by watering around the plants, but not over them. Feed every 10-14 days with a high-potash liquid fertiliser once the first fruits start to swell.

The fruits of marrows and squashes should be supported off the soil on a piece of wood, a tile or something similar. All three crops can be subject to powdery mildew disease, which produces a white covering on the leaves, especially in late summer. In mild cases this isn't a problem, but

Squashes are available in a wide range of shapes and sizes – including patty pans and turk's turbans.

when it really gets hold, plants can be damaged and produce lower yields. The disease is worse in hot, dry conditions when the plants are stressed at the roots. Keep the soil moist to prevent this, and remove badly affected leaves.

Harvesting

The approximate time between sowing and harvesting is 10-12 weeks.

For the best quality, harvest when the fruit is still quite small: courgettes at 10-13cm (4-5in) long, marrows at 25cm (10in). Picking courgettes regularly while they are small (this can mean every day) will ensure a long cropping period.

To grow marrows for overwintering, let the fruits mature on the plant and remove before the first frost strikes.

Yield: **Courgettes:** up to 20 fruits per plant; **Marrows and summer squashes:** 3-4 fruits per plant.

Harvest courgettes by carefully cutting off the young fruit with a sharp knife.

Pumpkins and winter squashes

These are big, beefy spreading plants and need a lot of room, which is great if you have soil to cover up but more of a problem if space is limited. Try growing smaller-fruiting types up solid supports like pergolas and wooden arches. You may need to support fruits individually in nets tied to the supporting structure.

Sowing

For the best results, sow seeds individually and on their sides, in mid- to late spring 1cm (½in) deep individually in 7.5cm (3in) pots of compost. Place the pots in a propagator or warm place at 18-21°C (64-70°F). Harden off before planting outside in late spring or early summer, after the risk of frosts has passed. The early start gives the longer growing season that these plants prefer. Even so, they may struggle in cooler regions. Outside, sow two or three seeds 2.5cm (1in) deep in late spring or early summer and cover with cloches, jars or plastic. Leave these in place for two weeks, or as long as possible, after germination. Thin the seedlings to leave the strongest one.

Growing

Pumpkins and winter squashes need a sunny, sheltered position and a fertile, moisture-retentive soil.

For best results, grow them in planting pockets (*see* page 73) spaced up to 1.2m (4ft) apart for trailing types. Put one plant or two or three seeds into the top of the mound and water in thoroughly; thin out to the best seedling after germination. Cover young plants with fleece if the weather turns cold.

Pinch out the tips of the main shoots of trailing varieties when they are 60cm (2ft) long or once three fruit have set. If you are trying to grow giant pumpkins, remove all but one of the fruits.

Keep the soil constantly moist by watering around the plants, not over them. Feed every 10-14 days with a high-potash liquid fertiliser once the first

Winter squashes are vigorous plants that need a lot of room to develop and grow in.

fruits start to swell. The fruits should be supported off the soil on a piece of wood, a tile or a sheet of glass to keep them clean and help ripen properly.

Pumpkins and squashes need plenty of water to crop well. The fruit can be used in numerous ways – from roasting and soups to cakes and pies!

Harvest

The approximate time between sowing and harvesting is 20-24 weeks. For overwintering, let the fruit mature on the plant and remove before the first frost strikes. Store at 27-32°C (81-90°F) for several days to 'cure' the skin before storing at about 10°C (50°F).

Yield: 3 or 4 fruit per plant.

Aubergines

Although aubergines can be grown outside, they rarely do well except in mild areas or during very good summers. For reliable, good crops, they are better grown in a greenhouse, polytunnel or growing frame.

Although deep purple is the standard colour, there are white, yellow, and greenish varieties. They are usually grown as oddities rather than for their culinary qualities. There are also types with spherical or long, thin fruits.

Sowing

Sow at 18-25°C (64-77°F) in 9-10cm (3½-4in) pots of good compost. Prick out the young plants individually into 9cm (3½in) pots when they are large enough to handle. Grow seedlings on at 16-18°C (61-64°F).

For greenhouse cultivation, sow in midwinter to raise plants for a heated greenhouse or late winter for an unheated greenhouse. For outdoor cultivation sow in early spring.

Growing

Aubergines need a very warm, sunny, sheltered position outside, but they will crop more reliably if they are grown indoors. Try providing glass or polythene protection if growing outside.

Aubergine plants can become very large and will need tying to stakes or similar supports.

The soil should be rich and well drained with plenty of humus; they can also be kept in large pots.

Transfer plants to 20-23cm (8-9in) pots of good compost in mid-spring in a heated greenhouse or late spring in an unheated one, or in very late spring and early summer if growing outdoors. In the ground, space plants 60cm (2ft) apart. Warm the soil under polythene or cloches two weeks before planting out and keep young plants covered with cloches or frames for a further two weeks. Growing through black polythene will help produce a more reliable crop and increase yields.

Stake plants with sturdy bamboo canes and tie them in as they grow. Remove the main tip or growing point when plants are 30cm (12in) high to produce bushier plants that will bear more fruit.

Water regularly and feed with a high-potash liquid fertiliser once the first fruit has set. Under cover, mist the foliage regularly with tepid water to discourage red spider mite (*see* page 217) and help flower set.

When five or six fruits have set, remove any other flowers, as plants are unlikely to be able to support any more than this. Only varieties producing very small or round fruit may be able to produce further reliable crops.

Harvesting

The crop will take 18-20 weeks from sowing to harvesting. Cut the fruits when they've reached a good size.

Yield: 4-6 aubergines per plant.

Aubergines are ready to harvest when the skin has developed a good colour and is shiny.

AT A GLANCE

Aubergines, or eggplant, are now becoming popular vegetables to grow on the allotment, thanks mainly to new varieties more suited to the British climate and the popularity of Mediterranean-style food and cooking.

ALLOTMENT ADVICE:
what I wish I'd known

Towards the end of summer/early autumn, remove any fruit that forms as it is unlikely to ripen and this will help existing, developing fruit reach maturity. Covering plants with fleece on cool evenings at this time of year can also help the fruit develop and ripen.

TRIED AND TESTED RHS VARIETIES

'Black Beauty', 'Long Purple', 'Mohican' (AGM), 'Moneymaker'

Sweetcorn

Sweetcorn is a fast-maturing, tender vegetable, so make sure it isn't hit by cold weather and late frosts in spring. Late planting will not affect the yield since it needs a relatively short growing season. In cold regions, grow a tried and tested variety, known for its tolerance of colder weather. Some varieties are grown for mini-cobs or 'baby corn' which are eaten whole. Because these are harvested before pollination, they can be grown quickly in a standard row.

Sowing

Sow seeds individually from mid- to late spring at 18–21°C (64–70°F) in deep pots, large modules, or root trainers at a depth of 2.5cm (1in) – slightly deeper for baby corn varieties to encourage extra rooting. Plants dislike root disturbance.

In mild areas you can sow seeds direct outside from late spring to early summer in soil pre-warmed for two weeks under cloches or clear plastic covers. Sow two seeds 2.5cm (1in) deep spaced 38–45cm (15–18in) apart; carefully remove the weakest seedling. Leave the cloches or plastic over the plants until the plants have grown and touch the top.

For an early crop, or in cold regions, sow seeds in small pots and grow on under cover.

Growing

Sweetcorn must be grown in a sunny position that is sheltered from strong wind. The plants are wind-pollinated, so they should be grown in blocks rather than rows. Set the plants 38–45cm (15–18in) apart. The minimum size for good pollination is a block of four by four plants; bigger blocks will give better pollination and cropping. Set mini-cob types 10–15cm (4–6in) apart in rows 20cm (8in) apart and harvest when the flowers begin to show: each plant will produce five or six cobs.

Plant out indoor-raised plants at the very end of spring or start of summer. Stake the plants if growing particularly tall cultivars or if the position is windy, and when roots appear at the base of the stem cover them over with soil to improve stability. When the male flowers (tassels) at the top of the stem open, tap them to help shake the pollen on to the female flowers (silk) below; poor pollination results in poorly filled cobs.

Water well in dry weather; this is vital while the plants are establishing and flowering and the cobs are swelling. Give liquid feed when the cobs begin to swell.

Harvesting

The approximate time between sowing and harvesting is 14–18 weeks. Test for

Sweetcorn is ready to harvest when the tassels have turned brown and start to fade.

ripeness when the tassels have turned chocolate brown. Peel back the husks at the top of a cob and squeeze a grain with your thumbnail: if the liquid that squirts out is watery then the cob is unripe, if the liquid is creamy the cob is ready. Twist the ripe cobs carefully from the stem.

Yield: 1 or 2 cobs per plant.

AT A GLANCE

Once regarded as a luxury, sweetcorn is now common on allotments, mainly due to new, more reliable varieties better suited to our climate. Supersweet and extra tender sweet varieties have also emerged, with a higher sugar content that takes longer to turn starchy, making them super-succulent.

ALLOTMENT ADVICE:
what I wish I'd known

Supersweet varieties must be grown away from other varieties, or cross-pollination will reduce the sweetness. If growing these, ask neighbouring plot-holders what they are growing and keep yours as far as possible from standard varieties.

TRIED AND TESTED
RHS VARIETIES

Standard: 'Kelvedon Glory', 'Sundance' (AGM)
Supersweet: 'Earlibird' (AGM), 'Early Extra Sweet', 'Ovation' (AGM), 'Sweet Nugget'
Extra tender sweet: 'Lark' (AGM), 'Swift' (AGM)
Baby corn: 'Mini Pop', 'Minor'

Peppers

Closely related to the chillies opposite, peppers have a tangy sweetness rather than heat, and are often called sweet peppers. All peppers pass through the green stage on their way to red, yellow, orange, or even purple.

Sowing

Sow at 18-21°C (64-70°F) in pots in a propagator or on a warm windowsill. Transplant into 7-9cm (3-3½in) pots when two true leaves have formed and grow on at 18°C (65°F).

To raise plants for greenhouse cultivation sow from late winter to mid-spring. For outdoor cultivation sow in mid-spring, and harden off for 10-14 days before planting outside.

Growing

Outside plants need a sunny warm site with fertile, moisture-retentive soil that drains well enough to warm quickly in spring. Pre-warm heavier soils under cloches or polythene.

Plants are ready to plant on once the roots fill the pots. Transfer them to 23-25cm (9-10in) pots of good compost in mid-spring in a heated greenhouse, late spring in an unheated one, and as late as early summer for outdoors: plants can be kept in growing bags

Make sure you keep pepper plants well watered while the fruit is developing and swelling.

or pots, but will need to be carefully watered. In the ground, space plants 45cm (18in) apart, planting out in late spring to early summer and keeping young plants covered for two weeks.

Stake plants with canes and tie in as they grow. Pinch out growing tips when plants are 20cm (8in) tall to encourage bushiness, but this will delay cropping.

Water regularly and feed with a general fertiliser, switching to a high potash one when the first fruit has set. Mist the foliage regularly, especially indoors, with tepid water to discourage red spider mite and to help flower set.

Harvesting

The approximate time between sowing and harvesting is 18-20 weeks. Pick the fruit when it is green, swollen, and glossy for the highest yield: leaving it on the plant to ripen usually reduces the crop.

Yield: 5-10 peppers per plant.

You can leave peppers to ripen on the plant, but it will reduce the overall yield.

AT A GLANCE

Growing sweet peppers at home has increased in popularity over recent years, mainly thanks to more reliable varieties. Although crops are better, earlier, and more reliable under cover, growing outside will produce good crops in a warm, sunny summer. The fruits can be picked green or left on the plant to ripen and colour, developing a sweeter flavour.

ALLOTMENT ADVICE:
what I wish I'd known

At the end of the summer, you can help unripe fruits finish ripening by lifting the plants whole and hanging them upside down under cover, preferably in a polytunnel or greenhouse.

TRIED AND TESTED
RHS VARIETIES

'Ace' (AGM), 'Ariane' (AGM), 'Bell Boy' (AGM), 'Californian Wonder', 'Corno di Toro Rosso' (AGM), 'Gourmet' (AGM), 'Gypsy' (AGM), 'Mohawk' (AGM), 'Redskin' (AGM)

Chilli peppers

Taste-wise, chilli peppers couldn't be more different from their sweet relations (*see* opposite). The heat is concentrated mainly in the pith. A far wider range is available as seeds than as produce in shops, and they are not hard to grow.

Sowing

Sowing is the same as for sweet peppers. Hot chillies are best sown in late winter, as long as you can provide the heat needed for germination. This is because seeds can take a long time to germinate and without heat may rot.

Growing

Growing is the same as for sweet peppers, including pinching out the growing tips when plants are about 20cm (8in) tall to encourage bushiness; side-shoots can be further pinched back to encourage lots of small chillies. Warmer, drier conditions produce hotter chillies.

Harvesting

The approximate time between sowing and harvesting is 18-20 weeks, or up to 24 weeks for very hot chilli varieties.

Yield: Up to several dozen per plant, depending on type and variety.

Chilli peppers are a great crop to grow as the seed range is wider than any crops you can buy.

AT A GLANCE

The popularity of Indian, Thai and Mexican cuisine has raised the profile of chillies and just about everyone seems to have one or two chilli plants growing somewhere on their plots - some grow dozens.

Chilli growing has almost reached cult status, with a degree of bravado attached to eating the hottest chillies. Because of this, there are now seed companies that offer explosively hot chillies. Their heat is measured in Scoville units, and you may now find these mentioned on seed packets or in the catalogues: a mild pimento scores 100, while the hottest chilli reaches 1,000,000.

Chillies can be eaten or cooked fresh and dried or frozen for storing and future use. They will more than likely become hotter if treated in either way.

ALLOTMENT ADVICE:
what I wish I'd known

Chilli plants, especially those of very hot chillies, will do better grown under cover as this helps develop the heat and flavour; too much watering dilutes it. In late summer they should be brought inside to ensure good ripening; for these reasons they are best grown in containers.

TRIED AND TESTED
RHS VARIETIES

'Apache' (AGM), 'Cayenne', 'Demon Red' (AGM), 'Etna' (AGM), 'Fiesta' (AGM), 'Filius Blue' (AGM), 'Fuego' (AGM), 'Habanero' (AGM), 'Hungarian Hot Wax' (AGM), 'Jalapeno', 'Joe's Long Cayenne', 'Navaho' (AGM), 'Prairie Fire' (AGM), 'Super Chili' (AGM), 'Thai Hot Dragon'

The onion family

Basic techniques

The onion, or *Allium* family is made up of onions – both bulbing onions and the slender spring onions used raw in salads or as a garnish – and the closely related shallots, garlic, and leeks. If you choose your cultivars and sowing times well, you can be harvesting something from this group in almost every month.

The onion family prefers to grow in an open, sunny site. This is essential for those crops that produce bulbs – onions, shallots, and garlic – to ensure good ripening towards the end of the growing season. If the bulbs don't ripen properly they can rot, especially in storage. Leeks and spring onions are harvested green, so aren't so fussy and will tolerate some shade, but in the case of leeks make sure the site isn't in deep shade during winter.

Sowing or planting?

Members of the onion family are either grown from seed or, in the case of garlic, bulbing onions, and shallots, from young, immature bulbs, which for the first two crops are called sets.

Sets have been specially prepared for planting out and are the easiest way of growing onions and shallots. They are quicker to mature than plants grown from seed (especially important where the growing season is short or weather conditions poor) and are easier to grow. Plants grown from sets can 'bolt', flowering and running to seed early, if growing conditions aren't right at planting time and for the few weeks afterwards, but nearly all sets are heat treated these days to prevent this from happening.

Soil preparation

Soil preparation before planting can be critical, so pay attention to this during the winter or previous autumn before sowing or planting.

You'll always get much better results growing on fertile soil, but if you overdo it and the soil is too rich the plants will

not grow well. They can produce poor yields, bolt, and be more susceptible to diseases. Never use fresh manure or other organic matter: always make sure it is well rotted, and apply in autumn or winter to give it time to break down and settle into the soil. An application of a balanced general fertiliser at the rate of 50g/sq m (2oz/sq yd) at sowing or planting out time is usually all the feed that's needed, although an application of sulphate of potash in early to mid-summer can help ripening and improve the flavour.

Growing

There are a number of reasons why members of the onion family flower and go to seed early, but it's usually due to either over-rich soil or a check in their growth. This check can come about from planting out too early in the year, when the weather conditions aren't right, or allowing the plants to dry out during times of critical developments in growth.

The foliage of the members of the onion family is thin and upright and doesn't produce a dense canopy.

5

1) *Plant onion sets in rows in well-prepared soil, spaced regularly for good airflow.*
2) *Young leeks should be planted in 15cm (6in) deep holes made with a dibber.*
3) *Sow onion seeds thinly in rows (drills) made in well-prepared soil.*
4) *When onions are ready to harvest, carefully lift the roots with a garden fork.*
5) *Onions and shallots for storage should be strung and hung or kept in containers that allow plenty of air circulation.*

As a result, weeds can easily get established and become a problem among the crop. These crops are also shallow rooted, so weed competition will starve them of food and water and greatly reduce yields. So if there's one thing you need to do on a regular basis, it's hoe, hoe, and hoe again to keep weeds away. Always hoe carefully to ensure you don't accidentally damage any bulbs, as this can lead to rotting.

All onion crops except for leeks can be 'intercropped', sown or planted with sweetcorn or other later crops.

Diseases to watch out for

With good growing conditions and fair weather, the onion family tends to escape the ravages of pests and diseases, but there are three fungal diseases that you need to be aware of. These diseases make crop rotation essential for the onion family, as is good hygiene for your tools and your boots.

White rot affects garlic, onions, and shallots. Not only does this disease reduce your yields and sometimes completely kill the plants, it also affects storage, and bulbs with the disease soon rot away. If the foliage turns yellow and wilts, look for white, fluffy growth on the bulbs themselves. If you spot infected bulbs, lift them and destroy them immediately. Unfortunately, you'll also have to avoid growing members of the onion family in that area of soil for eight to nine years, as the disease can remain dormant for that long.

Downy mildew has also become a problem for onions in recent years, due to changes in weather patterns. This disease is always worse after an extended period of cool, wet weather. First the leaf tips go yellow, often in spots and patches. Then a fine whitish layer develops on these patches, and soon becomes a dull brown to purple shade. These are the spores that will spread to other plants. Picking off the yellowing, affected leaves can sometimes save the crop if done early enough, but infected plants rarely store well, and if they make it to cropping size should be used fresh rather than stored. If you don't mind using chemicals, you can spray with a fungicide based on mancozeb as a preventative measure. Other control methods involve spacing out the plants to ensure good airflow around them and avoiding the use of high-nitrogen fertilisers, especially when the crop is growing. The spores of downy mildew can remain in the soil for up to four years.

Finally, onion rust can affect onions and leeks. This disease produces bright orange pustules on the leaves. Remove affected leaves and destroy them and try growing a resistant variety.

Onions

Most people grow bulbing onions from young, immature bulbs called sets (*see* page 88), although a greater range of varieties is available as seed and this is a much cheaper way of growing them. Seeds and seedlings are more likely to be attacked by onion fly. A good crop of spring-sown or planted onions can be stored for many months, and will often keep you going for almost a whole year.

But let's not forget salad, or spring, onions. These baby relatives of bulbing onions bring a fresh, oniony taste to salads and make perfect garnishes for soups and other meals. They are very quick to mature and take up hardly any room on the plot. You may also want to grow pickling onions or silverskin onions, which are mainly harvested at a very small size as cocktail onions.

Sowing & planting

If starting from seed, sow 1cm (½in) deep in rows 20–23cm (8–9in) apart from late winter through to mid-spring. Start sowing as soon as the soil is warm enough and workable; a minimum soil temperature of 5°C (41°F) is needed for germination.

For an earlier crop or in cold regions, it is better to sow seed in cell trays, modules, or cell trays indoors with gentle heat. Seed of overwintering onions is sown in late summer at the same depth and spacing.

Thin the young seedlings in stages, first to 5cm (2in) apart and then to 10cm (4in) apart. Lift the thinnings carefully so as not to disturb the remaining plants; the scent released when thinning can attract onion fly.

If starting from onion sets, plant them 10cm (4in) apart in rows 20–23cm (8–9in) apart from mid- to late spring. Overwintering onion sets are planted in early autumn at the same spacing. Push the sets gently into well-worked, soft soil

Salad onions will produce small bulbs if left in the ground to develop further.

so that the tip is just showing, and equally gently firm the soil around them. Birds can be a problem, lifting the sets, so carefully remove the loose skin at the top of the set before planting.

Sow salad onion seed 1cm (½in) deep in rows that are only 10cm (4in) apart. Thin out the seedlings if necessary to 2.5cm (1in) spacings. Silverskin onions are sown in mid-spring in well-drained soil. Sow thinly, as the seedlings shouldn't be thinned, and don't feed the plants.

Growing

Grow in an open, sunny site where good air circulation will help to keep fungal problems (*see* page 89) at bay. Plant in well-prepared soil that was improved with compost or well-rotted manure during the previous autumn or winter.

Water if the weather is dry in early and midsummer, and give an occasional feed with a balanced liquid fertiliser if necessary. A light feed of sulphate of potash in early summer will help ripen the bulbs ready for storage, but much watering after midsummer will hinder ripening. Overwintered onions benefit from a light feed with a balanced granular fertiliser in early spring.

Mulching the soil will help conserve soil moisture and keep down weeds. Keep competition from weeds to a minimum, hoeing regularly or hand-pulling established weeds. Remove any flower spikes as soon as they are seen.

Stop watering and feeding once the onions have swollen and the foliage starts to yellow, and remove any mulch or built-up soil around the bulbs to expose them to the sun.

Harvesting

The approximate time between planting onion sets and lifting is 20 weeks. Onions can be harvested when their foliage turns yellow and starts to topple over. Bending over the foliage or gently lifting the bulbs to break the roots is no longer recommended and can affect

Growing onions through a planting membrane will help suppress weed growth.

Don't bend over the tops of onions, but allow them to fold over naturally.

storage. Leave the plants for two to three weeks and then carefully lift with a garden fork on a dry day.

Storage

It is best to remove the tops once the plants have been lifted. Cut off the top 5-7.5cm (2-3in) above the neck to speed up drying and reduce the likelihood of rot. Cut off the roots and remove loose or split skins, but don't remove too many layers or it will hinder ripening.

Onions for storage must be firm, disease free and dried for two to three weeks, either laid out in the sun or over wire mesh in a shed. Check regularly for any bulbs with damage or soft, spotted, or thick necks. These won't store and should be used straight away.

Once dry, store in trays with slatted bases, net bags, or old tights for good air circulation, or tie an onion rope. Store in a cool, dry and shady place.

Yield: 3-3.5kg from a 3m row (7-8lb from a 10ft row).

A good crop of onions can be dried and stored for use over several months.

AT A GLANCE

Bulbing onions are among the most versatile and frequently used vegetables in the kitchen, and are reliable and fairly easy to grow, especially if started from sets. They are rich in vitamins, minerals, and antioxidants - the more pungent the onion, the higher its antioxidant levels.

ALLOTMENT ADVICE: what I wish I'd known

Growing one crop of bulbing onions from seed and another from sets will give an extended cropping period. If you also grow overwintering or Japanese onions, these will fill the early summer gap.

TRIED AND TESTED RHS VARIETIES

Onion from seed: 'Ailsa Craig', 'Bedfordshire Champion', 'Golden Bear' (AGM), 'Hygro' (AGM), 'Kelsae', 'Marco' (AGM)
Onion from sets: 'Centurion' (AGM), 'Hercules' (AGM), 'Setton' (AGM), 'Sturon' (AGM), 'Stuttgart Giant'
Red onion: 'Red Baron' (AGM)
Overwintering onion: 'Imai Yellow', 'Senshyu Semi Globe Yellow'
Salad onion: 'Guardsman' (AGM), 'Ishikura' (AGM), 'North Holland Blood Red - Redmate', 'Ramrod' (AGM), 'White Lisbon' (AGM)

Garlic

There are lots of garlic varieties, which are categorised into two major types: soft-necked and hard-necked. These descriptions relate to the stalk that grows up from the garlic bulb. Soft-necked garlic has a strong flavour and stores well because it has several protective outer layers of papery skin. Hard-necked garlic is milder tasting and best used soon after harvest, as it doesn't keep well.

Sowing & planting

It is best not to plant garlic cloves bought from a supermarket. They are not certified disease-free, as those from a garden centre or mail order supplier should be. They are also often imported from quite different climates, and may not be suited to our climate.

Break up the bulbs and plant the individual cloves just below the surface, spacing them 15cm (6in) apart in rows 30cm (12in) apart.

Birds may be a problem, pulling up the newly planted cloves, so remove any loose skin at the top of the clove before planting. Check the cloves regularly for a few weeks after planting to make sure they haven't been disturbed.

Plant individual garlic cloves carefully in well-prepared soil, burying them so that only the tips are visible.

Growing

Garlic grows best in well-prepared, light, and fertile soil. Add sand if necessary. Plant it in a sunny position, as warmth is needed to ripen the bulbs.

Because weeds can be a problem, requiring regular hoeing and the risk of damaging the bulbs, some garlic fans grow their plants through planting membranes or black polythene.

Water occasionally but thoroughly during dry spells in spring and early summer. Stop watering once the bulbs are large and well formed, as too much water at this stage can encourage rots to develop and will reduce the storage qualities. Remove any flower spikes that form – although they seldom do.

Garlic suffers only a few problems and then rarely but rust and white rot are two of them (*see* page 89).

Harvesting

The green leaves can be cut when young and used as a garnish or in salads. The bulbs are harvested once the leaves and stems have turned yellow. Carefully lift them with a fork or hand fork. Lay out the bulbs to dry in an airy place. When they are 'rustling' dry, remove any dry soil and outer dried skin layers. They can then be stored in a net bag or pair of old tights, or you can plait the stems to form the classic rope.

Garlic is now a very popular allotment crop and one that is easy to grow.

'Top sets' of garlic cloves may form on the stalk, above the main cloves, in spring. Gather and use these in the same way as you would the main bulb.

Yield: Each clove will produce one bulb, with 8–12 cloves depending on the cultivar and conditions.

AT A GLANCE

Growing your own garlic is now highly popular, reaching almost cult status among some allotment holders. It is a very healthy vegetable, full of vitamins and minerals, and some people swear by it to ward off attacks of cold and flu.

ALLOTMENT ADVICE:
what I wish I'd known

Garlic generally needs a spell of cold weather, normally one to two weeks at 0-4°C (32-40°F), to prepare itself for making the new crop of bulbs. This means it is best planted in late autumn to early winter, but some varieties can also be planted in spring. It's an easy vegetable to grow: simply pop a clove into the soil and wait a few months and you'll be rewarded with a bulb of up to a dozen or more cloves.

TRIED AND TESTED RHS VARIETIES

'Arno' (AGM), 'Cristo' (AGM), 'Early Wight' (AGM), 'Germidour' (AGM), 'Long Keeper' (AGM), 'Purple Wight', 'Solent White' (AGM)

Shallots

Until recently, shallots were always grown by planting sets – single bulbs that bulk up to give an impressive crop of clusters of bulbs – but now shallot seed is also available.

Sowing & planting

If starting from seed, sow from early to late spring 1cm (½in) deep in rows 25-30cm (10-12in) apart. You can make successional sowings if you want to harvest over a long period. Each seed produces a single shallot.

Sow thinly, about 2.5cm (1in) apart and then thin seedlings to anything from 2.5-10cm (1-4in) apart, depending on how large you want the individual shallots to develop.

For an earlier crop or in cold regions, it is better to sow in modules or pots indoors with gentle heat and then plant out, after hardening off, in mid-spring.

If starting from sets, plant 15cm (6in) apart in rows 23-25cm (9-10in) apart from late winter to early spring.

Each individual shallot plant produces a cluster of bulbs that can be used fresh or pickled.

Growing

Grow in an open, sunny site on well-prepared soil that was improved with compost or well-rotted manure the previous autumn or winter.

Water if the weather is dry and give an occasional feed with a balanced liquid fertiliser if necessary. Stop watering and feeding once the bulbs have swollen and the foliage starts to yellow.

Keep the competition from weeds to a minimum by hoeing or hand-pulling them. Mulching the soil will help conserve soil moisture. Remove any flower spikes as soon as they are seen.

Harvesting

The approximate time between planting sets and lifting is 18 weeks, while shallots grown from seed will be ready in late summer. The foliage of shallots will start to turn yellow in midsummer. When it has yellowed, lift the clusters of bulbs on a dry day, separate them, and allow to dry in a cool, dry place.

Yield from sets: 4.5kg from a 3m row (10lb from a 10ft row).

Allow the tops of the plants to die down before carefully lifting and harvesting the bulbs.

AT A GLANCE

Shallot growing is very similar to onion growing – the plants are grown and harvested much in the same way. But shallots are even easier to grow, especially from sets: just plant and wait for the crop. They are also a quick growing, early maturing crop, usually ready in mid-summer, thereby freeing up ground that can then be used for follow-on crops.

ALLOTMENT ADVICE:
what I wish I'd known

Modern seed-raised varieties of shallots tend to be bigger than those raised from sets. Save yourself hours of skinning ready for pickling by selecting one of these varieties, as the larger shallots are easier to skin.

TRIED AND TESTED
RHS VARIETIES

Shallot: 'Golden Gourmet' (AGM), 'Hative de Niort', 'Jermor' (AGM), 'Pikant' (AGM), 'Topper'
Shallot seed: 'Ambition', 'Matador' (AGM)

Leeks

Although leeks occupy the ground for a long time, this is normally a time when little else is growing. They are rewarding, as they can be harvested over a long period from autumn into early spring.

Outdoors, leeks are sown and raised in a seedbed and then transplanted to their final growing positions when they are large enough to handle. This means they can be transplanted into an area that has already been used for earlier crops.

Sowing

Sow thinly, 1cm (½in) deep in rows 15cm (6in) apart in a seedbed. The main sowing period outdoors is early and mid-spring for crops to mature in autumn or early winter. A minimum soil temperature of 5°C (41°F) is needed for germination. You can also sow outdoors in early summer for a crop that matures

Carefully weed around leek plants; an onion hoe is a useful tool for doing this.

the following spring. Thin out seedlings to approximately 4–5cm (1½–2in) apart as soon as they are large enough to handle without damage.

For an early crop that matures in late summer or early to mid-autumn, sow indoors in seed trays in a heated propagator or on a windowsill in mid- to late winter. Transplant the seedlings to root trainers or module trays and continue to grow them indoors before hardening off for ten days and planting outside in mid-spring.

Growing

Leeks prefer a sunny site, but will tolerate light shade. The soil should be well-cultivated and not prone to being

waterlogged in winter. For bumper crops you will need to have improved the soil by digging in plenty of compost or well-rotted manure the previous autumn. If this is not possible, you can still add organic matter a few weeks before planting out, providing it is not too rich in nutrients. Add a little balanced fertiliser before planting out and rake into the soil.

The plants are ready to transplant when they are about 15–20cm (6–8in) high and the thickness of a pencil. Water them well the day before transplanting. After lifting, prepare them for planting out by trimming off the root tips and the tops of the leaves.

Make holes 5cm (2in) wide and 15cm (6in) deep with a dibber. They should be 15cm (6in) apart in rows 30cm (12in) apart. Drop a plant into each hole and fill the hole with water to settle the roots. Top up with water as necessary for the plants to establish, but don't fill the hole with soil. If you have a lot of plants, try dropping two or three into each planting hole. You'll get smaller leeks, but the overall yield should be about the same. To increase the length of white stems, blanch the plants by drawing up dry soil around the stems

A good crop of leeks will keep you in green vegetables for several of the winter months.

Leeks should be carefully lifted with a garden fork to ensure the stems don't break.

in stages, but try not to allow soil to fall between the leaves. Once established, water only during extended dry periods, giving the plants a good soaking every 10–14 days.

Keep weeds at bay throughout the growing period by carefully hoeing and hand-pulling weeds between plants.

Harvesting
The approximate time from sowing to harvest is 30 weeks for the early varieties, 45 weeks for the later or maincrop varieties. To extend your harvesting period, start lifting 'baby leeks' when the plants are still quite small. Most leeks are left until the stems have become reasonably thick. Gently lift them from the soil using a fork.

Leeks can be left in the ground, even through winter, and lifted when needed.

Yield: 4.5kg from a 3m row (10lb from a 10ft row).

Leek plants won't mind a little winter frosting, but may need lifting if bad weather persists.

Stem and perennial veg

Asparagus

Most modern asparagus varieties are all-male F1s; these are more vigorous than older varieties and do not self-seed all over the place. Although plants need plenty of space, once established they should crop for up to 20 years and need little in the way of regular care.

Sowing & planting

Asparagus can be raised from seed, but takes three years to reach cropping size. It's usually better to buy dormant one-year-old plants or 'crowns'. Crowns are more expensive, but crop a year earlier.

Soak seeds for 24–48 hours in tepid water before sowing. Sow singly into modules in late winter and plant out in early summer. Alternatively, sow outside in mid-spring in a well-prepared seed bed 5cm (2in) deep, 7.5cm (3in) apart in drills 30cm (12in) apart. Germination is slow. When large enough to handle, thin young plants to 30cm (12in) apart, and grow on for a season.

Next spring the young plants can be moved to their permanent growing place; this is also when you plant bought crowns, having skipped all the sowing.

Growing

Prepare the soil well before planting in early to mid-spring to guarantee good crops for many years to come.

Start by digging and forking over the area where you want your asparagus bed, removing all stones and perennial weeds and adding plenty of humus-building organic matter in the form of well-rotted manure or compost.

For best results, especially on heavy soil, dig a trench 30cm (12in) wide and 20cm (8in) deep. Work in some well-rotted manure into the soil at the bottom of the trench, then add some of the excavated soil to make a 7–10cm (3–4in) high ridge down the centre of the trench. Place the crowns on top, carefully spreading out the roots, spacing them 30–45cm (12–18in) apart. Leave 45–90cm (18–36in) between rows and stagger the plants within them. Carefully cover the crowns with 5–7.5cm (2–3in) of soil, leaving the bud tips just visible. Water in and mulch with 5cm (2in) of well-rotted manure, and gradually fill in the rest of the trench as the plants grow up through the soil.

Asparagus beds must be kept weed free, and weeding is best done by hand as the shallow roots are easily damaged by hoeing. Adding a 5–7.5cm (2–3in) mulch annually discourages weeds, feeds plants, and helps retain moisture.

Apply a general granular fertiliser at the rate of 100g/sq m (3oz/sq yd) in early spring and repeat once harvesting has finished.

Allow the foliage to yellow in autumn before cutting it down to 2.5cm (1in) above the soil surface.

Harvesting

Resist picking in the year you plant and the following year. The second year after planting, pick from mid-spring for six weeks; in subsequent years you can

The first asparagus spears of the year are always a welcome sight.

pick for eight weeks. To harvest, cut individual spears with a sharp knife 2.5cm (1in) below the soil when they are 15–20cm (6–8in) long. It's important to cut each stem at this time.

Yield: Up to 25 spears per plant.

Weed carefully around asparagus plants; the developing spears are easily damaged.

AT A GLANCE

The delicately flavoured young shoots of asparagus are one of the great luxuries of the vegetable plot – simply steamed and served with melting butter. Much of the mystique surrounding its cultivation is unwarranted. This is one of the most sought-after vegetables, but not difficult to grow if you pay attention to planting, and then simply keep the plants well fed and weed free.

ALLOTMENT ADVICE:
what I wish I'd known

On windy sites, run twine on canes along either side of the row for support. This should prevent the top growth breaking and damaging the crown.

TRIED AND TESTED
RHS VARIETIES

'Backlim' (AGM), 'Connover's Colossal' (AGM), 'Gijnlim' (AGM), 'Jersey Knight (Improved)', 'Pacific Purple'

Celery

To ensure a good crop of celery, the plants must be regularly watered during dry periods.

If you want to grow easy celery, then choose self-blanching or green varieties. If you have the time and space and fancy growing celery in the old-fashioned way, go for 'trench' varieties. You will be rewarded for this extra effort, as these varieties have better flavour.

If you want to avoid stringy celery, the plants must never receive a check to growth, so transplant, harden off and water properly at all times.

Sowing

Sow from early to mid-spring in seed trays or pots and germinate at 15°C (59°F). Germination can be slow.

Transplant seedlings when large enough to handle individually into 7.5cm (3in) pots or module or cell trays. Make sure seedlings grow strongly and don't receive a check to growth. Plants will be ready to plant outside when they are 7.5cm (3in) tall or have five or six leaves.

Growing

Whichever type of celery you grow, the site must be open and sunny and the soil moisture-retentive. It is often best to grow all types above a trench dug the previous autumn and filled with plenty of organic matter. Leave the trench 8–10cm (3–4in) deep for trenching celery, fill it level for self-blanching types.

Make sure plants are fully hardened off before planting out in late spring to early summer. Plant 23cm (9in) apart, arranging self-blanching varieties in a block to allow the plants to shade each other to help blanching.

Water regularly during dry weather and apply a balanced liquid feed every fortnight during the summer. A light dressing of a high-nitrogen fertiliser once the plants are established will help improve crops.

Mound soil around trench types in late summer, and complete earthing up in early autumn to make a mound with only the foliage tops showing.

Harvesting

The approximate time between sowing and harvesting is 25 weeks for self-blanching varieties and 40 weeks for trench varieties. Water well before lifting and trimming the whole plant. Lift self-blanching celery from late summer until the first frosts, and the hardier trench varieties from mid-autumn onwards.

Yield: Up to 5.5kg from a 3m row (12lb from a 10ft row).

Sow celery seed indoors in pots or trays of good compost and help germinate with heat.

AT A GLANCE

Celery is considered a difficult crop to grow, mainly because traditional varieties need a lot of attention – they need blanching so have to be grown in trenches or with collars. Luckily, modern self-blanching varieties reduce the strain, effort, and time needed.

ALLOTMENT ADVICE:
what I wish I'd known

Trench varieties need blanching, starting in late summer, but they don't necessarily have to be grown in a trench. These days they are often grown on the flat, like self-blanching types, and blanched with collars. When you would normally start to earth up, simply wrap the plants with corrugated cardboard or similar material and tie it loosely around the stems. In frosty, cold weather cover the tops with straw or fleece.

TRIED AND TESTED
RHS VARIETIES

Trench: 'Giant Red', 'Granada' (AGM), 'Octavius' (AGM), 'Victoria' (AGM)
Self-blanching: 'Celebrity' (AGM), 'Golden Self Blanching', 'Lathom Self Blanching' (AGM), 'Loretta' (AGM), 'Tango' (AGM)

Celeriac

Celeriac is often avoided on allotments as it can be tricky to get a good crop.

Sowing

Sow from late winter to mid-spring at 15°C (59°F) in pots or trays of compost. When they are large enough to handle, transplant the seedlings singly into 7.5cm (3in) pots or cell or module trays. Better still, to prevent root disturbance, sow two seeds in a pot or module and pinch out the weakest seedling. Grow on the young plants at a minimum temperature of 10°C (50°F) and harden them off before planting out from mid-spring onwards, if it is warm enough.

Growing

Like celery, celeriac needs a moisture-retentive soil that doesn't dry out. Ensure the soil has plenty of organic matter to hold on to any available water.

Plant out 30cm (12in) apart in rows 40-45cm (16-18in) apart. Don't bury the crown – the base of the stem should be at soil level. Mulch around plants.

Water every week or so in dry weather. Remove any sideshoots as they form, and from midsummer onwards remove a few lower leaves to expose the crown. In early autumn draw a little soil around the swollen stem base to keep it white.

Harvesting

Sowing to harvesting takes 30–35 weeks. Start lifting in early to mid-autumn. If your soil is well drained, roots can be left in the ground until needed in most areas. Cover plants in the ground with straw or compost to protect against frost.

Yield: 3-3.5kg from a 3m row (7–8lb from a 10ft row).

Celeriac tastes like celery and is a versatile crop – it can be cooked in several ways.

AT A GLANCE

Becoming more popular in the kitchen, celeriac is useful for adding celery flavour to winter cooking. The roots can be cooked as a hot vegetable or made into a tasty, warming soup, or grated raw and added to salads. It can be used as a celery substitute, and is much easier to grow. The leaves can also be used as a garnish or in salads.

ALLOTMENT ADVICE:
what I wish I'd known

Although the mature plants are hardy enough to leave in the soil into winter, young celeriac plants are very sensitive to cold weather and checks to their growth. They are often planted out at the very end of spring or the start of summer, but this should be delayed if the weather is cold. Keep them growing on strongly under cover until the weather conditions improve.

TRIED AND TESTED RHS VARIETIES

'Brilliant', 'Diamant' (AGM), 'Giant Prague', 'Monarch' (AGM)

Chard and leaf beets

These crops are similar to spinach but easier to grow. They are less likely to go to seed in dry weather, and one sowing will produce an abundant, reliable crop for many months.

Mainly grown for picking over the summer, leaves can be harvested during autumn and winter and sometimes beyond if the plants are protected.

Keep chard well watered in dry periods to ensure a good crop and prevent bolting.

Sowing

These crops are sown direct. Sow seeds thinly, 2.5cm (1in) deep and 10cm (4in) apart in rows 38–45cm (15–18in) apart from late spring to midsummer. Late spring is the main time for sowing.

Thin out the seedlings to 30cm (12in) apart, or 38cm (15in) apart for spinach beet, when large enough to handle.

Growing

Grow in a sunny position, although plants will tolerate light shade. Plants need well-prepared, moisture-retentive soil, but any reasonable soil will usually produce a good crop.

Water every two weeks during prolonged dry periods; mulching will help conserve soil moisture.

Keep the soil free of weeds and feed with a high-nitrogen liquid fertiliser fortnightly during the summer if needed.

In mid-autumn, cover plants for overwintering with cloches or protect the crown with straw or similar material and cover with fleece.

Harvesting

The approximate time between sowing and harvesting is 12 weeks. Pull off the outer leaves when they are large enough to use, and harvest regularly. The thinnings can also be used whole.

Yield: Up to 3–3.5kg from a 3m row (7–8lb from a 10ft row).

The colourful and tasty stems of chard make an attractive sight on any allotment plot.

AT A GLANCE

Leafy chard, leaf beets, and spinach beet are easy to grow, tasty, and full of goodness. The varieties of chard with coloured stems are the most popular, thanks to their glowing, ornamental shades. They now supersede the white-stemmed types, commonly known as Swiss chard.

ALLOTMENT ADVICE:
what I wish I'd known

These crops can be sown more closely, scattering seeds thinly in a wide drill, and used as cut-and-come-again salad crops when leaves are 5cm (2in) long. Don't cut too close to the ground; a longer 'stump' will give the plants a better chance of sprouting again. The leaves have a very short shelf life once picked, so visit the plot on the day you want them.

TRIED AND TESTED
RHS VARIETIES

Chard: 'Bright Lights' (AGM), 'Bright Yellow' (AGM), 'Charlotte' (AGM), 'Fordhook Giant' (AGM), 'Lucullus' (AGM), 'Rhubarb Chard' (AGM), 'Rainbow'
Spinach beet: 'Perpetual Spinach' (AGM)

Peas and beans

Basic techniques

Peas and beans (legumes) are important crops to grow. Not only are they tasty side-dish vegetables, but they provide a rich source of protein and can be used in many ways in the kitchen.

They need an open, sunny position that is sheltered from strong winds; they are insect pollinated, and the shelter will ensure the insects can do their job properly.

All prefer an alkaline to neutral soil (pH7 and greater). If your allotment is on acidic soil you will need to add lime in late winter for best results.

Legumes need plenty of soil moisture, otherwise the crops are poor or the pods become small, dry and tasteless. The best way to ensure they never go short of water at the roots is to dig a trench approximately 30cm (12in) deep in autumn and fill it with moisture-holding material. Typically this is garden compost, but even shredded newspaper and un-rotted garden or kitchen waste can be added. Top off the trench with soil at least a fortnight before sowing or planting out to give the contents time to settle. Even then, you should water well during dry periods, especially when the plants are in flower and the pods are developing, to ensure bumper, succulent crops. It even pays to mulch the soil around the plants; you can use grass clippings, but keep them well away from the plant stems.

Legumes should be picked regularly. Not only does this ensure the crops are at their best - picked young they have the finest flavour and don't have time to become tough - but it also allows the plants to continue to flower and so crop over the longest period possible.

The cropping period can also be extended by choosing varieties that crop at different times (early and maincrop peas, for example), by sowing at different times of the year (as with autumn- and spring-sown broad beans), or by sowing seed indoors with a little gentle heat, in a propagator or on a

warm windowsill, for example, to start some plants off early.

Sowing

Seeds can be sown directly into the soil at the right time of year, but they can also be sown in pots or cell or module trays and given protection from the elements by growing on in a greenhouse, cold frame or conservatory or on a light windowsill. They can be planted outside after being hardened off, or gradually acclimatised to outdoor conditions over a period of 10-14 days.

This will provide an earlier crop than sowing directly outside. In fact, you'll usually find that sowing indoors at any time of year and then planting out the young plants will give much better results than sowing seed directly into the soil on the plot.

Pea and bean seeds don't like to be sown in a cold, damp soil, so when sowing outside cover the soil with cloches or clear plastic sheeting a fortnight or so before sowing. Broad beans need a minimum soil temperature of 5°C (41°F) for good

5

6

1) *For an earlier crop, bean seeds can be sown under cover in cell or module trays.*
2) *Sow two runner bean seeds at the base of each support; if both seeds germinate remove the weakest seedling.*
3) *Carefully train young runner plants around their supports and tie in the stems with soft string.*
4) *Runner beans can be grown up wigwams of bamboo canes to make an ornamental feature in a small space.*
5) *Peas and beans need a regular and plentiful supply of water to ensure good crops of juicy pods.*
6) *Pick French beans regularly when they're young and tender to ensure the plants crop for as long as possible.*

Crops to grow

The usual legumes grown on allotments are peas – including mangetout and sugar snap types as well as podding types – broad beans, French beans, and runner beans. But there are a couple of others you might like to try too.

Soya beans have been increasing in popularity, and are now more reliable croppers; the variety 'Ustie' has been specifically bred to suit the British climate. They produce lots of downy, weatherproof pods in autumn. The plants are also pest and disease free. The beans must be soaked and then boiled for at least an hour before eating to destroy inhibitors for protein digestion contained in them.

If you love the taste of asparagus, then the asparagus pea is well worth trying – it's also very ornamental. Small, sprawling plants produce attractive, sweet pea-like, deep red flowers followed by curious winged pods. These have the flavour and consistency of asparagus and should be picked when they're about 2.5cm (1in) long. Don't leave them until they're bigger, as they become tough and stringy with age.

Both soya beans and asparagus peas are best sown in pots or modules in mid-spring and planted out in late spring or early summer, after the fear of frosts has passed.

germination, peas need 10°C (50°F) and runner and French beans need 12–13°C (54–55°F).

Always sow a few extra seeds at the end of the rows to produce plants you can dig up and transplant to fill in any gaps left by seeds that don't germinate.

Feeding needs

Legumes produce their own nitrogen, thanks to a symbiotic relationship with a soil-dwelling *Rhizobium* bacteria. As a result, they do not need feeding with high-nitrogen fertilisers; in fact, this can reduce both growth and yield, so use balanced or high-potash fertilisers only. A light dressing of a balanced granular feed at sowing or planting out time is usually all that's needed. A high-potash liquid feed (such as a tomato fertiliser) can be used during the growing season to improve yields.

Nitrogen is released back into the soil as the plant roots decompose, so rather than digging up the spent plants, cut them off at ground level. Their top growth is also a good nitrogen-rich addition to the compost heap.

Peas

Dried peas, canned peas, even bought fresh peas and those frozen within hours of leaving the field just can't beat the flavour of freshly picked, home-grown ones. That's because as soon as they are picked the sugars they contain start to turn to starch and they quickly lose their sweetness and flavour. This means that peas should be cooked and eaten as soon as possible after they've been picked. Although, of course, they can be frozen straight away, too, if you have too may to deal with. Podding peas can sometimes be a bit tricky to grow, but they're worth bearing with.

Types of pea

Podding or shelling pea varieties are classed by when the pods are mature (earlies, second earlies and maincrops) and the shape of the pea. Round pea varieties tend to be hardier, and so are best for early sowings and will tolerate poor growing conditions, but they lack the sweetness of wrinkled ones.

The flat-podded mangetout peas are eaten pod and all before the peas have developed in them. Sugar snaps are also eaten whole, but after the peas have swelled. Both mangetout and sugar snaps are generally easier to grow than podding peas, and they are well worth considering if you've had problems growing peas in the past.

Sowing

First early varieties are sown in autumn and protected over winter, or from early spring to the very start of summer; second earlies and maincrops are sown from early spring into early summer.

To ensure you get a succession of crops over the longest period possible, one option is to sow an early variety every three to four weeks until midsummer. Another is to make one or two sowings each of an early, a second early, and a maincrop variety, which will then mature at different times. I know plenty of allotment holders who do both.

Sow pea seeds in a shallow, flat-bottomed trench spacing them evenly 7.5cm (3in) apart.

Never sow in cold, wet soil, as the seeds will rot. If you need to make an early start, warm the soil for a few weeks first by covering with plastic sheeting. Or you can sow the seeds indoors in small pots, modules, or root trainers. Another popular method is to use short lengths of plastic guttering. Drill some drainage holes first, fill with compost, water and allow to drain, then sow the seeds. Once the plants are big enough and outdoor conditions are right, you simply slide the plants from the guttering into a guttering-shaped trench dug in well-prepared soil.

The easiest way to sow outdoors is to dig out a flat-bottomed trench 5cm (2in) deep and 20-25cm (8-10in) wide. Lightly fork over the bottom of the trench, water the soil and then sow the seeds evenly, approximately 7.5cm (3in) apart, lightly pressing them into the soil. Fill the trench with soil and lightly firm down. If you need a second row, make a second trench spaced away from the first by the expected height of the crop.

The pods are ready to pick once they are well filled, but before the peas get too big.

Mice and slugs can be a problem outside, especially with early sowings, so make sure you provide protection from them.

Growing

Choose a sheltered position that gets plenty of sun. For the best results, make sure the soil is well dug and has plenty of added moisture-holding material, such as compost, or grow above a pre-dug, prepared moisture-retaining trench (*see* page 104).

Early sowings can be susceptible to frost and cold and should be covered with fleece if these conditions are likely.

Water well during dry periods, especially during flowering and pod set, giving the soil a good soaking once or twice a week. Mulch the soil around the plants to preserve soil moisture.

Unless growing dwarf varieties, you need to provide some support for the plants. One of the easiest and most natural ways of supporting peas is to insert twiggy branches alongside the plants when they're 7.5-10cm (3-4in) high. Pea netting supported by stout

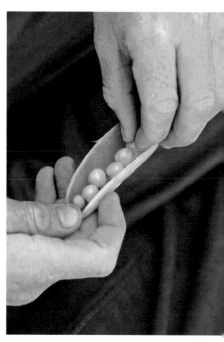

Mangetout are a very productive crop, as you eat the pods as well as the immature peas.

canes is an alternative, but it's tricky to untangle the plants from it at the end of the growing season; chicken wire is a better alternative. Lightweight wooden trellis and willow panels are attractive alternatives, especially when growing peas as ornamental features. Whatever you choose, make sure it's sturdy, as a row of peas in full leaf can catch the wind and end up several yards from where they were growing!

There is one pest you need to be careful of: pea moth. You'll only notice its presence when it comes to shelling your peas and you find that the maggot has got to them first. Female moths lay their eggs just as the flowers fade and the pods are developing, and this is the time to do something about it. Very early and very late crops usually escape attack, but cover mid-season crops with small-gauge, insect-proof mesh.

Harvesting

The approximate time between sowing and harvesting is 11–13 weeks for earlies, 13–14 weeks for second earlies, and 16 weeks for maincrops. Podding peas are ready to pick when they are well filled, when the pod is still fresh and green and hasn't started to dry out. Pick regularly, or the plants will stop producing. Start picking at the bottom of the plants and work upwards.

Pick mangetout peas when the pods are about 7.5–8cm (3–3½in) long and the peas are just starting to develop. Sugar snaps are picked at roughly the same time, but when the peas have developed within their pods.

The young tips and shoots of the plants can be picked and are an added treat eaten raw in salads. Pick the shoots before the leaves open out.

Yield: 4.5kg from a 3m row (10lb from a 10ft row).

AT A GLANCE

Peas are one of those crops that often fail to make it to the table – eating them fresh off the plant as you pick them is one of the delights of summer. By growing different varieties and sowing at different times of the year, you can be picking succulent fresh peas from early summer until mid-autumn.

ALLOTMENT ADVICE:
what I wish I'd known

Providing the soil is warm, peas get off to a flying start and can grow trouble free. They are subject to two major problems: powdery mildew in dry conditions, and pea moth.

Keep the plants well watered at the roots (don't wet the foliage) to avoid the first, and use mesh to protect against the second.

TRIED AND TESTED
RHS VARIETIES

Early: 'Early Onward' (AGM), 'Little Marvel' (AGM)

Maincrop: 'Cavalier' (AGM), 'Hurst Greenshaft' (AGM), 'Kelvedon Wonder' (AGM), 'Onward' (AGM)

Mangetout: 'Delikata' (AGM), 'Oregon Sugar Pod' (AGM)

Sugar snap: 'Sugar Ann' (AGM)

Broad beans

There's nothing quite like the flavour of the first broad beans of the year. They are the first beans to crop on the allotment, and with successional sowings you can have fresh broad beans from late spring into early autumn.

Broad beans are the least fussy of the legumes, being more tolerant of poor soils, but still benefit from lots of organic matter added to the soil before sowing or planting. They also make attractive, ornamental plants, with sweetly scented white flowers that act like a magnet to pollinating insects.

Sowing

In mild areas and on sheltered allotment sites you can sow hardier varieties, such as 'Aquadulce', in the autumn for a really early, late-spring crop.

For the earliest crops, sow in mid- to late winter under cloches or indoors in pots, large module trays or root trainers; harden off plants for 10–14 days before planting outside. Sowings made outside in winter and early spring do better if the soil is pre-warmed by covering with plastic sheeting two weeks beforehand.

The main outdoor sowing period is early and mid-spring. Sow 5cm (2in) deep and 20cm (8in) apart; dwarf varieties, like 'The Sutton', can be sown 15cm (6in) apart. Broad beans are best sown in double rows, with the rows 20cm (8in) apart. If a second double row is needed this should be sown 60cm (2ft) away from the first; 45cm (18in) for dwarf varieties. Sow extra seeds to produce plants you can transplant to fill in gaps left by seeds that don't germinate.

Successional sowings will provide a bountiful crop over a long period. Wait until the plants from one sowing reach a height of around 15-20cm (6-8in) before making the next sowing. Sowing in late spring extends the crop throughout the summer months and into autumn.

Growing

Choose a position that gets plenty of sun and is sheltered from strong winds, as plants with a heavy crop are prone to wind damage.

Grow broad beans in well-prepared soil that has had plenty of well-rotted organic matter added.

Autumn or early sowings can be susceptible to frost and cold and should be covered with fleece if these weather conditions threaten once the young plants have emerged.

Taller varieties need support. Strong, twiggy branches can be used, but better supports are made by inserting a stout cane or stake at each corner and in the middle of the double row. Run string around the supports and the plants at 30cm (12in) intervals from the ground.

Water well in dry periods, especially during flowering and pod set, soaking the soil once a week when needed.

Harvesting

The approximate time between sowing and harvest is ten weeks. You can start picking when the pods are immature, around 7.5-10cm (3-4in) long, and cook them whole. Mangetout varieties are available if you like this idea.

Sow broad beans evenly in a trench. Standing them on end will help prevent rotting.

When picking pods to shell, wait until the beans start to be visible through the pod, but don't leave them too long. Once the scars on the beans turn black, they become tougher and will have lost some of their sweet flavour. Start picking from the base of the plants and work upwards.

Yield: 9kg from a 3m double row.

Opposite, clockwise from top Protect young plants from cold weather by covering them with fleece; tall varieties will need staking to prevent them from blowing over; harvest when the beans are still young and fresh; double-pod the beans for the best taste.

AT A GLANCE

Broad beans are a versatile crop – eat them fresh, dry them or freeze them – that taste fantastic picked at the right time and eaten straight from the plot. They're easy to grow and can produce huge yields over a long period, especially when sown in autumn and in spring.

ALLOTMENT ADVICE:
what I wish I'd known

Broad beans are often attacked by black bean aphids in summer, which target the young shoots. To reduce the damage – and produce an earlier crop – pinch out the top 7.5cm (3in) of the stems when the first pods start to form. Don't throw these succulent tops away: they are excellent lightly steamed as a vegetable.

TRIED AND TESTED RHS VARIETIES

Autumn-sowing: 'Aquadulce' (AGM), **Autumn- or spring-sowing:** 'Aquadulce Claudia' (AGM)
Spring-sowing: 'Bunyards Exhibition', 'Express' (AGM), 'Imperial Green Longpod' (AGM), 'Jubilee Hysor' (AGM), 'Masterpiece Green Longpod' (AGM), 'Meteor' (AGM), 'The Sutton' (AGM), 'Witkiem Vroma' (AGM)

Runner beans

Shop-bought runner beans can be tough, stringy, and tasteless. Growing your own and picking them at their peak will show you exactly how runner beans are meant to taste, and there are plenty of stringless varieties, which are even more succulent.

The vast majority of runner beans are climbers that need substantial supports to hold them up. However, there are dwarf varieties that need no support and which are perfect for small or very windy areas and for growing in containers.

Sowing

Sow seeds outdoors in late spring and early summer 5cm (2in) deep. To produce an earlier crop, sow in 7.5-10cm (3-4in) pots in mid-spring indoors with a little heat and plant out the young

Before sowing, check through the seeds and only sow those that are intact.

plants in late spring or early summer, depending on when the frosts have passed. Always harden off the plants for 10-14 days before planting outside.

Growing

Although they prefer a sunny position, runner beans will tolerate a little shade.

For best results make sure the soil is well dug and has plenty of added moisture-holding material, such as compost, or better still grow above a pre-dug trench (*see* page 104).

The plants need sturdy supports to climb up. The traditional method is to grow them individually up two rows of 2.4m (8ft) tall bamboo canes, with the bottom 30cm (12in) inserted into the soil. The canes are spaced 20-23cm (8-9in) apart within the row, and the two rows 45cm (18in) apart. The two rows are then tied near their top to a horizontal cane, forming a row of inverted Vs. If you slope the bamboo canes so that they meet in the middle (like Xs) and tie them here, so that the tops of the canes extend beyond the row, you will find picking is easier and the yield is usually better.

Alternatively, grow them up a wigwam of canes, which takes up less room and makes an ornamental feature. Dwarf varieties, such as 'Hestia', don't need

Runner beans can also be grown up wigwams made from lengths of willow stems.

any support and can be grown 20-23cm (8-9in) apart. Loosely tie the plants to their supports after planting; after that they should climb naturally. Re-train and tie in any shoots that become wayward, and remove the growing point once the plants reach the top of their support.

Keep an eye out for slugs and blackfly that may attack the plants.

Flower set

Runner bean flowers sometimes fail to set, resulting in no beans. There are a number of causes for this, and a number of solutions.

Ensure the soil is constantly moist and doesn't dry out; mulch the soil in early

The traditional way to grow runner beans is to support them on a framework of bamboo canes.

AT A GLANCE

Runner beans are an allotment staple – the distinctive frames of bamboo canes stick out like shining beacons on almost every plot. And it's not surprising – what other vegetable yields such an enormous crop over such a long time, looks so wonderful, and gives rise to so many lengthy discussions on what to do with the armfuls of delicious veg produced?

Start picking the beans when they are young and before they begin to swell.

ALLOTMENT ADVICE:
what I wish I'd known

In some years, poor flower and bean set can lead to little or no crop. In others, you will have more than you can cope with.

TRIED AND TESTED
RHS VARIETIES

'Achievement' (AGM), 'Celebration' (AGM), 'Desiree' (AGM), 'Enorma' (AGM), 'Kelvedon Marvel', 'Lady Di' (AGM), 'Liberty' (AGM), 'Painted Lady', 'Polestar', 'Prizewinner', 'Red Rum' (AGM), 'Rotblühende' (AGM), 'Scarlet Emperor', 'White Achievement' (AGM), 'White Emergo' (AGM), 'Wisley Magic' (AGM)'

midsummer. Misting the foliage and flowers regularly in the early morning or evening – especially during hot, dry weather – will increase humidity around the flowers and help improve set. Flower set is much better in alkaline, chalky soils. If your soil is neutral or acidic it pays to water the crop once with hydrated lime.

Another way to improve flower set is to pinch out the growing tips of the plants when they are 15–20cm (6–8in) high. The flowers formed on the resulting sideshoots usually set better.

If you regularly have problems, it would be worth growing pink- or white-flowered varieties, which usually set more reliably than red-flowered types.

Harvesting
The approximate time from sowing to harvest is 12–13 weeks. Start harvesting when pods are 15–20cm (6–8in) long and before the beans begin to swell.

It is vital that you pick regularly to prevent any pods reaching maturity; once this happens plants will stop flowering and no more pods will be set. If you pick regularly, plants will crop for up to eight weeks or more.

Yield: 17kg from a 3m row (30lb from a 10ft row).

French beans

Although French beans are not as productive as their close family member the runner bean, they have a more refined texture and taste, and rarely have the problem of not-setting pods. This is a varied group, encompassing flat- and round-podded beans, some grown for their pods, others for their beans. There are two main types: dwarf bush and climbing. The former only grow to around 40–45cm (16–18in) high, making them a perfect choice where growing space is tight and there isn't room to erect support poles for climbing beans. Some varieties produce coloured pods, which make them useful additions to ornamental allotments, and good choices among these include 'Kingston Gold' and 'Purple Teepee'.

Sowing
French beans are tender plants, so succumb to frost damage; bear this in mind when considering sowing dates and planting out times. Young plants can also be adversely affected by cold temperatures, so cover them with fleece until the weather warms up.

The main outdoor sowing period is late spring and early summer; you can also sow dwarf French beans in mid-spring under cloches or similar protection for an earlier crop. Both dwarf and climbing varieties can be sown in midsummer to extend the season as late as mid-autumn.

Sow dwarf varieties 5cm (2in) deep and 10cm (4in) apart in rows 38–45cm (15–18in) apart. This sowing distance is tighter than usually recommended (15–23cm/6–9in), however, this closer spacing means that the plants can support themselves better and the yield per row is much higher. If growing at this closer spacing, pay particular attention to feeding and watering.

You will get better results, especially in early spring and on cold, exposed sites, by sowing indoors in small pots or root trainers and planting out when the young plants are 7.5–10cm (3–4in) tall; always harden off the plants for 10–14 days before planting out to acclimatise them to outdoor conditions. But don't plant out until all fear of frost has passed. If your plot is in a cold, exposed area, or you're taking a risk for a slightly earlier crop, you should use cloches, fleece, or similar protection.

Growing
Choose a sunny position, with a well-prepared soil that has had plenty of well-rotted organic matter added.

The dwarf bush types may not need supporting, but short twiggy branches

French beans can produce huge crops of tasty pencil-thin pods.

can be used to support the plants and will help keep the pods off the ground. Alternatively, grow them in blocks, where neighbouring plants will provide some support and a little protection.

Climbing varieties are best grown up 2.1-2.4m (7-8ft) tall bamboo canes, arranged in a wigwam or a double row. Space the canes 20-23cm (8-9in) apart and grow one plant up each cane. Tie in the young plants as they grow; they can become unwound from their supports in windy conditions. Pinch out the tips of climbing varieties once they reach the top of their supports.

Water well during any periods of prolonged dry weather, especially when the flowers are setting. Mulch around the plants in early to midsummer to help conserve soil moisture.

Harvesting

The approximate time between sowing and harvesting is 9-13 weeks. Begin picking the pods when they are 10cm (4in) long. Pods are ready when they snap easily and before the beans can be

Yellow-podded varieties of French bean are also available.

seen through the pod. Picked regularly, plants will crop for several weeks.

Young pods are eaten whole or sliced. Haricot beans within mature pods can be eaten fresh or dried for storage, so there is no wastage of pods that have been left on the plants too long at the end of the growing season.

Once all the pods have been picked, water the plants well and feed with a liquid fertiliser. You may get a further

Harvest the pods regularly to ensure the plants continue cropping when they have reached a suitable size.

crop later in the year. The pods will be smaller, but still worthwhile.

Yield: Bush: 3.5kg from a 3m row (8lb from a 10ft row).
Climbing: 5.5kg from a 3m row (12lb from a 10ft row).

AT A GLANCE

Once regarded as inferior to the staple British summer bean, the runner, French beans are now more popular than ever. This is strange, since the tasteless wonders flown in from the other side of the world melt into insignificance against French beans grown on the allotment, and picked and eaten on the same day. Dwarf bush and climbing varieties are available – it is worth growing both, as they produce very different types of pods, some with wonderful colours.

ALLOTMENT ADVICE:
what I wish I'd known

You can increase the cropping period to more than five months by making

successional sowings from late spring to midsummer. After the initial cropping, water and feed plants well for a secondary crop.

TRIED AND TESTED RHS VARIETIES

Climbing: 'Algarve' (AGM), 'Blue Lake', 'Cobra' (AGM), 'Diamant' (AGM), 'Hunter' (AGM), 'Kingston Gold' (AGM), 'Musica' (AGM)
Dwarf: 'Annabel' (AGM), 'Delinel' (AGM), 'Ferrari' (AGM), 'Golden Teepee', 'Masterpiece', 'Nomad' (AGM), 'Orinoco Golden Bean' (AGM), 'Purple Teepee', 'Safari' (AGM), 'Sonesta' (AGM), 'Speedy', 'Sprite' (AGM), 'Tendergreen', 'The Prince' (AGM)

Planning your crops
Brassicas

Basic techniques

You either love them or you hate them, but the brassicas, or cabbage family, are important vegetables. They provide nutritious crops just about all year, but particularly from winter to early spring when very little else is available fresh.

Brassicas include the leafy cabbage and kale, cauliflower, Brussels sprouts, broccoli, and calabrese, plus the root crops kohlrabi, swedes and turnips. All share similar needs and problems, so they are nearly always grown together as part of a three- or four-year crop rotation, including the root brassicas (*see* pages 65–6). Choose the right varieties and sow at the right time, and you can crop all year.

Growing

Brassicas prefer a sunny site, although cabbages, Brussels sprouts, and kale tolerate light shade. In a rotation, plant them after peas and beans (*see* pages 104–13); they will benefit from the extra nitrogen in the soil from the breakdown of the legume roots. To grow and crop well, brassicas need humus-rich, alkaline soil, of pH6–7.5, with plenty of well-rotted manure or compost. Check your soil with a soil pH tester; if it is acidic, add lime before sowing or planting out.

Leafy brassicas also need the soil in their final growing area to be firm and reasonably well compacted to produce solid, firm hearts or heads. Walk over the soil with your weight on your heels before planting out or leave several months between digging and planting to give the soil plenty of time to settle.

If your site is exposed, it pays to earth up around the stems of overwintering plants – especially Brussels sprouts – or tie them to stout canes or stakes.

Raising from seed

All brassicas need a soil temperature of at least 7°C (45°F) to germinate. With leafy brassicas, you'll get better results if you can set aside a small area as a seed bed, sowing and growing them

on here before transplanting the young plants to their final positions.

If you don't have room for a seed bed, want to produce earlier crops, or find that seed-sown plants struggle when sown directly outside, then raise the young plants in cell or module trays in a greenhouse, conservatory, or cold frame, or on a windowsill. Providing gentle heat will give better results when sowing in winter or early spring. Sow two seeds per module and remove the weakest seedling if both germinate. Plants grown indoors will need to be hardened off or

acclimatised for 10–14 days before planting out. Gradually expose them for longer periods to the cooler outdoors. Start by putting them out in the day covered with fleece, then in the day without the fleece, then overnight with fleece, until finally they can tolerate being outside without protection. Once young plants are big enough, usually when they are a good size or have five or six true leaves, transplant them into their final growing places. Water them well the day before to reduce shock and lift them with as much soil as possible.

1) Sow brassica seeds thinly in rows (drills) made in well-prepared soil; you can place the seeds in the palm of your hand and gently tap them into place.
2) Plant out young brassica plants raised indoors in modules at the final spacing in lightly compacted soil, and plant firmly.
3) Brassica collars placed around the stems will help prevent damage from cabbage root fly.
4) Brassicas are the mainstay of the allotment during the winter months; many of them provide valuable crops at this time of year.
5) Brussels sprout plants are top heavy and can blow over in exposed areas, so support them with stout stakes.
6) Carefully tie in the plants to their supports to keep them steady in windy weather.
7) Cabbage white caterpillars can be very damaging on cabbages and other brassica plants.

or carpet underlay. They are simply discs with a radial slit to allow them to be fitted snugly around the stem; they must completely surround the stem to prevent the female laying.

Growing plants under fleece or fine-mesh netting will help prevent root fly attack and will also protect against the other two major pests: cabbage white caterpillars and pigeons. It also keeps off flea beetle, which can be a problem on young plants. Check plants regularly, daily if you can, for cabbage whites. Squash or remove clusters of yellow eggs and the caterpillars by hand as soon as you see them.

Remove yellowing leaves as soon as you see them; they may be affected with leaf diseases and this will help stop their spread. The main disease is clubroot, which affects water take up, reduces yields, and can ultimately kill the plant. There are a number of precautions you can take, and you may need them all. Follow a four-year crop rotation. Dig the soil over and lime it to ensure it is alkaline – clubroot is worse in waterlogged soil and needs acidic conditions. Start plants in pots, finishing in a 15cm (6in) pot, planting out only when they have a good root system.

Before transplanting add a general, balanced, granular fertiliser to the soil in the final growing position and lightly rake in. Some brassicas can be very sensitive to a lack of trace elements in the soil, especially boron and manganese, so using a fertiliser that contains these trace or micronutrients often gives even better results.

Transplant into a hole deep enough for the young plant's lower leaves to touch the soil. Puddle in by filling the hole with water a few times before filling it with soil and firming around the plant.

If young brassicas become stressed they will not perform well. Make sure they are well watered during warm, dry weather and keep weeds at bay.

Pests and diseases

Cabbage root fly is a major pest that attacks a wide range of brassicas. The females lay eggs around the stems, and the resulting larvae eat the roots. Look out for wilting plants that produce reddish leaves. To protect against attack, use brassica collars or make your own from 7.5cm (3in) diameter roofing felt

Cabbages

Although traditionally green, cabbages can also be red or purple and come in a range of shapes from round to pointed and open and flat. There are also spring greens – undeveloped spring cabbages that are grown closer together and picked early. They are usually sown in summer, but can be grown all year round.

There are very hardy, winter varieties able to stand up to the worst winter weather. Savoys, for example, are grown as winter cabbages.

Sowing

Sow thinly, 1cm (½in) deep in rows 15cm (6in) apart. Thin the young seedlings to

Some cabbage varieties can grow very large, so make sure you give them plenty of space.

7.5cm (3in) apart to give the young plants room to grow on unchecked.

Sow little and often to ensure a succession of crops and to prevent gluts. When you sow depends on the type being grown. Sow spring cabbage in mid- to late summer and transplant in autumn. Sow summer cabbage from late winter to early spring (with protection or indoors) until late spring and transplant in late spring or early summer; later sowings crop into autumn. Sow winter cabbage from late spring to early summer and transplant in early to midsummer.

Growing

Plant compact varieties 30cm (12in) apart, larger varieties up to 45cm (18in)

apart. Plant spring cabbages just 10cm (4in) apart in rows 30cm (1ft) apart – thin out to 30cm (1ft) apart in late winter to early spring and use the thinnings as spring greens.

Water well every ten days during dry weather and conserve soil moisture with a mulch. Irregular watering can lead to the heart splitting.

Occasional summer feeding with a liquid fertiliser will improve yields of summer and winter cabbages. Spring cabbages should be given a feed with a granular fertiliser in early spring.

There are a few problems that are common to all brassicas to look out for (*see* page 117).

Harvesting

The approximate time between sowing and harvesting is 32–36 weeks for spring cabbages and 20–36 weeks for other varieties.

Cabbages are harvested by cutting through the stem just above ground level with a sharp knife as and when they're needed.

Yield: Depends on type and variety, but up to 10kg from a 3m row of winter cabbages (22lb from a 10ft row).

Opposite *Different varieties of cabbage are available; with careful planning you can have some available to harvest almost all year round.*

AT A GLANCE

A well-grown, well-cooked cabbage can be a long-awaited treat – especially the first one of spring. One that has been boiled to death is a waste of growing time and space.

With a little planning it's possible to pick fresh cabbages nearly every day of the year. Cabbages are divided into spring, summer and winter types depending on when they're ready to use. Winter cabbages, and even some summer cabbages, can be lifted and stored if necessary.

ALLOTMENT ADVICE:
what I wish I'd known

For an extra crop, cut a 13mm (0.5in) deep cross in the stump of spring and summer cabbages, feed with a liquid fertiliser and you'll be rewarded with a cluster of much smaller cabbages in about five weeks.

TRIED AND TESTED
RHS VARIETIES

Spring (all pointed): 'Duncan' (AGM), 'Offenham 1 – Myatt's Offenham Compacta'

(AGM), 'Pixie' (AGM), 'Pyramid' (AGM)
Summer: 'Cape Horn' (AGM), 'Derby Day' (AGM), 'Elisa' (AGM), 'Greyhound' (AGM), 'Hispi' (AGM), 'Pyramid' (AGM), 'Spitfire' (AGM), 'Stonehead' (AGM)
Red: 'Ruby Ball' (AGM)
Winter: 'Celtic' (AGM), 'Deadon' (AGM), 'Huzaro' (AGM), 'January King 3' (AGM), 'Kilaton' (AGM)
Winter white: 'Marathon' (AGM)
Savoy: 'Endeavour' (AGM), 'Tarvoy' (AGM), 'Tundra' (AGM), 'Wintessa' (AGM)

Cauliflowers

There is some contention over whether some of the winter varieties here are cauliflowers or broccoli: different seed companies, for instance, list them as either one or the other – or even both. Strictly speaking most, if not all, are heading broccoli, but we cover them here because they look like and are treated like cauliflowers.

Traditionally, cauliflower heads or curds, are white, but there are varieties with purple, lime-green and even orange curds.

Romanesco types have an unusual shaped head and a fine taste and texture. They are ready in late autumn, and you don't have to harvest the whole head – just snap off the spears you need.

Sowing

Sow thinly, 1cm (½in) deep in rows 15cm (6in) apart. Thin the young seedlings to 7.5cm (3in) apart as soon as possible to give the young plants plenty of room to grow on unchecked.

The main sowing period is early to late spring. Summer varieties are sown in mid-spring, transplanted in early summer, and crop in late summer and early autumn. Achieve earlier summer crops by sowing under cover with gentle heat in mid- to late winter and transplanting in early to mid-spring. Autumn varieties are sown from mid- to late spring, and winter ones in late spring.

Growing

To grow perfect cauliflowers you will need a rich and deep soil in a sunny site. Any check to growth can cause small, deformed heads, so careful planting and watering throughout the growing season if conditions are dry are vital.

Space summer and autumn cropping types 60cm (2ft) apart and winter cultivars 75cm (30in) apart.

Water well in dry weather and conserve soil moisture with a mulch. Occasional summer feeding with a liquid fertiliser will improve results, as cauliflowers are a hungry crop.

There are a few problems that are common to all brassicas (*see* page 117).

Protect the curds of summer types from strong sun by bending a few leaves over them; doing the same with winter curds protects against frost and is important with less hardy varieties.

A home-grown cauli is hard to beat, but make sure you harvest them before the curd starts to open up.

Harvesting

The approximate time between sowing and harvesting is 18-25 weeks for summer varieties and up to 50 weeks for winter varieties. Start cutting when the heads are firm; if the florets start to separate, you've left it too late and the flavour will be weaker.

Yield: Up to 5.5kg from a 3m row (12lb from a 10ft row).

AT A GLANCE

Often regarded as being tricky to grow, these are certainly the fussiest of the brassicas, but with a little attention to detail you can grow perfect caulis.

By sowing different varieties you can have cauliflowers more-or-less all year round. Most produce curds in summer or autumn – the winter caulis are, in fact, just overwintered and mature in spring. Roscoff varieties for cutting in winter are not very hardy, and will only reliably crop in very mild winters or if they are grown in a polytunnel.

ALLOTMENT ADVICE:
what I wish I'd known

If space is at a premium on your plot, try growing the fast-maturing mini summer cauliflowers. Growing the standard varieties at closer spacings, just 30-45cm (12-18in) apart, will provide you with 'one-person' mini-curds.

TRIED AND TESTED RHS VARIETIES

Summer: 'Aviron (AGM)', 'Beauty' (AGM), 'Flamenco' (AGM), 'Mayflower' (AGM), 'Nautilus' (AGM)
Autumn: 'Aviso' (AGM), 'Belot' (AGM), 'Kestel' (AGM)
Winter: 'Aalsmeer' (AGM), 'Galleon' (AGM), 'Patriot' (AGM)
Coloured: 'Cheddar' (AGM), 'Graffiti' (AGM), 'Violet Queen' (AGM)

Broccoli

There are three main types of broccoli: the white and purple sprouting, and the green calabrese that forms a larger central head and is most often seen on our supermarket shelves. The sprouting types are hardy and are overwintered for harvest in spring, filling the gap between Brussels sprouts (*see* page 122) and spring cabbage (*see* pages 118-19), whereas calabrese is harvested in the autumn. New hybrids of interest are 'Tendergreen' and 'Tenderstem', and Chinese kale produces green sprouting broccoli spears on long tender stems.

Sowing

Sow thinly, 1cm (½in) deep in rows 15cm (6in) apart. Thin the young seedlings to 7.5cm (3in) apart to give the young plants room to grow on unchecked. Calabrese is best sown where it is to crop, thinly or at its final spacing.

The main sowing time is mid- to late spring, although you can sow in early spring in mild regions, preferably under cloches, and as late as early summer for late varieties.

Growing

These crops both prefer a fertile, well-drained, firm soil, but calabrese types will tolerate less fertile soils than the sprouting varieties. When the young broccoli plants are 10-15cm (4-6in) high, transplant them to their growing

Purple-sprouting broccoli can be harvested over a long period, when other greens may be scarce.

positions, leaving 45cm (18in) between plants. Harden off indoor-sown plants before planting out (*see* page 116) Thin directly sown calabrese to 30cm (12in).

Water well in any periods of dry weather and conserve soil moisture with a mulch. Occasional summer feeding with a liquid fertiliser will improve results.

There are a few problems to look out for that are common to all brassicas (*see* page 117).

Harvesting

The approximate time between sowing and harvesting is 42-45 weeks for purple and white sprouting varieties and 12 weeks for calabrese.

Harvest when the flower shoots (spears) are well formed, but before the individual flowers begin to open. Cut the central spear first. This is followed by a series of sideshoots, which can be picked regularly over four to six weeks.

Yield: 4.5-5kg from a 3m row (10-11lb from a 10ft row).

Calabrese is an excellent autumn cropper.

Brussels sprouts

Growing Brussels sprouts couldn't be easier. After harvesting, lightly steam the tight buttons for the best flavour.

Even though F1s grow better, the older Brussels sprout varieties have more flavour. For something a bit different, there are even red varieties, such as 'Red Bull' and 'Rubine'.

Sowing

Sow thinly, 1cm (½in) deep in rows 15cm (6in) apart. Thin the young seedlings to 7.5cm (3in) apart as soon as possible to give the young plants plenty of room to grow on unchecked.

Sow from early to mid-spring for winter to spring pickings. Early sowings may need to be covered with cloches in cold or exposed regions.

For an early crop in late summer or early autumn, sow under cover in late winter and plant out after hardening off.

Growing

Firm, water-retentive soil with plenty of humus is important for good Brussels crops, otherwise the sprouts 'blow', or open prematurely.

When the young plants are 10–15cm (4–6in) high, transplant to their growing positions 75cm (30in) apart; you can also plant short varieties 45cm (18in) apart for an earlier crop of smaller, tastier sprouts.

Water well in dry weather and conserve soil moisture with a mulch. A light feed of a granular high-nitrogen fertiliser in summer will help boost plants and an occasional summer feeding – especially a foliar feed – with a liquid fertiliser will also help.

There are a few problems to look out for that are common to all brassicas (*see* page 117).

As sprout plants are top heavy, they can blow over in exposed areas, so earth up soil around the stems or support them with stout bamboo canes or 2.5cm (1in) stakes.

Harvesting

The approximate time between sowing and harvesting is 28 weeks for early varieties and 35–36 weeks for late ones.

Start picking the lower sprouts when they are the size of a walnut and are still firm and tightly closed, and work your way upwards. Carefully snap them off with a sharp downward tug.

The flavour is usually better once the sprouts have experienced a touch of frost. Leave them on the plant and harvest them as you need them; if you have too many, freeze them promptly.

Yield: 4.5kg from a 3m row (10lb from a 10ft row).

Harvest by picking the lowest sprouts when they're the size of a walnut.

AT A GLANCE

Well-grown and (more importantly) well-cooked Brussels sprouts are certainly worth having. They can be picked over a long time, providing valuable winter vegetables when little else may be available. The plants are very hardy, and if you choose your varieties, sowing times, and plant spacings carefully, it's possible to have sprouts from early autumn until well into spring. The smaller the sprouts are when picked, the sweeter they are, but for the best flavour, add a touch of frost before picking if you can - this makes the sprouts even sweeter.

ALLOTMENT ADVICE:
what I wish I'd known

F1 hybrid varieties are usually the best choice; they produce a larger yield of better quality sprouts. The sprouts also hold for longer on the stem in good condition and so can be picked over a longer period.

TRIED AND TESTED
RHS VARIETIES

'Bosworth' (AGM), 'Cascade' (AGM), 'Diablo' (AGM), 'Maximus' (AGM), 'Montgomery' (AGM), 'Nelson' (AGM), 'Revenge' (AGM), 'Trafalgar', 'Wellington' (AGM)

Kale

There are four main types of kale. Curly kale is by far the most popular. Its leaves are frilly and curled, giving it an ornamental appearance. The newer F1 varieties are much sweeter than older varieties, which can be bitter.

Plain-leaved kale is taller and tends to be coarser than curly leaved varieties. Eat the young shoots in early spring rather than the autumn leaves. Rape kale provides young tender shoots in spring. Leaf-and-spear kale is a cross between a curly kale and a plain-leaved one. Pick the young leaves from late autumn and the leafy sideshoots in early spring, and then later pick the immature flower heads, which are cooked like broccoli.

Sowing

Sow thinly, 1cm (½in) deep in rows 15cm (6in) apart. Thin the young seedlings to 7.5cm (3in) apart to give young plants room to grow on unchecked. Sow rape kale in situ; it does not transplant well.

Sow in rows 15-23cm (6-9in) apart from early spring to early summer. For an early crop sow under cover in early spring and plant out after hardening off.

Curly kale is cold and frost hardy, nutritious and looks good on the winter plot too.

Kale is a great winter standby to grow on the allotment.

Growing

Kale needs rich, well-drained soil, but tolerates some shade.

Space plants 45cm (18in) apart. Water well in dry weather and conserve soil moisture with a mulch. A spring feed will improve results.

There are a few problems to look out for that are common to all brassicas (*see* page 117).

Harvesting

The approximate time between sowing and harvesting is 30-36 weeks.

Start to remove the young leaves from the top of the plant from mid-autumn. Sideshoots are formed after the main crown is harvested and these will be ready for use from late winter to late spring; pick shoots that are 10-15cm (4-6in) long and still young.

As a cut-and-come-again crop, harvest when the plants are 5cm (2in) high. Further young leaves will be produced that can be cut again.

Yield: 6.5-7kg from a 3m row (14-15lb from a 10ft row).

AT A GLANCE

Often a neglected crop, but one that is increasing in popularity, kale or borecole is a colourful and attractive addition to the winter plot. It is also an easy brassica: it tolerates very cold weather and frost better than most other brassicas, isn't generally troubled by birds, clubroot, or cabbage root fly, and will also tolerate a lightly shaded position.

When picked young and tender and lightly steamed, kale is a rich source of vitamins and iron. Fresh leaves can be steamed, braised, or quickly blanched and sautéed.

ALLOTMENT ADVICE:
what I wish I'd known

Kale can be grown as a cut-and-come-again crop. To treat it this way, sow the seed thinly where you want it to grow, in rows 23cm (9in) apart.

It can also be sown in pots or trays indoors to provide salad leaves all the year round.

TRIED AND TESTED RHS VARIETIES

Curly kale: 'Black Tuscany', 'Dwarf Green Curled', 'Nero di Toscana', 'Redbor' (AGM), 'Red Russian', 'Winterbor' (AGM)
Plain-leaved: 'Cottagers', 'Thousand Head'
Rape kale: 'Hungry Gap'
Leaf and spear: 'Pentland Brig'

Salads and leaves

Basic techniques

Summer just wouldn't be the same without a constant supply of delicious, crunchy salads. The sales of bagged salad leaves by supermarkets continues to increase every year. But, as with just about every vegetable, home-grown is best and you can pick at the peak of flavour and tenderness.

It's not only in summer that salads can be used for fabulous meals or side dishes. Many crops come into their own in autumn and even winter, and it is possible to produce crisp lettuce and other salad crops over a much longer period if you have a greenhouse, polytunnel, cold frame or even cloches to help extend the season. With a little forward thinking and choosing the right mix of types and varieties you can be picking crops for salads all year round.

Growing

Most salad crops are fast growing and quick to mature, so should be sown

Watercress

Although usually grown commercially in water, there are varieties that can be grown in the soil, providing it is given plenty of water. These will crop from early summer until around Christmas if protected with cloches or similar from autumn onwards. You can also grow watercress in a container stood in a saucer of water.

Sow in a shady place from late spring to early autumn and keep moist. Regular picking is essential for continuity.

Several companies sell watercress seed. Watercress 'Aqua' is one selection and should be sown from mid-spring for harvesting throughout summer, although some companies say it can be harvested year-round, except when frozen. Simply snip off the topmost shoots with scissors – the plant re-grows quickly from below. Always wash watercress thoroughly before eating.

successionally – little and often. Sow just enough for your needs every 10–14 days, rather than all in one go. This not only ensures the cropping period is as long as possible, it prevents gluts and gaps.

Because they're quick to mature, many salads make excellent catch crops between slower-growing, larger crops, making use of the otherwise wasted ground. The salads are harvested well before the main crop is ready. Just make sure the salads receive enough light and there are no major differences in the growing requirements.

Many can also be grown as cut-and-come-again crops by harvesting a few leaves regularly and allowing new ones to grow back, or cutting down close to ground level and allowing plants to re-shoot for a second or third crop.

For most winter salads, unless you live in very mild parts of the country, you will need to provide some form of protection. Some hardier crops will stand outside if protected by fleece or cloches. Others will need to be sown and grown indoors in a greenhouse or polytunnel. If you grow them in pots

5

1) *For best results always use a garden line to mark out your rows (drills) at the recommended spacing.*

2) *For earlier crops, sow a few seeds in each cell of module or cell trays and keep them under cover.*

3) *Thin out seedlings to the recommended spacing as soon as they are large enough to handle; most thinnings can be used in salads.*

4) *After thinning out, the plants will have more room to expand and develop fully to produce a good crop.*

5) *Carefully water young salad leaf plants; watering along the row at soil level rather than from above can help prevent problems with rotting.*

Micro leaves

The latest trend to hit salads is 'micro' leaves. Harvested when seedlings have formed their first true leaves, these crops bring variety to the salad bowl, have intense flavours, and can also be grown indoors all year round. Top chefs use them to dress plates, garnish soups, and bring interest to salads; at home, small quantities can pep up salads and add intense flavour to sandwiches.

As micro leaves are an indoor home project rather than an allotment one, we've just whetted your appetite; you'll need to find out more if you want to have a go yourself. But growing them is simplicity itself – the seeds can simply be germinated on a piece of blotting paper or kitchen towel and the seedlings cut once they've developed.

Lots of vegetables and herbs make excellent micro leaves; try beetroot, broccoli, chard, celery, peas, radish, mustard leaves and rocket, basil, coriander, and fennel.

you can bring them home and grow them on indoors or close to the house for protection, ready to pick whenever you need them. Or you can use growing bags for several sowings from autumn to spring, providing the compost is refreshed and fed for each crop.

Watering and care

Being fast growing, these crops should never receive a check to their growth or they quickly run to seed (bolt). Make sure the soil is kept moist and water regularly during sunny, dry periods.

In winter, reduce watering and water carefully trying to keep the leaves dry, otherwise diseases like grey mould (botrytis) can become a problem.

Although crops will need a fertile soil, don't overdo the feeding – especially with high nitrogen fertilisers, as this can result in soft, poorly flavoured growth. In autumn and winter, soft growth will also be more prone to cold damage. Use balanced feeds, or high-potash feeds that will toughen up the growth.

Whenever we think about salads it is our recognised favourites that always come to mind – rocket and lettuce being the obvious, ever-present choices – but there are lots of others. These add different textures and delicate, peppery or even spicy flavours to the salad bowl. Try Chinese cabbage, corn salad, endive, land cress, winter purslane, or Oriental vegetables – now very popular.

Lettuce

Lettuces are perfect 'filler' crops. You can fit a row in between other crops, as long as they have enough light. There are several different types of lettuce.

Butterhead lettuces have an open habit, are quick maturing, and tolerate poorer growing conditions. The soft, tender leaves quickly wilt after cutting, but the hearts have a lovely flavour.

The cos types have an upright growth habit, oblong head, and crisp, tasty leaves. Semi-cos are smaller, denser, and usually sweet tasting.

The crisphead types, which include the iceberg lettuces, produce large hearts of curled and crisp leaves and are more resistant than others to bolting (going to seed prematurely), but the flavour can be disappointing.

Unlike the other three types, loose-leaf varieties do not produce a heart. They are cut-and-come-again lettuce – you simply cut as many leaves as you want and leave the plant to continue growing, although they can be harvested whole. They are some of the most colourful varieties available and are highly ornamental.

Sow thinly by carefully tapping the seeds from the packet direct into the drill.

Cut-and-come-again lettuces take up little space and can be grown with other salad crops.

Sowing

A minimum soil temperature of 5°C (41°F) is needed for germination. Add a little general fertiliser to the soil before sowing and rake in.

Sow a short row every 10–14 days to ensure continuity of cropping. Sow seed thinly, 1cm (½in) deep in rows 30cm (12in) apart.

The time of sowing depends on cropping time. For summer and autumn crops, sow outdoors from early spring to midsummer. For an even earlier crop, sow indoors with gentle heat in late winter and plant out in early spring under cloches or plastic sheets; pre-warm the soil for two weeks first.

For an early winter crop, sow outdoors in mid- to late summer and cover the plants with closed cloches in early to mid-autumn; for a midwinter crop, sow in a heated greenhouse in early and mid-autumn and grow on in the greenhouse.

For spring crops, sow a hardy variety in early to mid-autumn, either in a cold greenhouse or outside under cloches in mild areas. Indoors they can be grown in growing bags or medium-sized pots. Pot growing is particularly useful, as you can bring them home one at a time and have them by the back door or on a windowsill to pick as and when needed.

Growing

Lettuce likes a sunny site and a moisture-retentive soil, but prefers light shade in the height of summer. Make sure the plants grow without any check, or they will run to seed (bolt) before they're ready to harvest. Plants that grow too slowly under poor conditions may also develop a bitter taste.

Start thinning seedlings when they're about 2.5cm (1in) high, and continue until the plants are 30cm (12in) apart for most varieties, 23cm (9in) for dwarf, compact varieties, and 15cm (6in) for loose-leaf types.

If you water the soil well the day before thinning and do it carefully, the thinnings can be replanted elsewhere to give a slightly later crop or dotted among other, later-maturing vegetables; water them in well after transplanting.

Later thinnings, when the plants are larger, can also be picked and eaten.

Alternatively providing the seed has been sown thinly, leave all the plants to grow and harvest them young as baby leaves, which does away with the need for any thinning!

Water when the soil is dry; the best time to water is in the early morning. There shouldn't be any need to feed while the crop is growing, but water the soil with a balanced liquid fertiliser if any extra feeding is necessary.

Early in the year sparrows can be a problem as they find young lettuces irresistible. Protect with fleece, chicken wire, or similar. Slugs will also take a liking to your lettuces, so protect them with your favourite control method.

Grey mould or botrytis can also be a problem in cool, damp summers or on autumn and winter crops. If growing in these conditions, increasing the spacing between plants will help reduce

Cos lettuce produce very crisp, crunchy leaves that can even be cooked by light steaming.

Harvest cut-and-come-again lettuce with scissors and then let the plants re-grow to produce further crops.

problems. Carefully clear away affected leaves as soon as you see them.

If plants receive a check to their growth or if they're not pulled when ready, they will bolt. The leaves are still edible, but the flavour will be stronger and more bitter than usual.

Harvesting

The approximate time between sowing and harvesting is 8-12 weeks, or six to eight weeks for loose-leaf varieties. Lettuce is ready when a firm heart has formed; the exception to this is the loose-leaf types, where individual leaves are harvested as and when needed once the plants are about 7.5-10cm (3-4in) high.

It's best to cut in the morning when the plants will be at their freshest. Cut lettuces rather than pulling; the stems will usually produce a second crop of new leaves providing the conditions aren't too hot and dry. Most lettuce will keep for a few days in the fridge.

Yield: From 8-9 (crispheads) to 18-20 (mini-lettuce) from a 3m (10ft) row.

Spinach

Some spinach varieties are ideal for spring sowing and others for autumn, but there are also easy-growing varieties that can be sown in either season.

Sowing

A minimum soil temperature of 7°C (45°F) is needed for germination; seed won't germinate above 30°C (86°F).

Sow thinly, 2.5cm (1in) deep in rows 30cm (12in) apart. Sow summer varieties every couple of weeks from early spring to the very start of summer. Sow winter varieties in late summer and early autumn. Thin seedlings to 7.5cm (3in) when about 2.5cm (1in) tall; a few weeks later harvest alternate plants.

Spinach can also be grown for salad leaves and even as a cut-and-come-again crop, in which case don't thin out the seedlings, but make sure you start cutting them as soon as they're ready.

Growing

Grow in a fertile, moisture-retentive soil with plenty of organic matter. Apply a general granular fertiliser two weeks before sowing. Keep well watered or plants will quickly run to seed.

Winter varieties generally need protection from mid-autumn. Cover with cloches or protect with straw or similar material and cover with fleece.

Mildew can be a problem, so choose a disease-resistant variety.

Harvesting

The approximate time between sowing and harvesting is 8-12 weeks.

Pick summer varieties between late spring and mid-autumn, and winter varieties from mid-autumn to mid-spring. Harvest the leaves continually once they're large enough to pick.

Yield: 2.5-4.5kg from a 3m row (5-10lb from a 10ft row).

For the best flavour, pick spinach leaves when they're young. They can then be added to salads.

AT A GLANCE

Spinach can be grown to produce a crop all year round, and at times when other greens might be in short supply. When prepared and cooked properly – pick and use fresh, and steam rather than boil – it is a tasty, versatile crop. Young leaves can even be used raw in salads. Some varieties can be overwintered for an early spring harvest.

ALLOTMENT ADVICE:
what I wish I'd known

Winter varieties need a sunny position, but summer varieties prefer a little shade – try growing between rows of taller crops – otherwise they may run to seed. Choose a variety that is resistant to bolting.

To prevent the leaves tasting bitter, make sure the soil is rich and contains plenty of organic matter.

TRIED AND TESTED
RHS VARIETIES

'Campania' (AGM), 'Emilia' (AGM), 'Fiorano' (AGM), 'Giant Winter', 'Lazio' (AGM), 'Medania' (AGM), 'Monnopa' (AGM), 'Scenic' (AGM), 'Tetona' (AGM), 'Tornado' (AGM), 'Toscane' (AGM), 'Triathlon' (AGM)

Chicory

The chicons of forced chicory are a winter treat, but need a little effort to produce.

'Heading' chicory include radicchio and sugarloaf, which are grown much like lettuce. 'Forcing' chicory (or Witloof or Belgian) are blanched or lifted and forced in a greenhouse to produce plump, leafy heads called chicons in winter.

Sowing

Sow thinly, 1cm (½in) deep in rows 30-35cm (12-14in) apart. Sow forcing chicory in late spring and early to mid-summer. Sow heading varieties from early to mid-spring for summer crops or late spring to midsummer for autumn.

When seedlings have three true leaves, thin forcing types to 15-23cm (6-9in) and heading types to 25-30cm (10-12in) or leave unthinned for salad leaves.

Growing

Water thoroughly in dry weather and give a liquid feed fortnightly in summer.

Plants may bolt if they become dry or receive a check to their growth.

Harvesting

The approximate time from sowing to harvesting is 8-12 weeks for heading types, 25-26 weeks plus forcing time for forcing types. Cut the heads of hearting types when ready; give protection to those kept in the soil over winter.

Lift forcing types in late autumn. Cut back leaves to 2.5cm (1in). Pack roots horizontally in sand in a cool shed until needed. To force, plant five in a 25cm (10in) pot of moist compost with the crown exposed. Cover with a black polythene bag or pot with no drainage holes and keep at 10-15°C (50-60°F). The chicons are ready when 15cm (6in) high.

Yield: About 2.5kg from a 3m row (5-6lb from a 10ft row).

Radicchio is a colourful addition to the allotment plot and adds a slightly bitter taste to salads.

Allotments in France

True French allotments date to the end of the 19th century, when factory owners set up *jardins ouvriers* or 'worker gardens'. The land was donated or rented out by factories to their employees to grow their own food so that they could have a 'taste of nature'. This was a cynical but successful move by the factory owners, as it meant the employee became dependent on his place of work in order to keep the allotment, and was less inclined to complain about conditions and wages.

After the Second World War, there were around 800,000 such allotments and the name changed to *jardins familiaux*, 'family gardens', or allotments. Small areas of land were given to the local population by the town councils as a way of encouraging subsistence and in an effort to reduce the gap between the lower classes and the richer population. By the 1970s only 150,000 survived but, much as in the United Kingdom, their popularity is on the rise again.

In the urban allotments of the Île-de-France region (Paris and its immediate surrounds), unique shed architecture plus a cross-purpose use for sport and play sit alongside the traditional garden use, with community involvement and importance given to the visual as well as structural planning of the sites - very different from British allotments.

Edible flowers

You'll see flowers growing on allotment plots for cutting, but growing them for the kitchen is becoming more popular. Some have a good, strong flavour – often peppery or fruity – while others are subtler. Others just look attractive.

They have other uses on the allotment too. Many attract pollinating insects, vital for good crops of beans for instance. Others attract beneficial insects, such as hoverflies, which help to keep down aphids and other pests.

Picking and preparing
Most flowers will wilt quickly when picked, especially on hot days, so try to pick either early in the morning or in the evening when it's cooler. Even though they may be used as individual petals, always pick the flowers whole and keep in a plastic bag until you can get them home and prepare them in the kitchen. In a plastic bag inflated with air and sealed, they can be kept in the fridge for several hours, but it's usually better to use them as soon as you can.

Lay them out and work through them individually, in most cases removing the petals from the flowerhead.

Annuals
Annuals are the easiest flowers to grow, treated like an annual vegetable crop and sown in rows. Most will also self-seed if you leave one or two plants to produce seedheads.

English or pot marigold
(*Calendula officinalis*)
A hardy annual producing flowers that are usually orange, although there are other colours available. The single-flowered varieties are the best choice. Deadhead plants to provide a succession of flowers. The petals add colour to salads.

Cornflower (*Centaurea cyanus*)
The flowers have a slightly sweet, clove-like flavour. Suitable as a garnish.

Nasturtium (*Tropaeolum majus*)
A half-hardy annual with flowers ranging from yellow to red. Both the leaves and the petals have a peppery taste; flowers can be used whole. Even the fresh seedheads can be picked and pickled to use like capers.

Tagetes (*Tagetes tenuifolia*)
A half-hardy annual whose flowers can be yellow, orange, red or a combination of these colours. The petals have a distinctive, zesty lemon flavour. Don't use the blowsy French or African marigolds sold for the border.

Heartsease (*Viola tricolor*)
The delicate flowers of this wildflower can be used whole. They have a sweet, fragrant flavour. Even cultivated violas and pansies can be used; winter-flowering pansies provide flowers from autumn through to spring. The leaves are also edible when steamed or boiled.

Flowers from crops
The flowers from a couple of crops can be eaten, making use of something that would normally die or be thrown away.

Courgette and squash flowers (*see* pages 78–9) are excellent stuffed, especially with feta cheese, and deep-fried in a light batter. Using the male flowers doesn't interfere with cropping. Pick before they are fully opened and remove the central parts before using.

Flowers of all the onion family (*see* pages 88–95) are edible. They tend to be stronger flavoured than the leaves, and go well with salads and in egg dishes and soups.

Rocket flowers (*see* page 139) taste similar to the leaves, so can be used in the same way especially in salads. Nearly all flowers from herbs can be used in the kitchen.

Herb flowers
Basil Flowers are milder than leaves, and suitable for salads or pasta dishes.

1

Borage Cucumber taste suitable for cold soups, sorbets, and drinks, such as Pimms, gin and tonic, or iced tea.

Chive The mild onion flavour is suitable for salads, egg dishes, and soups.

Dill Flowers have a stronger flavour than the leaves. Use like the leaves; suitable for seafood and dressings.

Fennel Flowers have a mild aniseed flavour. Use like the leaves; suitable for desserts and garnish.

Lavender Sweet flavour; use as a garnish and in savoury or sweet dishes.

Marjoram Flowers are milder than the leaves; use as the leaves.

Mint Use as the leaves, particularly in marinades and dressings, but sparingly.

Oregano Flowers are a mild version of the leaves, and used in the same way.

Rosemary Milder version of the leaves, especially good with meat and seafood.

Sage Flowers are milder than leaves; suitable for salads, bean and vegetable dishes, and as a garnish for pork dishes.

Thyme Milder than the leaves; use in salads, rice and pasta dishes.

Others to try

Carnations and dianthus Flowers have a mildly sweet, spicy flavour, and are suitable for desserts and salads.

Day lilies (*Hemerocallis*) Slightly sweet; use for desserts, stuffing or deep-frying.

1) *The flowerheads of chives are just as useful as the leaves.*
2) *Nasturtium flowers add a spicy flavour to salads.*
3) *Try courgette flowers lightly fried in a golden batter.*
4) *Borage flowers have a delicious cucumber taste.*
5) *Pot marigolds (calendulas) will brighten up any salad.*

Roses All are edible; the flavour of the petals depends on type and colour, but they're generally fruity. They're suitable for garnishing desserts and salads and are excellent in syrups and jellies.

Salad leaves and Oriental vegetables

SALAD LEAVES

As well as the classic lettuces (*see* pages 128–9) there are a host of other leaves useful for salads, grown in broadly the same way.

Chinese cabbage

Chinese cabbage is often sold as Chinese leaves. The green heads can be cooked like cabbage, stir-fried, or served raw in salad.

Sow thinly from late spring to late summer, once a month for successional crops, in well-prepared soil, 1cm (½in) deep in rows 38cm (15in) apart.

Thin seedlings to 30cm (12in) apart for large heads or 15cm (6in) apart for cut-and-come-again salad leaves. Don't bother transplanting thinnings; they are likely to run to seed. Keep the soil constantly moist to prevent the remaining plants bolting.

Chinese cabbage is fast growing and can be ready for cutting in as little as six to seven weeks, and ready to harvest from late summer to mid-autumn. You can cut the head and leave the stump to produce more, smaller heads, or use as cut-and-come-again leaves.

Chinese leaves are a crispy alternative or addition to lettuce in the salad bowl.

Corn salad

Often called lamb's lettuce, corn salad can withstand frost, which makes it the perfect choice for winter and early spring salads. It forms small rosettes of bright green, succulent leaves.

Sow 1cm (½in) deep in rows 15cm (6in) apart. Sow at fortnightly intervals from late summer to late autumn for a winter crop, and in early spring for a late-spring crop. When large enough to handle, thin out seedlings to 10cm (4in) apart. Water the young plants during dry spells.

Plants can be ready to crop from 50 days after sowing. Start by pulling up every other plant and then pick a few of the outer leaves at a time from the remaining plants.

Endive

Endive is grown as a cut-and-come-again crop and is usually blanched to reduce its bitter content. Sow thinly, 1cm (½in) deep in rows 30cm (12in) apart from late spring to late summer. Thin seedlings to 23cm (9in) apart.

Water thoroughly in dry weather and give a liquid feed fortnightly in summer. Start blanching about 12 weeks after sowing. Make sure the leaves are dry and loosely tie together. Cover with a black plastic pot with the drainage holes covered. Blanching takes about 10–20 days, and is faster in summer than winter. Sever the head with a knife when the leaves are creamy white.

Land cress

Land cress, sometimes called American cress, is a tasty watercress substitute. It provides a continuous supply over a long period and is easy to grow. Ready to eat seven to eight weeks after sowing,

Oriental vegetables add a range of spicy flavours to salads or can be cooked.

it provides pickings through the winter if covered with a cloche or similar.

Sow seeds thinly, 1cm (½in) deep in rows 15cm (6in) apart from early spring to late summer. Plants for overwintering can be sown in late summer and early autumn in rows 30cm (12in) apart.

Land cress does best in a cool, moist soil and part shade. When large enough to handle, thin seedlings to 10cm (4in) apart. Keep plants well watered, especially sowings made in the spring.

Cut plants regularly while they are fresh and young, as this will encourage further growth.

Winter purslane

Winter purslane is an attractive winter salad crop also known as claytonia or miner's lettuce. It can also be lightly boiled or steamed.

Plants do best in a slightly shaded position. Sow thinly, 1cm (½in) deep in rows 15cm (6in) apart. Sow in midsummer outdoors or late summer and early autumn in a cold greenhouse. Seeds can also be sown in spring. When large enough to handle, thin seedlings to 5–10cm (2–4in) apart.

Keep the soil moist during dry periods. Outdoor sowings may need cloche protection during bad weather.

Leaves can be cut as needed from early autumn to midwinter, or sometimes until as late as early spring.

Others to try

Buckler-leaved sorrel Bright green, arrow-shaped leaves with a sharp citrus flavour used to perk up salads. Although this is a perennial, plants develop a woody centre and are then best replaced. As this plant self-seeds quite quickly that isn't usually a problem.

Good King Henry A perennial that grows to around 30-60cm (1-2ft) high. The leaves taste like spinach and can be cooked as spinach or eaten raw in salads. Even the young shoots are very good, tied together in bundles and cooked and eaten like asparagus. The flower buds can be sautéed in butter. Being hardy, it can be picked through the winter if given some protection.

Red orach A quick-growing annual with deep maroon-red, arrowhead-shaped leaves. It goes to seed quickly, so sow little and often; the younger leaves have the best taste and colour.

ORIENTAL VEGETABLES

Oriental vegetables are becoming more and more popular. There are numerous ways of using them - from adding to salads, stews and soups to stir-fries and as a lightly steamed vegetable.

Here are some of the more popular and available ones that add subtle - or not so subtle - flavours to food.

Ceylon spinach

Ceylon spinach is a tender, fast-growing climber that will easily reach 3m (10ft). The leaves are picked and used in much the same way as normal spinach, often steamed, used in stir-fries, and lovely in quiches or similar dishes.

Buckler-leaved sorrel has a sharp citrus flavour and is useful for perking up salads.

Red orach is a colourful addition to mixed salads and has a bitter, sweet taste.

Sow the seeds in pots of compost indoors with heat at 21°C (70°F) in late winter to early spring. Plant outside in late spring or after the last frosts, after hardening off. Take care not to disturb the roots when transplanting.

Plants will grow in full sun or light shade. The soil must be rich and well drained, but plants need regular watering during dry periods.

Harvest at about 10-12 weeks, when the plants have reached a good height and have produced plenty of leaves. Don't be too greedy: over-picking can prevent the plant producing more leaves and causes it to run to seed early.

Pick salad and Oriental vegetables when the leaves are still young and tender to ensure the best flavours.

Chinese mustard greens

There is a wide range of Chinese mustards or mustard greens that can be grown and some are highly ornamental. Less bitter types are used in salads, when young, for their peppery taste while others are pickled.

Sow seeds thinly from mid-spring to late summer 1cm (½in) deep in rows 25–45cm (10–18in) apart. Some types can be sown all year round in a warm greenhouse or on a windowsill.

Keep well watered until seedlings appear. When large enough to handle, thin seedlings to 10–30cm (4–12in) apart. Sowings made in late summer will carry on cropping into winter if protected.

Harvest young leaves as required, picking a few at a time from each plant.

Chopsuey greens

Chopsuey greens are wonderful for the aromatic flavour of their deeply cut, bright green foliage; the petals of the

When grown as a cut-and-come-again crop, salad leaves can be grown close together and so you can grow lots of different types.

flowers can also be used in cooking. They are either steamed like spinach, used in stir-fries, or eaten raw in salads.

Sow thinly, 2.5cm (1in) deep in rows 15cm (6in) apart from mid-spring to early autumn. Thin seedlings to 7.5cm (3in). Keep well watered in dry periods.

The smaller the plant the milder the flavour, so start harvesting when they are around 13–15cm (5–6in) high – around six weeks after sowing. Continue to harvest leaves until you're ready to enjoy the flowers; the leaves become bitter once the plants flower. They also quickly wilt once picked, so it is best to harvest them as required.

Japanese mustard spinach

This is also known as komatsuna, and the young leaves, stalks, and flower shoots are used in salads and stir-fries.

Sow thinly, about 2.5–5cm (1–2in) apart from late spring to late summer. After a couple of weeks, thin out to 20–45cm (8–15in) apart.

Keep the soil consistently moist; water well during dry and hot periods. Feed occasionally with a liquid fertiliser.

Harvesting can start from around 30 days after sowing, any time from when the plants are 10cm (4in) high. Cut them

about 2.5cm (1in) above ground level so that plants can re-shoot to produce further crops. Up to three cuttings per plant can be harvested over several months – or you can cut leaves as and when you need them.

Japanese turnip

Kabu or Japanese turnip is crunchy with a mild flavour, and is perfect raw or used in soups or stir-fries.

Sow seeds 1cm (½in) deep in rows 23cm (9in) apart from early spring to early summer. Thin out plants until they are eventually 15–23cm (6–9in) apart. Water well during dry weather, or the roots will be small and woody.

Pull the turnips when the size of a golf ball for eating raw or the size of a tennis ball for cooking.

Mibuna and mizuna

Mibuna plants grow to about 30cm (12in) high, producing tight clusters of long, narrow leaves. These have a light mustard flavour, and are excellent in a salad or lightly cooked and seasoned as a side dish. One of the most versatile cut-and-come-again vegetables, it's very easy to grow and can be cut four or five times a year.

Some Oriental vegetables, such as mustard spinach, can be used in stir-fries or steamed.

Mizuna produces a large head of finely dissected, feathery leaves up to 25cm (10in) high. It has a peppery cabbage flavour. Use the leaves raw in salads or cooked in stir-fries or soups, and the young flowering stems like broccoli. It is hardy and grows best in moist conditions.

Sow at intervals throughout summer outside, or under cover in early autumn. You can sow directly where the plants are to grow, or in a seed bed and then transfer plants to their growing position, or in pots or module trays then plant out.

Both crops are harvested in more than one way. Plants to be used when young should be 10-15cm (4-6in) apart, those to be cut frequently for their leaves 20cm (8in) apart, and those for larger plants 30-40cm (12-16in) apart.

Grow in a sunny position, although plants will tolerate light shade in summer. There is a risk of bolting in very hot, dry conditions, but also if sown too early when conditions are too cold. Keep plants well watered in dry periods.

From three to six weeks after sowing, the heads can be harvested whole by cutting at the base with a sharp knife; large plants will need six to eight weeks. Alternatively, cut individual leaves from plants regularly so that a fresh crop is continually produced. Eat on the same day for the best flavour.

Pak choi

Pak choi is very attractive used in salads or stir-fries as a baby leaf. When semi-mature or fully grown, it's cooked in a variety of Oriental dishes.

It grows best in a sunny position in a fertile soil. Sow thinly, 1cm (½in) deep in rows 30-38cm (12-15in) apart from late spring to midsummer; the older you want to harvest, the wider the spacing. Make earlier and later sowings for baby leaves under protection in mild areas. Gradually thin to 7.5-10cm (3-4in) for baby leaf, 20cm (8in) for semi-mature plants and to 25-30cm (10-12in) for mature plants. Keep plants well watered to avoid bolting and blandness.

Pak choi is ready to harvest in 30 days as baby leaves, or 45-75 days as semi-mature to full-size heads.

Texel greens

These have a mild mustard flavour and are used as salad greens or in stir-fries.

Sow thinly, 13mm (0.5in) deep in rows 23cm (9in) apart from late spring to late summer, or under cover in late winter to early spring, and in autumn for very early and extra late crops. Once seedlings are large enough to handle, thin to 5-10cm (2-4in) apart. Keep the soil weed free and water well during dry conditions.

They grow fast; you can harvest the whole plant, but if you pick a few young leaves at a time they crop all summer.

Grow a range of types for a mosaic of colours, leaf textures and flavours.

AT A GLANCE

Bags of salad leaves are expensive to buy in supermarkets and because they're washed and ready to eat, they have a short lifespan in the fridge. By growing your own, you can pick the exact quantity and combination of colours and flavours you want for each meal.

In recent years, we have started to eat a wide range of other salad crops, including Oriental salads, which add superb and often subtle flavours to our salads. Many of the Oriental types can also be used in stir-fries and most can be sown at high density.

ALLOTMENT ADVICE:
what I wish I'd known

Salads don't have to be restricted to the summer. There are several salad crops available that will provide tasty leaves in spring, autumn, and winter, making the humble salad not so humble all year round.

TRIED AND TESTED
RHS VARIETIES

Chinese cabbage: 'Green Rocket', 'Kasumi' (AGM), 'One Kilo' (AGM), 'Tah Tsai', 'Wong

Bok', 'Yuki' (AGM)
Chinese mustard: 'Green-in-the-Snow (Kai-Choi)'
Chopsuey greens: 'Shungiku'
Corn salad: 'Cavallo' (AGM), 'Verte de Cambrai'
Endive, curled: 'Jeti' (AGM), 'Pancalieri' (AGM)
Endive, frisée: 'Frisée Glory' (AGM), 'Wallone' (AGM)
Komatsuna: 'Torasan'
Pak choi: 'Canton Dwarf', 'Cantong White', 'Hanakan', 'Joi Choi', 'Tatsoi'
Purslane: golden and green summer purslane, winter purslane

Rocket

This peppery, loose-leaved salad is a fast-maturing and easy-to-grow crop.

Sowing

A minimum soil temperature of 7°C (45°F) is needed for germination. Sow thinly, 5mm (¼in) deep in rows 15–23cm (6–9in) apart. If growing as single plants, thin the seedlings out to 15cm (6in) when they're large enough to handle. If growing as a cut-and-come-again crop, only thin very overcrowded plants.

For a very early crop, sow under cover in a cold greenhouse or in a cold frame from late winter to early spring; be prepared to cover these crops with fleece in very cold weather. Regular outdoor sowings can begin as soon as the soil is workable and continue until the end of midsummer. Later sowings can be made under cover until early autumn for a winter crop.

Sow little and often, about every 10–14 days, to ensure a successional supply throughout the summer.

Growing

Keep the soil moist to prevent premature bolting. As autumn

Rocket is easy to grow, but don't let it dry out or it will run to seed prematurely.

approaches, cover with fleece and you can crop right through to first frosts.

Harvesting

Time from sowing to harvesting is six to eight weeks as plants, or four to five weeks as a cut-and-come-again crop.

Rocket is best when young. Pick leaves as needed or cut plants back to 2.5–5cm (1–2in) when about 15cm (6in) high. Pinch out flower buds to prolong cropping.

Yield: About 9–10 bunches from a 3m (10ft) row.

Carefully harvest the leaves with scissors, leaving the plants to re-shoot and produce further crops.

AT A GLANCE

Although often sold as part of salad-leaf mixtures, rocket is also well worth growing on its own for the lovely pepper flavour it adds to salads. Leaves can also be lightly steamed as a delicious spinach substitute.

Late summer sowings will continue cropping into the winter if the plants are covered by cloches or similar protection.

ALLOTMENT ADVICE:
what I wish I'd known

Rocket is prone to very rapid bolting (running to seed prematurely), especially in the height of summer, and particularly if allowed to dry out. Growing in light shade at this time of year or covering crops with fleece to provide shade may help delay bolting. Wild rocket is more bolt-resistant, but it has a slightly different, although still delicious, flavour.

TRIED AND TESTED
RHS VARIETIES

Few varieties are available; rocket is often just sold as 'annual', 'cultivated', 'salad', or 'wild'. Three worthwhile ones you may find are 'Apollo', 'Skyrocket', and 'Voyager'.

Herbs

Basil *Ocimum basilicum*

A half-hardy herb grown as a tender annual, basil brings the Mediterranean to your food in summer. It is possibly the most popular herb in the world, with different types used in the cooking of many cultures, and originally from India.

Sweet basil, with its large green leaves and distinctive smell of cloves, is the type we associate with Italian cuisine.

Sowing

Sow basil seeds in spring in pots or modules under cover; sow directly into the soil in late spring or early summer, when all risk of frost has passed.

Growing

Choose a moist, well-drained, sunny site. Thin or transplant seedlings to 30–45cm (12–18in), so they have plenty of space to produce leafy plants. Depending on the cultivar, they may reach up to 60cm (24in) high if given plenty of warm sun and sufficient but not excessive moisture and space. Pinch out the shoots to get a bushier plant and delay flowering. Try to avoid the temptation to pick the odd leaf.

Keep an eye out for aphids and slugs, plus powdery mildew.

On the allotment you can leave some to flower – they will be enjoyed by beneficial insects – although this will shorten the productive life of the plant.

Harvesting

You can harvest your basil by taking the whole plant before it flowers, when it's about 25cm (10in) tall. Alternatively take a stem, leaving at least two leaves at the base so that new branches can form. For smaller amounts, you can take a few single leaves throughout the growing season, but plants may become 'leggy'.

Basil is wonderful used fresh or dried. You can use it in many ways, from soups to curries, or simply alongside tomatoes in a simple salad. Use it as fresh as possible, adding it to meals at the last minute to get the punchiest effect. If your crop is unexpectedly successful, make your own pesto – not hard, and much better than bought.

Common or sweet basil is one of the most popular culinary herbs in the world.

AT A GLANCE

There is such a huge choice available with this adaptable plant. You can grow basil in a pot on a windowsill if nowhere else, but on the allotment you have space to try the many different varieties: Thai, Greek, lemon, cinnamon, green ones, purple ones, the list goes on.

ALLOTMENT ADVICE:
what I wish I'd known

Basil resents having wet leaves or sitting in saturated soil overnight. Water at the base rather than overhead, early in the day at a time when it is not in full sun.

TRIED AND TESTED RHS VARIETIES

Sweet: 'Cinnamon' (purple-leaved, cinnamon-scented, attractive flowers), 'Lettuce Leaved' (large-leaved, needs more space than others)
Purple: *Ocimum basilicum* var. *purpurascens* 'Dark Opal' (beautiful, highly aromatic leaves contrast with other ingredients); *O. basilicum* var. *purpurascens* 'Red Rubin' (very strongly scented deep purple leaves, bred for pot production)
Thai: *Ocimum basilicum* x *citriodorum* 'Siam Queen' (cinnamon-aniseed leaves, purple flower bracts)

Bay *Laurus nobilis*

Highly versatile in the kitchen and an evergreen ornamental, bay, sweet bay, or laurel bay makes a beautiful conical tree or large shrub. It was sacred to the ancient Greeks and Romans who used the traditional laureate wreath, a crown of bay leaves, to recognise those who excelled in their field. Its distinctive leaves are dark green and glossy, long and pointed, with a sweet, aromatic scent. There are variegated and wavy-leaved versions, but the simple species is grown for culinary purposes.

Where to grow

In the right situation bay can make a large tree, but it is very tolerant of clipping. Before planting, check that it will be acceptable on your allotment, as some sites have regulations about trees. Think also about any shade it might cast on to yours or your neighbouring plots.

A frost-hardy evergreen, bay tolerates temperatures to just under freezing, so it will thrive if your allotment is in an area that does not experience prolonged frosts. If your area experiences severe

Harvest bay leaves as required to impart flavour to slow-cooked dishes or boiled meats.

winters, grow bay in containers that can be brought under cover if necessary. In the ground, it prefers fertile, moist soil and is happiest in partial shade, sheltered from cold, drying winds.

Planting

Bay does best if you plant it in the spring and refrain from taking leaves for the first year or two while it establishes. To propagate your own, take semi-ripe cuttings in summer or sow seed in containers in a cold frame in autumn.

Growing

Though hardy, it may benefit from some protection from harsh weather in exposed areas. It is relatively trouble free but may be troubled by bay sucker, scale insects, tortrix moth caterpillars, powdery mildew and leaf spot.

Harvesting

Harvest as required. When cooking, be aware that fresh leaves have a stronger flavour than dried ones. Use bay in soups, casseroles, sauces, stews and

Bay makes an elegant tree with attractive, dark green, glossy leaves.

stocks as part of the classic *bouquet garni*, which releases the flavours of the herbs slowly throughout the cooking process. Some desserts also feature bay.

To dry bay leaves, collect them in the summer and hang in a warm, dry place. Use within a year. If you have a surplus, they are said to be good at deterring weevils from flour and dried produce.

> ### AT A GLANCE
>
> Make a real feature with your bay tree. If you start with a young, single-stemmed specimen you could have a go at making a bare-stemmed, and elegant, standard.
>
> ### ALLOTMENT ADVICE:
> what I wish I'd known
>
> In the right conditions bay can become quite a large plant – as much as 12m (40ft) tall and 10m (33ft) wide.

Borage *Borago officinalis*

Beautiful nodding, starry blue flowers adorn this hairy herb all summer long. It can set seed and germinate quickly where it likes the soil, year after year, and is considered a nuisance by some. But for many more it's an easy favourite that attracts beneficial insects.

Sowing

Borage has a large tap root and resents the disturbance of transplanting, so it's best to sow the seed directly where you want it to grow, from mid-spring to midsummer. Sow widely and thin out seedlings to allow space for the plants to expand, as they can grow to 60-100cm (24-39in) high and 45cm (18in) wide. If you must sow and transplant, sow in modules or pots under cover in early to mid-spring. Sow two seeds per module or plant pot, pinch out the weakest seedling, and plant out the individual plants when they reach 10-15cm (4-6in). This method works fairly well as long as the root disturbance is minimal.

Growing

Borage will thrive in moist, well-drained soil in full sun and will also do well in poorer soils and partial shade.

Getting the level of moisture right is important. In very dry conditions it may develop mildew, while in very soggy soil root rot may be a problem. Be prepared to give the plants a little support as they can become top heavy.

Use cucumber-flavoured borage flowers to decorate salads and summer drinks.

Harvesting

Borage takes one of its common names, starflower, from its five pointed petals. They are usually blue but occasionally pink, and there is also a white form.

Use borage flowers fresh as a garnish on dishes or frozen into attractive ice-cubes, especially popular in summer wine- or gin-based drinks. They can also be crystallised or candied for desserts.

Borage leaves have a cucumber-like flavour that can also go in summer drinks, or be added in small amounts to salads. Use the leaves dried, fresh or frozen. They are best harvested in spring or early summer, just as the flowers appear.

Managing water

All crops need water. If you have a shed, greenhouse or other suitable structure, you have the potential to capture your own supply by collecting rain water in butts, close to your crops and reducing the arm ache of lugging cans. If you have doubts about the toxicity of rain water due to algae or anything else, do 'cress test' by watering separate lots of cress seed with tap and butt water; if both germinate equally well there is no problem. Regardless, it should be fine for established crops in the soil. (This is also a useful technique if you are worried about potential contamination of soil or manure).

Managing water means managing the need for water, which you can do by using mulches around your crops. Whether you lay a sheet mulch or apply a layer of organic mulch, try to conserve ground water by putting it down on wet soil. Avoid watering in the heat of the day, when much will evaporate, and direct water right at the roots of the plants rather than over the foliage. A good soaking a couple of times a week will be better for the plants than a light watering every day. And while some crops benefit from regular watering, such as celery, other crops, such as carrots, make less of a demand for water.

AT A GLANCE

What a beauty: it looks good, the bees love it, it makes a useful green manure, and it almost grows itself – every year. Borage is also one of the best known sources of gamma-linolenic acid (GLA), which may have anti-inflammatory properties, and is grown commercially and sold as starflower oil.

ALLOTMENT ADVICE:
what I wish I'd known

Do deadhead this enthusiastic seeder promptly if you want to stay in control.

Chives *Allium schoenoprasum*

The smallest member of the onion (allium) family, chives have a delicate flavour that makes them suitable for many dishes. Pink to purple pompon-shaped flowers bloom in the summer above narrow, tube-like green leaves. As chives always grow in clumps, they tend to be referred to in the plural rather than the singular. About five or six plants grow in a clump, and they may reach as high as 45cm (18in) tall.

Sowing and planting

Propagate by seed or divide clumps in spring or autumn. For seed, sow into a pot in spring and plant out 10cm (4in) apart in late spring, but avoid taking a harvest in the first season.

Growing

Chives prefer a fertile, moist soil and full sun. They are hardier than other members of the onion family grown as vegetables (*see* pages 88–95), and can tolerate wetter conditions. Cover with a cloche to prolong their season of use to Christmas and for early spring supplies.

Keep weeded and water well in dry spells. Chives are generally pest free, but if you see little rust-coloured spots on the leaves you have trouble. Rust spores will wash into the soil, so dig the plant up immediately and bin or burn it – do not compost. Avoid planting chives, mint (*see* page 150) or tarragon (*see* page 154) on the spot for three years. Divide clumps every two or three years,

as they can bulk up quickly and may become squashed. Replant clumps about 25cm (10cm) apart. You might even find your chives self-seeding freely. As with many other herbs, this happy-go-lucky arrangement adds to the beauty of an allotment plot and will attract the bees, but if they become a nuisance, remove seedheads promptly.

Harvesting

Harvest a clump at a time with scissors; this will encourage regrowth and a continual supply of fresh, green leaves.

Chives are often used snipped into salads, potatoes or omelettes, or used as a flavoursome garnish to soup. The pretty flowerheads, if picked soon after opening, are also popular as an edible garnish. Flowers and leaves freeze well.

It is easy to grow chives. Cut a whole clump at harvest time and let it regrow.

AT A GLANCE

Ornamental, easy to grow, and tasty, every allotment should have a clump of this hardy, herbaceous perennial.

ALLOTMENT ADVICE:
what I wish I'd known

In free-draining allotment soil, chives can often self-seed prolifically if you don't pick off the flowers. If they become a nuisance, gather them all up and use them in the kitchen (or share them), or simply hoe them off as you see them.

TRIED AND TESTED
RHS VARIETIES

Common: 'Forescate' (pink-flowered), *A. schoenoprasum* f. *albiflorum* (white-flowered)
Garlic, Chinese: *Allium tuberosum* (similar to ordinary chives, but with flat rather than round leaves, white flowers, and a mild garlic flavour)

Coriander *Coriandrum sativum*

A popular culinary herb, particularly in Asian cooking, this highly aromatic herb is great for a beginner on the allotment, because it is easy to grow and if you miss the leaves you can still use the seeds. The leaves, which look similar to flat-leaved parsley (which is a fairly close relation), are sometimes called cilantro, and are used as a herb; the seeds have a distinctive, lemony flavour and are used as a spice or condiment.

Sowing

Sow directly where plants are to grow, for best results. Sow into moist, shallow drills and thin out to 5cm (2in) apart for leaf production, 20-25cm (8-10in) apart for harvesting the seed. Alternatively sow seed in modules, but transplant seedlings quickly before the taproot develops, otherwise they tend to bolt after being transplanted. The round seeds are large enough to make sowing and spacing relatively easy.

Sow again at monthly intervals between early spring to late summer. Once the flowering stems appear, the leaf production will diminish rapidly. In mild areas you can keep up supplies over winter by sowing in the autumn and keeping the plants in full sunlight.

Growing

Coriander grows best in light, well-drained soil in a semi-shaded position. It does less well in damp or humid conditions, so should give the best results in a dry summer, but take care to ensure that it isn't allowed to dry out. Coriander has a very strong tendency to run to seed almost at once if it gets stressed by transplanting or drought, so keep it well watered and cosseted.

Harvesting

Coriander is a triple-value crop: you can take leaves, flowers and seeds one after the other. Plants usually grow to 50-70cm (20-28in) tall if they flower, but leaves should be harvested well

before this. Start picking them when the plants are young, about 10-15cm (4-6in) tall, and bright green. Add them to stews and salads, or try using them in Moroccan and Indian dishes.

If your coriander does decide to bolt, you can use the flowers in salads. The

Coriander leaf has a distinctive flavour.

seeds themselves are what we use as a spice in Thai and Indian cuisine, and carrot and coriander soup is one popular, tasty dish that uses both the leaves and the seeds.

AT A GLANCE

Coriander has been cultivated for over 3,000 years. Its pretty, ferny foliage has a distinctive aroma, which can divide opinion, and it produces pretty white flowers. The leaves freeze well if chopped first, and can be dropped into your cooking straight from the freezer. The seeds are simply dried.

ALLOTMENT ADVICE:
what I wish I'd known

Coriander often does well from an autumn sowing, being less likely to dry out and bolt.

Sow directly into damp drills, as it dislikes being transplanted.

TRIED AND TESTED RHS VARIETIES

Most coriander seed on sale is by species, but there are types bred for bolt-resistance: 'Santos' is a good allotment variety; 'Confetti' has dainty, filigree leaves good for garnish and bunching, and is slow to bolt; 'Calypso' has a slightly different flavour from ordinary coriander but is slow to bolt and great as a cut-and-come-again crop.

Dill *Anethum graveolens*

AT A GLANCE

Dill has long been used not just for its aniseed flavour but as an aid to digestion: it's particularly well known as an ingredient in the 'gripe water' given to babies suffering from colic, and has also been taken for insomnia, hiccups and tummy upsets. Add its ornamental value, and who would be without this herb?

ALLOTMENT ADVICE:
what I wish I'd known

Dill leaves have a sharp flavour that is slightly reminiscent of parsley, whereas the seeds are almost bitter.

TRIED AND TESTED RHS VARIETIES

Dill 'Dukat' (high-yielding standard leaf dill, slow to bolt).

Delicate filigree foliage and yellow flowers attract both the human eye and beneficial insects, making dill a striking and useful addition to an allotment plot. It is a pungent perennial with an aromatic aniseed flavour that has a history of use going back 5000 years.

Sowing and planting

Sow seed directly in late spring, or sow in pots or modules and transplant while young to minimise root disturbance, which may induce bolting. Give each plant 25–30cm (10–12in) of space and plant seedlings after the threat of frost has passed. Sow every three weeks for a constant supply of fresh leaves.

Growing

Grow in well-drained, sheltered, poor soil in sun or partial shade. Dill can reach up to 1m (3ft) high. Dill, fennel (*see* page 148) and coriander may cross-pollinate, so keep them separated. Plants under stress may bolt, so keep them well watered. At the end of the year, dig up and compost

The feathery foliage of dill looks pretty and tastes great with fish.

the plants, removing seedheads first: seeds remain viable for up to three years, so dill may become a nuisance if allowed to self-seed. Slugs can be a problem on young growth and, if too crowded, aphids may become an issue.

Harvesting

Cut the leaves at any time during the growing season to use fresh; harvest them just before flowering for drying. Gather the seeds in summer and dry them for pickling or infusing. Use dill in fish dishes such as gravadlax, alongside leaf vegetables and in salads, in which the flowers make an attractive addition.

Comfrey, an allotment holder's friend

Comfrey is a deep-rooted herbaceous perennial that seems to soak up nutrients, especially potassium (potash), from the depths of the soil and store them in its leaves. It grows densely and is propagated by root cuttings. This means it can be difficult to eradicate, so select its site with care. Happy in full sun or partial to nearly full shade, it is perfect for a damp spot. Russian comfrey, *Symphytum* x *uplandicum* 'Bocking 14' has the most potassium. To use it, make 'comfrey tea': cut the plants down when they flower and put them in a water butt – about 6kg (13lb) of leaves to 90 litres (20 gallons) of water. (For smaller amounts, scale down to a bucket with a lid.) After about four weeks you can drain off liquid feed to use undiluted. It truly stinks, but is fantastic stuff for all your plants, especially tomatoes, potatoes, beans, and soft fruit. A less pungent way of using it is to put leaves in the compost heap, where they activate or speed up composting as well as adding nutritional value. You can also use them to line planting trenches, or in mulch around crops like sweetcorn or cabbages, and they're a favourite with chickens too (*see* pages 208–9). Nettles have similar qualities, being high in nitrogen and potassium, and possibly having insecticidal and fungicidal properties too.

Fennel *Foeniculum vulgare*

Herb, leaf or sweet fennel is not to be confused with Florence or bulb fennel. Tall, graceful herb fennel is popular for its ornamental appeal as much as its aromatic leaves and seeds. It's easy to grow and relatively trouble-free, and produces clouds of finely divided, feathery foliage with a faint liquorice flavour. The closely related Florence fennel or finnochio (*Foeniculum vulgare* var. *dulce*) is grown as a tender annual for its bulbous base of crunchy, swollen stems, and eaten as a vegetable.

Sowing

Sow in early spring in pots or modules and transplant out at 50cm (20in) spacings (20cm/8in for Florence fennel) while the plant is still young to minimise root disturbance and risk of bolting. Fluctuations in temperature and its sensitivity to day length can also induce premature flowering, so try sowing Florence fennel, which is frost tender, after the longest day of the year to enjoy a late summer or autumn harvest.

Growing

Fennel tolerates poor conditions, but to get the best from it, grow it in moist, drained soil in full sun or partial shade. It can reach 1.5–1.8m (5–6ft) tall. Picking the flowers will prolong the supply of leaves, but the seeds are also useful. Keep it away from dill (*see* page 147) to avoid cross-pollination.

Sow Florence fennel in early spring at a minimum of 15°C (59°F) in modules and transplant when seedlings have no more than four true leaves. Keep the swelling bulbs well watered, weed-free and earthed up a little to make the bulbs sweet and white. If aphids descend, squash or hose them off.

Harvesting

Harvest the leaves at any time to freeze or use fresh. Take unripe seeds to use in dishes, or collect ripe seeds for drying. Use as an accompaniment to oily fish or pork, pasta and salad dishes. The seeds are used as a spice and to make tea.

For Florence fennel, the approximate time from sowing to harvesting is at least 12 weeks. Cut at ground level from early summer to autumn, once they are sufficiently swollen. Bulbs keep for

The attractive aniseed-flavoured foliage of bronze fennel can be used in a similar way to Dill in cooking for flavouring.

about a week if refrigerated. Slice them into salads raw, cook in casseroles, or cut into wedges and roast.

AT A GLANCE

Originally from the Mediterranean and a feature of Italian cuisine, fennel is now widespread. Leaves, seeds, and bulb have the same liquorice-aniseed flavour.

ALLOTMENT ADVICE: what I wish I'd known

Fennel is a hardy perennial and will die back each winter, leaving its seedhead stems rattling in the wind until they are cut or blown down. If it is happy on your allotment and the seeds are left for the birds, expect seedlings to pop up all over the place in the following year. The bronze fennel is slightly less rampant than the green.

TRIED AND TESTED RHS VARIETIES

Sweet: *Foeniculum vulgare*
Bronze: *Foeniculum vulgare* 'Purpureum'
Florence: *Foeniculum vulgare* var. *dulce* 'Sirio', 'Victorio' (AGM)

Marjoram *Origanum species*

Sweet marjoram (*Origanum majorana*) and wild marjoram (*O. vulgare*) are two of the main types of what is commonly called oregano in the kitchen. Sweet marjoram is said to have the best flavour and has a good, bushy habit.

These make great plants for the allotment, with clouds of pink flowers in summer that are a real magnet for bees. Native mainly to Mediterranean areas, marjorams now grow wild in many parts of the world under assorted common names and are often used in cooked tomato dishes.

Sowing and planting

Sow the seed into plugs in early spring, with some bottom heat if available.

These healthy, green marjoram leaves are at a good stage for harvesting.

Germination is erratic, and can take several weeks, so be patient. Keep young seedlings slightly moist. Prick out and pot on before planting out in early summer. Sweet marjoram is usually sown afresh or self-seeds each year; wild marjoram can be grown from cuttings, and the only way to propagate the forms like 'Aureum' is to take softwood or basal cuttings in spring, or divide in spring or after flowering.

Growing

Marjoram species thrive in poor to moderately fertile, well-drained soil in plenty of sunlight, with *O. majorana* in particular preferring alkaline conditions. Some, especially the golden-leaved varieties, will tolerate partial shade.

Marjoram species are half hardy perennials, but avoid growing them in cold, wet conditions. They may suffer frost damage, and some may need care to survive a harsh winter.

To keep the plants compact, and to minimise self seeding, trim straggly plants back. The flowers come in a range of pinks and purples, and attract bees and beneficial insects.

Harvesting

Harvest leaves as required, or take whole stems for preserving, ideally just before the flowers open. Delicious in soups, pasta dishes, and most meat dishes, add fresh leaves towards the end of cooking for the best flavour.

Wild marjoram is best used as a dried herb, while sweet marjoram is better fresh. Whole stems can be frozen and the leaves crumbled off them, or you can infuse the leaves in oils and vinegars.

AT A GLANCE

These warm, aromatic herbs are native to the Mediterranean and southwest Asia, and have been widely used for millenia. They are easy to grow and preserve well.

ALLOTMENT ADVICE:
what I wish I'd known

Don't bother putting in a lot of effort to grow marjoram in a bed or pot: let it self seed to fill gaps and corners of your plot and soften path edges. It particularly likes the dry, alkaline conditions beside paths made with high-lime-content materials like cement.

TRIED AND TESTED RHS VARIETIES

Sweet marjoram: *Origanum majorana*
Pot marjoram: *Origanum onites*
Wild marjoram or oregano: *Origanum vulgare*
Golden marjoram: *Origanum vulgare* 'Aureum' is not too vigorous, with pink flowers and brightly coloured leaves

Mint *Mentha species*

Mint has a wide range of uses and over 120 named varieties. We're all familiar with spearmint and peppermint, but there are also lemon, lime, and grapefruit mints; chocolate mint; Corsican, Russian, and Moroccan mints; plus an array of colours including red and silver, and leaf shapes from pointy to round.

Planting

Mint is unreliable from seed. Buy plants or take root cuttings and divisions from friends – there is usually plenty to share. Lift a plant and gently pull it into pieces, each with some large, fleshy roots, and pot up the sections into fresh compost. Or find the nodes where new roots and shoots develop. Cut a root 5mm (¼in) or more thick into sections 5-7cm (2-2½in) long, each with at least one node. Lay the root cuttings on compost in pots or 25cm (10in) apart in trays of compost, water in, and you should see new growth in two or three weeks. Do this in autumn and put it somewhere light and warm for early spring harvests.

Growing

A moist but not waterlogged position in partial shade is ideal; mint appreciates bright light but shelter from midday sun, and tolerates most soils. Mint is invasive so consider carefully before you plant it into the ground. Keep the

running roots within bounds by growing it in a raised bed or a sunken pot – but suckers and runners seek out any escape route, so put tough weed-control fabric over any holes. Or grow it in a large container of soil-based compost, as long as you can keep it well watered and repot every year. Most mints reach 50-100cm (20-39in) although the smallest barely reaches 1cm (½in).

Lift and divide every few years to keep mint young and fresh. Half way through the season it can look weary and moth-eaten. Trim, water, and feed to rejuvenate it for a few more months.

Mint comes in many attractive forms though it is best to keep them separate.

Mint may suffer from powdery mildew if it gets too dry, and from rust (*see* chives, page 145). Mint rust can be devastating so buy new stock from a reputable source, and never propagate from infected stock.

Harvesting

Pick mint throughout the growing season and use immediately or freeze. Use in mint sauce (for lamb), mint tea, in desserts, or add it to salads.

AT A GLANCE

There are many different types of mint, used for all sorts of medicinal and culinary purposes. It's worth finding a specialist supplier and taking a good sniff of what's available. All of them are easy to grow.

ALLOTMENT ADVICE:
what I wish I'd known

If you're growing a number of different types of mints in containers, don't be tempted to put them all in together. Some will become dominant over others and they lose their

individual flavours and end up smelling and tasting the same.

TRIED AND TESTED RHS VARIETIES

There are many mints available: check the RHS Plant Finder for a comprehensive list.
Peppermint, English mint: *Mentha* x *piperita* (favoured for menthol oil)
Spearmint, garden mint, common mint: *Mentha spicata* (still the most widely grown type of mint)
Apple mint: *Mentha suaveolens* (has a

minty apple flavour, soft, round, hairy leaves, and is lovely to boil in with potatoes)
Bowles' mint: *Mentha* x *villosa* var. *alopecuroides* (a hybrid of spearmint and apple mint, and one of the best for culinary use, but highly vigorous)
Japanese mint: *Mentha arvensis* var. *piperascens* (has distinctive, glossy, green-veined leaves and lilac ball-shaped flowers; makes bushy growth with lots of runners; for Thai food or tea, it has a powerful minty flavour, especially raw)

Parsley *Petroselinum crispum*

Parsley is widely used as a garnish, but is also an essential flavouring for many savoury dishes. It is biennial, but usually grown as an annual, and comes in both a curly leaved (common parsley) and a flat-leaved (French parsley) form. There is even a form grown for use as a root vegetable (Hamburg parsley).

Sowing and planting

Sowing indoors is most reliable. Sow in modules in late winter or early spring under cover but without heat. Seed can be slow to germinate. Alternatively sow thinly direct in the ground at the end of late spring or early summer, to avoid the first generation of carrot root fly (*see* page 60), because parsley is in the same family as carrots. Try later sowings direct after midsummer, and cover with a cloche for overwintering.

Harden off and plant out sowings made under cover in mid-spring or late spring, when the soil has warmed up.

Flat-leaved parsley has a strong flavour and is a favourite in the kitchen.

Curly or crisped-leaved parsley is traditionally used as a garnish.

Allow 8–15cm (3½–6in) between plants for regular parsley, or 20cm (8in) intervals for Hamburg parsley.

Growing

Grow in fertile, moist but well-drained soil. For a summer crop, a partially shaded site is fine; for overwintering find a site in full sun.

Keep weed free and top dress with a nitrogen-rich fertiliser to maximise leafy growth. Remove flowerheads. An orange tinge to the foliage indicates carrot root fly damage; cover early sowings with a cloche or fine-mesh netting to reduce the chance of attacks. Beware slugs.

Harvesting

Harvest when there are at least eight to ten leaves on the plant, and do so regularly to encourage a continual supply. Freeze, use fresh, or dry using a microwave. For Hamburg parsley, dig up the roots in autumn.

Rosemary *Rosmarinus officinalis*

Easy to grow and long lived, rosemary is a popular herb and frequently a feature on allotment plots. It is grown for its aromatic, narrow leaves and two-lipped tubular flowers that can be blue, pink or even white. There are rosemary varieties which are upright and others with prostrate habits, all with long, needle-like leaves that grow from a stiff woody stem. This herb is a staple of European cuisine from British roasts to Mediterranean dishes.

Sowing and planting

Late spring is the optimum time to sow seed, but it is a real challenge to grow rosemary this way. Plants are easily propagated from cuttings instead. This is the only way to be sure of getting a plant with exactly the same habit or flower colour as the parent plant.

Take softwood cuttings in spring, or semi-ripe cuttings in summer from non-flowering shoots. They will root well in gritty, moist compost and be ready for planting out in the autumn. Alternatively, layer established branches in summer, slightly wounding the bark and pinning the shoot into the soil until it roots, then severing it from the parent. Plan to replace plants every five to six years.

Growing

This shrubby perennial thrives in an open, sunny site in well-drained soil. It originates from rocky Mediterranean areas and doesn't need overly fertile soil conditions. In colder climes, it does benefit from some shelter, and growing it in pots that can be brought under cover never hurts. It may reach up to 1.5m (5ft), depending on the variety, but on average gets to about 80cm/32in).

Rosemary is susceptible to honey fungus and rosemary leaf beetle. This is a metallic-green purple-striped beetle, 8mm (⅜in) long, that lays sausage-shaped eggs on the underside of the leaves from autumn to spring. The soft-bodied striped grubs feed on the leaves.

Harvesting

Pick leaves all year round, or take sprigs in summer and hang upside down to dry. Rosemary is used traditionally with roast lamb and fish, and for barbecues.

Aromatic rosemary is a delightful shrubby herb.

Snip off a sprig of rosemary for the Sunday roast, or prepare to take cuttings.

AT A GLANCE

Rosemary can form large bushes, and takes clipping well, so could become a focal point of an allotment plot. Clipping is best done after flowering, and of course gives plenty of material for propagation or use in the kitchen; any excess can be dried or freezes well. Its name translates as 'dew of the sea', and has nothing to do with either a rose or the name Mary.

ALLOTMENT ADVICE:
what I wish I'd known

Unlike almost any other plant on the allotment, rosemary will not appreciate being planted into a moist, nutrient-rich soil. Which means one less barrowload of compost is required!

TRIED AND TESTED RHS VARIETIES

'Miss Jessop's Upright' (AGM, pale blue to white flowers), 'Severn Sea' (AGM, bright blue flowers), 'Sissinghurst Blue' (AGM, deep blue flowers), 'Tuscan Blue' (deep blue flowers)

Sage *Salvia officinalis*

A beautiful plant cultivated in the garden as well as a useful culinary herb, sage is easy to grow and propagate. The large, oval, soft, felty leaves are usually grey but can come in a variety of colours, and the plant bears spikes of lilac-blue flowers in early summer. Sage is a hardy perennial, an evergreen subshrub that has a woody base, and can grow to 80cm (32in) tall and over 1m (3ft) wide, depending on variety.

Sowing and planting

Seed can be sown in spring into modules, and will germinate faster with some warmth. Alternatively, wait until the threat of frost has passed and sow

The pretty, purple leaves of Salvia officinalis *'Purpurascens' make it a decorative shrub.*

directly into prepared ground, eventually thinning seedlings to spacings.

You can also take softwood cuttings of any sage, including the cultivars and variegated species, in late spring or early summer, and they should root within four weeks. If you grow more than one, space 45–60cm (18–24in) apart, but a single plant will probably be all that you need, unless you are keen to grow a range of varieties.

Growing

Grow sage in light, free-draining neutral or alkaline soil in plenty of sunlight. It does less well in heavy soil. The intensity of the flavour may vary according to the fertility and richness of your soil.

Trim back sage in spring and again after flowering to prevent the plant

becoming straggly. Protect plants from winter weather in their first year; after this the common sage is generally hardy. Coloured forms can be less hardy.

Leaf hopper can cause a coarse, pale mottling to develop on the upper leaf surface during summer. In very hot weather watch out for powdery mildew.

Harvesting

Harvest sage leaves at any time and use fresh for the best flavour. It dries well; pick leaves for drying before flowering.

Sage goes well with poultry and fatty meats, traditionally in sage and onion stuffing or Lincolnshire sausages, and is part of the classic French bouquet garni used in stews and casseroles. Sage petals can be also be used in salads.

AT A GLANCE

There are numerous coloured forms of this attractive shrubby perennial, and all of them can be used in the kitchen. However, the plain green form is the hardiest, which is worth remembering in cooler areas. Sage has medicinal and antiseptic qualities that have long been recognised as reflected in its name – Salvia comes from the Latin *salveo*, 'I save' or 'I heal'.

ALLOTMENT ADVICE:
what I wish I'd known

Sage looks attractive beside a path but it will gently sprawl out with time, so give it plenty of space or keep it well trimmed.

TRIED AND TESTED RHS VARIETIES

Common or garden: *Salvia officinalis* is also available as a broad-leaved form.
Purple or red: *Salvia officinalis* 'Purpurascens' (AGM)
Tricolor: *Salvia officinalis* 'Tricolor'

Tarragon *Artemisia dracunculus*

Tarragon is traditionally associated with French cuisine and it is used especially to enhance chicken and fish dishes with its aniseed-like flavour. There are two types, French tarragon and Russian tarragon. French tarragon is the one known as the 'king of the herbs', while Russian tarragon is a hardier but poorly flavoured plant in comparison, and not particularly recommended. Other names include 'biting dragon' or 'dragon plant', reflecting its botanical name of *dracunculus* (meaning 'little dragon'). It's an apt name, given its fiery nature – this herb need only be used sparingly. French tarragon is native to southern Europe and is not completely hardy, whereas Russian hails from Siberia and is able to tolerate harsher conditions.

Planting
French tarragon will not come true from seed and must be propagated by division or cuttings.

After the frosts have finished in spring, dig up the plant and carefully pull the runners apart. On these there are nodules (nodes) which are easy to spot, and from where new growth will shoot. Pot up lengths of roots 8-10cm (3½-4in) long and bearing at least one node into pots of seed compost, and place somewhere warm and airy. Once they are well rooted, harden off and plant out 60cm (24in) apart.

Growing
French tarragon needs well-drained, light, sandy soil in a warm, dry, sunny and sheltered position. It dislikes damp conditions, and if the soil is too rich it can become lank and prone to dying off over winter. It is not completely hardy anyway, and will need some winter protection with straw, fleece or thick mulch when it goes dormant. French tarragon reaches 80-90cm (32-36in) in height. It spreads by underground runners, but isn't vigorous enough to ever become troublesome. Replace the plants every three to four years to maintain the best flavour for kitchen use.

Russian tarragon is a far more vigorous plant that can grow to about 1.5m (5ft). It is less aromatic than French tarragon, but still sometimes grown because it is hardy enough to survive a Siberian winter, and produces more leaves earlier in the season. Russian tarragon also tolerates most growing conditions.

Although relatively free of pest and disease problems, French tarragon has recently started to develop rust more frequently. Inspect new plants carefully, and check any you already have, looking for rusty coloured spots on the underside of the leaves. If you have it, dig the plant up, remove all foliage, and bin or burn – do not compost. Avoid planting tarragon, chives (*see* page 145) or mint (*see* page 150) on the affected area for a minimum of three years.

Harvesting
Wait at least ten weeks before harvesting the first sprigs from newly planted tarragon. Snip established plants any

Tarragon is a large herbaceous perennial with small but highly flavoured leaves.

time for immediate use. Young growth has a finer, stronger flavour.

For winter use, freeze or dry the leaves. Freezing is the better option, with leaves picked midsummer. Pick young sprigs and lightly bruise them to make tarragon vinegar, one of the key components of béarnaise sauce.

In the kitchen this herb partners parsley, chervil and chives in the classic French *fines herbes* seasoning and goes well with chicken, fish, eggs, stocks and casseroles, oranges and lemons. French tarragon is strong, so add sparingly towards the end of cooking to prevent it from becoming too overpowering.

For the finest flavour, carefully snip off sprigs of young tarragon.

AT A GLANCE

French tarragon is great for growing in short rows between other crops, such as lettuce, lamb's lettuce, red orache, chives and rocket, to create a pretty and productive patch.

ALLOTMENT ADVICE:
what I wish I'd known

If you buy a tarragon plant make sure (nibble a bit) that you are getting French rather than Russian tarragon, as it is only the former that is really worth growing.

Thyme *Thymus species*

Thyme is a delightfully aromatic and colourful herb that may be upright or creeping in habit. The flowers attract beneficial insects and the tiny leaves enhance the flavour of many dishes. It is a short-lived perennial subshrub hailing from the Mediterranean. There are many species and cultivars to choose from. *Thymus vulgaris* (common thyme) is the most used in the kitchen, but others such as *T. citriodorus* (lemon thyme) are often used too.

Sowing and planting

Sow seed, directly once the soil has warmed in the late spring or early summer and thin seedlings to approximately 20cm (8in). Alternatively, sow in trays in early spring and provide bottom heat. Most thymes, however, are best propagated by taking softwood cuttings 5–8cm (2–3½in) long in early spring or summer. Propagate mature, woody thyme plants by layering.

Growing

Thyme will thrive in relatively poor, preferably alkaline soil, especially if it is stony, as it likes to grow in very well-drained conditions.

Thyme grows woody quickly, so trim the plant after flowering to keep it compact and promote fresh, tender growth. The species may self seed if the flowerheads persist. Thyme will rot off if it becomes too wet, and in rich soil soft growth may encourage aphids.

Harvesting

Snip off small sprigs as required for immediate use all year round, or cut larger quantities for drying or freezing before the plant flowers. This aromatic herb is one of the ingredients of a *bouquet garni*, and is used in meat, poultry, and fish dishes, stews, casseroles, and Italian cuisine.

Small, shrubby thyme comes in many colours and flavours – attractive and tasty!

AT A GLANCE

As a drought-tolerant herb, thyme is usually very easy to grow on a sunny allotment. It brings a bit of Mediterranean magic to the plot and kitchen, and is attractive in its many different forms.

ALLOTMENT ADVICE:
what I wish I'd known

Thyme can really take its time if you propagate it by seed. But it is easy to take 'lazy' cuttings if you see aerial roots growing from the stems.

TRIED AND TESTED RHS VARIETIES

Common, garden: *Thymus vulgaris* (standard culinary thyme, typical flavour, strong green growth), 'Silver Posie' (pretty, variegated cultivar)
Lemon: *Thymus citriodorus* (large, lemon-scented leaves), 'Golden King' (golden leaves)
Broad-leaved: *Thymus pulegioides* (good for kitchen and useful as a groundcover plant)

Tree fruit

Basic techniques

Fruit trees are hopefully going to be a permanent feature on your allotment so it is worth spending time understanding the basics. Learning to plant a tree properly, pruning it correctly, and understanding issues such as pollination and fruit thinning will maximise yields and allow you to enjoy the fruits of your labour for many years to come.

Planting

You can buy fruit trees bare-rooted or in a container. Trees in containers can be planted all year round, although autumn is the best time, as the soil is warm and they won't need much watering. Bare-root trees are cheaper but are only available in late autumn. They are usually a healthier tree, as their roots haven't been restricted by a pot. The same planting principles apply to both, apart from staking.

If the tree is in a pot, gently prise it out and tease out the roots so that they aren't wrapped around each other. Dig a hole larger than the diameter of the roots and place the root ball into the hole with the top of the root ball level with the ground. Backfill the hole with the soil taken from it, mixed with compost and a bit of bone meal. Firm the soil in around the roots, water, and then mulch around the base of the tree ensuring the mulch doesn't come into contact with the trunk.

Freestanding trees will need staking. Bare-root trees do best with a stake driven into the ground before planting. Container-grown trees need a diagonal stake at about 45 degrees driven in after planting – this avoids damaging the larger root ball. Use a tree tie to attach the tree to the stake; a pair of old tights also makes a nice flexible tie that stretches as the tree grows. Tie a knot in the tights between tree and stake to prevent the tree from rubbing on the stake. Never use string on the trunk of the trees, as this cuts into the trunk when it sways in the wind.

Pruning

Pruning is the key to successful fruit growing. Your tree will be healthier and produce more fruit. Different trees require pruning at different times; check this book for details of when to prune.

Why prune? Firstly it restricts size. On an allotment space is at a premium, so keep your trees as compact as possible. Good pruning also creates a stronger structure: unpruned branches can become heavy and end up snapping if overburdened with fruit and sideshoots. Secondly, pruning reduces congestion

and overcrowding in the centre of the tree, creating a more open canopy. Fruit needs sunlight to ripen effectively, and if there are too many branches they will create shade, so the tree will form sideshoots at the expense of fruit.

Thirdly, pruning is an opportunity to remove dead, damaged, and diseased wood. Fruit trees are prone to canker, so diseased growth should be removed. Disinfect pruning tools after cutting out any diseased wood.

Fourthly, the removal of older branches can re-invigorate a tree and

5

1) *When planting, ensure the rootstock union is above the level of the soil.*
2) *Mulch around the base of fruit trees in late winter with well-rotted manure.*
3) *Pruning back to a bud encourages shoots to develop further down the branch.*
4) *Thin out fruitlets to ensure the remaining fruits develop fully.*
5) *Early flowering fruit trees such as peaches need assistance with pollination.*

for your final pruning cut; they tend to crush the end of a branch, rather than cut it. Use them for chopping up your prunings into small pieces once removed from the tree.

PRUNING TECHNIQUES

Using your tools properly should mean cleaner cuts, healthier plants, easier working, and fewer accidents.

Pruning with secateurs

Make pruning cuts just above a bud and gently sloping away from it. If the cut is right up against the bud it will damage it; too far away and the remaining stub will die back, encouraging disease. To get the cut close to a bud, keep the thin blade closest to the main body of the tree and the 'beak' part of the secateurs on the side that is being removed.

Pruning with a saw

You may inherit an overgrown fruit tree on an allotment. Overgrown branches will need to be removed with a saw if a tree is to stand any chance of producing high yields of healthy fruit. Remove any large branches in sections so that the weight of the branch doesn't tear it.

When making the final cut, first underscore the branch. This means cutting about a quarter of the way through the branch from the bottom, and prevents the weight of the falling branch ripping a tongue of bark away from the trunk. Then make the final cut from the top all the way through, ensuring that the swollen collar at the base of the branch is kept intact.

encourage new, healthy shoots. Don't over-prune though, because this can over-stimulate a tree, meaning it produces too many new shoots at the expense of blossom and, of course, fruit.

Finally, formative pruning can sculpt your fruit trees into beautiful shapes such as espaliers, cordons, and fans.

Pruning tools

You need to ensure that the tools you're using are sharp. Blunt tools will damage the wood you are cutting into. Always wear gloves when pruning: some plants exude irritant sap or have protective hairs that you may discover too late.

Use secateurs to cut any shoots of less than pencil thickness. Use a pruning saw for thicker branches.

Pruning saws come in various sizes, but their long, slim blade makes them suitable for getting into tight, restricted spaces between shoots. Compact saws that fold up like a penknife are handy for keeping in your pocket when working on the allotment.

Loppers are ideal for reducing the weight on a branch, but don't use these

Thinning

Most fruit will benefit from thinning (or the removal of some of the fruitlets) during summer. It means that trees can supply a higher level of nutrients, water, and sugar to the remaining fruit, giving them a better quality, colour, and sweetness. Thinning also enables the fruit to develop evenly on the tree without being squashed or squeezed by the surrounding fruit. More air is able to circulate, which helps to reduce the chances of fungal diseases, and more sunlight can enter the canopy encouraging the fruit to ripen.

TREE SHAPES

Fruit trees are wonderfully versatile and can be trained into all sorts of attractive shapes. Quite apart from the crops they produce in small spaces, their all-year-round ornamental structure can create an amazing-looking allotment .

The best thing of all though is that training a fruit tree is very easy once you have mastered the basics. Don't tell your neighbouring allotmenteers this, though – if you keep quiet, they will think you are a gardening guru with such beautifully trained trees.

These are some of the shapes more commonly found in gardens and on allotments. However, many more are possible, and with a bit of imagination and basic technical know-how you can train a tree into almost any shape.

Single cordon

Cordons are grown as a single stem with a series of short fruiting spurs growing off them. They take up hardly any space, with trees being planted as closely as 30cm (12in) apart from each other, and this makes them ideal for packing lots of different varieties into a small area. With careful selection of varieties, you can spread out the period of fruit production throughout the season, instead of having one large glut produced from one large tree.

Cordons are usually grown at an angle of 45 degrees (known as oblique cordons) as this slows down the vigour of the plant and encourages fruit to grow evenly from all the sideshoots along the main trunk, rather than all at the top. They will need to be grown on dwarfing rootstocks (*see* individual profiles for details) and varieties that are inclined to produce short fruiting 'spurs' should be favoured over 'tip' bearers. Cordons do need to be trained on to a series of two or three wires stretched between posts.

Double cordon

This is a highly ornamental way of growing fruit trees on the allotment. Double cordons are basically one tree with two main stems that are grown upright to form a goblet shape.

Espalier

Perhaps one of the trickier ways to grow a tree, an espalier is very rewarding as it adds an architectural quality to your garden. It consists of training tiers of parallel branches from a central stem: there can be as many tiers as you like,

1) *You can expect heavy crops of apples from an espalier.*
2) *Espaliers make a beautiful feature on the allotment when in blossom.*
3) *Fans are a great way of training fruit in a small space.*
4) *Stepover apple trees are ideal for edging areas on the allotment.*

Stepover

This is a beautiful way to edge your herb section or divide different areas of vegetables in the allotment. Stepovers are simply miniature espaliers with just the single tier. Some are double-sided, with branches going in opposite directions from a central trunk. Others just go in one direction, meaning that more fruit varieties can be successfully squeezed into your plot.

Apples grown on dwarf rootstocks are the most suitable trees for this type of training; others are too vigorous.

Open-centre bush or goblet

This is a tree grown on a short trunk with four or five branches growing off it with an open centre. Picking from them is easy when the tree is grown on a dwarfing rootstock.

Pyramid

Pyramids have a central stem and are pruned into a conical, Christmas-tree shape. This allows an even distribution of sunlight to reach the whole tree, and suits spur-forming trees.

Half-standard or standard

This tree is a bit like a lollipop shape, with a long clear trunk and a head at the top. Half-standards are simply half the size. Some allotments might not allow you to grow trees to such a large size, so check with the authorities.

If you have a large plot, or two or three plots, then these forms can be useful for producing fruit and adding height – and slinging a hammock up between two trunks to relax in the shade from the midday sun.

but it usually ranges from two to four. It is possible to train your own tree into this shape, but if you don't feel ready for that, it is simpler to buy a ready-trained tree. Once the main shape has been established the maintenance of the shape is much easier. Espaliers take up more space than cordons, but they do make excellent screens and fencing for dividing up plots of land. Like a cordon, an espalier needs to be trained on wires stretched between posts. They are ideal for apples and pears and other trees that produce spurs.

Fan

The name tells you exactly what this tree form looks like. All fruit trees can be trained into a fan, but it's most commonly used for cherries, peaches, plums, and figs.

Fans can be as high and wide as the rootstock and variety allow, although most people aim to grow them to about the height and width of a standard fence panel. Like the espalier, the fan is a highly ornamental method of dividing two areas on an allotment – as long as you are sure about the position.

Pollination

Apple blossom

Crab apple blossom

Cherry blossom

Most fruit trees require cross-pollination from another tree flowering at the same time to produce fruit. This is usually carried out by pollinating insects, such as the honey bee. Pollination requires the same type of tree – an apple for an apple or a pear for a pear – but they have to be different varieties that flower at the same time. So one Worcester Pearmain apple tree could not pollinate another, but it would pollinate a Fiesta apple tree.

When buying a tree, check the label for pollination. If it is self-fertile then you don't need to worry and can get away with just the one tree, although pollination is still usually better if other trees are about. If the tree needs a pollinator, then you will need to buy another variety in the same 'group'. Plant centres will have lists of pollination groups.

Do look around your neighbouring allotments to see if they have another tree that will be able to pollinate your tree: this will save you money in having to buy a second tree, and space, which is always at a premium on a plot. Bees will travel as far as two or three miles, so travelling to another neighbouring allotment should be no problem for them.

The key to good pollination is attracting insects. Consider having a beehive on your allotment, think before you spray, and grow a wide range of flowers that will attract pollinating insects to visit your allotment (*see* box opposite). If you have a greenhouse, leave the door open during sunny days so that bees can get to the flowers. Red mason bees are also effective pollinators and can easily be encouraged on to the allotment if you create a home for them to move into. Ready-made homes can be bought from garden centres, but it is easy to make one by bundling together about 10 hollow stems (bamboo is fine), each at about 20cm (8in) long, and tying them together with string. Hang the cluster of stems from the shed in a sunny spot. One advantage of red mason bees is that they fly in cooler conditions than honey bees (useful for early flowering fruit trees such as peaches) and they are non-aggressive and very rarely sting. Even when they do sting, it is nowhere near as painful. The downside is that they don't produce honey.

POLLINATION GROUPS

Each of these fruit trees has been divided into pollination groups, depending on the time its individual varieties flower. Choose trees from the same or adjacent groups, as flowering periods usually extend into each other.

Apples

Traditionally there are seven pollination groups for apples. Just to complicate things, triploids (marked with a 't') produce sterile pollen, so three trees are needed for all to be pollinated.

Group 1 'Gravenstein' (t), 'Lord Suffield', 'Stark Earliest, 'Vista-bella'

Group 2 'Adam's Pearmain', 'Baker's Delicious', 'Beauty of Bath', 'Bismark', 'Cheddar Cross', 'Devonshire Quarrenden', 'Egremont Russet', 'George Cave', 'Golden Spire', 'Idared', 'Irish Peach', 'Kerry Pippin', 'Keswick Codlin', 'Lord Lambourne', 'McIntosh', 'Michaelmas Red', 'Norfolk Beauty', 'Reverend W. Wilks', 'Ribston Pippin', 'Saint Edmund's Pippin'

Group 3 'Arthur Turner', 'Blenheim Orange' (t), 'Belle de Boskoop'(t), 'Bountiful', 'Bramley's Seedling' (t), 'Charles Ross', 'Cox's Orange Pippin'**, 'Discovery', 'Elstar', 'Falstaff', 'Fiesta', 'Fortune', 'Granny Smith', 'Greensleeves', 'James Grieve', 'John Standish', 'Jonagold' (t), 'Jonathan', 'Katja' (syn. 'Katy'), 'Kidd's Orange Red'**, 'Lane's Prince Albert', 'Langley Pippin,' 'Merton Russet', 'Miller's Seedling', 'Peasgood's Nonsuch', 'Queen', 'Red Devil', 'Redsleeves', 'Reinette du Canada', 'Rosemary Russet', 'Scrumptious', 'Spartan', 'Sturmer Pippin', 'ST Wright', 'Sunset', 'Tom Putt', 'Tydman's Early Worcester', 'Wealthy', 'Worcester Pearmain', 'Wyken Pippin'
** not compatible although in the same group

Group 4 'Annie Elizabeth', 'Ashmead's Kernel', 'Autumn Pearmain', 'Chivers' Delight', 'Claygate Pearmain', 'Cornish Aromatic', 'Cornish Gilliflower', 'Cox's Pomona', 'D'Arcy Spice', 'Delicious', 'Duke of Devonshire', 'Ellison's Orange', 'Gala', 'George Carpenter', 'Golden Delicious', 'Golden Noble', 'Howgate Wonder', 'Joybells', 'Laxton's Superb',

Pear blossom

Plum blossom

Damson blossom

'King's Acre Pippin', 'Lady Henniker', 'Lord Derby', Mannington's Pearmain', 'Pixie', 'Tydeman's Late Orange', 'Winston', 'Yellow Newtown'
Group 5 'Coronation', 'Gascoyne's Scarlet' (t), 'King of the Pippins', 'William Crump', 'Mother', 'Newton Wonder', 'Royal Jubilee', 'Suntan' (t), 'William Crump', 'Woolbrook Pippin'
Group 6 'Bess Pool', 'Court Pendu Plat', 'Edward VII'
Group 7 'Crawley Beauty' (flowers exceptionally late; partially self-fertile, but crab apples nearby should increase yields)

Cherries
There are six pollination groups for sweet cherries and five for acid cherries. Some varieties are self-fertile (sf), setting fruit on their own; others are partly self-fertile (psf), setting some fruit on their own but more if cross-pollinated; and some are totally self-infertile (si) so won't crop unless cross-pollinated.
Sweet cherries All cherries listed in this book are in group 4: 'Bigarreau Napoléon' (si), 'Lapins' (sf), 'Stella' (sf), 'Summer Sun' (sf), 'Sunburst' (sf)
Acid cherries 'Morello' (sf) is in group 5

Pears
There are three groups for pears.
Early 'Louise Bonne of Jersey', 'Packham's Triumph'
Mid 'Beurré Hardy', 'Black Worcester', 'Concorde', 'Conference', 'Durondeau', 'Jargonelle' (t), 'Joséphine de Malines', 'Merton Pride' (t), 'Fertility', 'Williams' Bon Chrétien'
Late 'Beth', 'Catillac' (t), 'Doyenné du Comice', 'Glou Morceau', 'Improved Fertility', 'Onward'

Plums, damsons, and gages
Can be self-fertile (sf), partly self-fertile (psf) or self-infertile (si).
Group 1 Gage: 'Jefferson' (si)
Group 2 Gage: 'Denniston's Superb' (sf)
Group 3 Plums: 'Czar' (sf), 'Laxton's Delight' (psf), 'Opal' (sf), 'Pershore' (sf), 'Sanctus Hubertus' (psf), 'Victoria' (sf) Bullace: 'Small Damson' (sf) Gage: 'Golden Transparent' (sf)
Group 4 Bullace: 'Golden' (sf) Damsons: 'Farleigh Damson' (psf), 'Prune Damson' (sf) Gage: 'Cambridge Gage' (psf), 'Oullins Gage' (sf)
Group 5 Plum: 'Blue Tit' (sf), 'Marjorie's Seedling' (sf)

Beneficial insects
Insects are an integral part of an allotment, enticed by the open space, shelter, and abundant flowers. We rely on them to pollinate many of our favourite crops, and some eat the less welcome visitors.

Any plants allowed to flower, either as a crop or self-sown at the margins, will lure both pollinating insects such as bees and aphid-eaters like lacewings, ladybirds, and hoverflies. The larvae of these insects do the most eating, and a ladybird larva looks nothing like the adult, so it's worth knowing what friendly beasts look like at all stages.

Grow a range of flowers to attract different pollinators: think of chives, borage, thyme, lavender, sage, phacelia, and comfrey; or you could sow a patch of poached egg plant for bees and hoverflies. Marigolds (_Tagetes_ and _Calendula_), asters, nasturtiums, and chrysanthemums attract the aphid-eaters. Choose open, single flowers over multi-petalled doubles that hide their nectar.

Be aware of other invertebrates, like the speedy hunting centipede and black beetles that devour soil pests. Encourage them to work for you by looking after the soil.

Apples

If you are to grow one type of fruit on your allotment, then this has to be it. Apples are engrained into our history, heritage, and culture, ranging from Eve's temptation in Eden to the formulation of the laws of gravity when one fell on Newton's head (reputedly a 'Flower of Kent'). And with names such as 'Bloody Ploughman', 'Catshead', and 'D'arcy Spice', how can you resist giving a bit of space to these delicious fruits?

Apples are not only versatile in the kitchen, being made into anything from cider to apple pie; they're just as adaptable in the garden, where they lend themselves to shapes including fans, espaliers, stepovers, and cordons (*see* pages 160–1).

They are by far the easiest of fruit to grow and can be cultivated in the tiniest of spaces thanks to extremely dwarfing rootstocks. With careful selection of varieties you can have an apple a day all year round, so it's hardly surprising that there are over 2,000 apple varieties to choose from, providing a whole range of exciting flavours, colours, and textures.

Choosing a tree

When choosing which apples to grow, don't just go for those that are familiar names on the supermarket shelves, such as 'Granny Smith' and 'Cox's Orange Pippin'. If you like those, you can buy them anywhere. Try sourcing more unusual varieties that are local to your area. Not only will you be helping to conserve the heritage of the surrounding area, but chances are they'll be more suited to the soils and climate on your plot and better adapted to combat local pest and disease problems.

Consider, also, how you want to grow the tree. Avoid varieties that bear most of their fruit in the tips of their branches (known as tip bearers) if you are planning to grow restricted forms such as cordons, espaliers, and stepovers. Otherwise when the new growth is pruned back to two buds in late summer,

Apples are one of the easiest fruits to grow on the allotment.

the fruit bud will be lost. Tip-bearers to avoid include 'Bramley's Seedling' and 'Worcester Pearmain'. Choose varieties that readily produce spurs (known as spur bearers) – fortunately this includes most of the apple varieties available.

It is easiest and fastest to grow a ready-trained tree. It's possible to train your own, and cheaper, but you will have to wait two or three years before harvesting your first crop.

Pollination groups

Almost all apple trees require another tree to pollinate it to produce fruit. Even the varieties described as self-fertile will crop more reliably if there are other trees growing nearby. Take a look at the pollination groups (*see* pages 162–3) to find out which trees need which 'friend'. Be aware that some apple trees, such as 'Bramley's Seedling', produce sterile pollen, so while they can be pollinated

by another tree that is flowering at the same time, they will be no good for pollinating it in return. Check with your fruit tree supplier if you are unsure.

If space is really restricted, it might be worth considering growing one tree with two or three varieties grafted on to it, commonly known as a family tree.

Rootstocks

If apples were grown on their own roots, they would mostly develop into enormous, vigorous trees completely unsuitable for allotments. Centuries ago it was discovered that apple varieties can be grafted on to specially selected roots (rootstocks) that control the size or vigour of the tree. Many allotments these days have rules to restrict the size of trees that can be grown on a plot, and if you are hoping to have room to pack lots of other tasty fruit and veg into your space, it is important that the tree you choose is not grown on too vigorous a rootstock.

Almost all apple trees that are bought from plant centres or nurseries will be on these specially selected rootstocks and there is a whole range to choose from – more for apples than any of the other fruit trees we grow.

The guides to size below will vary depending on variety and type of soil. On heavier and more fertile soils the trees will grow much bigger, but on very poor ground a very dwarfing rootstock might lead to a weak tree.

M27 Extremely dwarfing, suitable for stepovers or growing trees up to the size of 1.8m (6ft).

M9 Very dwarfing, suitable for trees grown in pots, stepovers, or producing a free-standing tree of 2-2.5m (6-8ft).

M26 Semi-dwarfing, the best rootstock for a pot and suitable for cordons and espaliers. Free-standing trees will reach about 2-3m (6-10ft).

MM106 Semi-vigorous, and possibly too vigorous for a free-standing tree on an allotment, unless you have a lot of space. Reaches 5m (15ft).

Where to grow

Apples are the tough nuts of the fruit world, and are by far the best adapted type of fruit tree to our climate. They should grow happily on any allotment. Tolerant of a wide range of conditions, they should ideally be given a sunny aspect with a well-drained, loamy soil, but some cooking varieties will tolerate a certain amount of shade. Because they are so versatile to train, they can be planted as stepovers to edge areas of the allotment, or a row of oblique cordons makes a really attractive 'living screen' between two areas. All that is

needed to grow a row of cordons is three horizontal galvanised wires, spaced 60cm (24in) apart and stretched between two posts or just attached to a fence panel or shed wall.

Apple trees can also be grown in containers, but they will need to be watered almost every day during the summer, so this is only an option if you plan to be on the allotment every day. Plunging the container in the ground is one method of alleviating this need for watering, but it will still need to be done at least a couple of times a week.

Planting

Planting an apple tree is exactly the same as planting any other fruit tree. Most importantly, make sure that the graft or bud union is kept above the soil. This is easy to spot: it is the slightly swollen area just above the rootball.

Apples can be grown in small spaces when grown on dwarf rootstocks such as M27.

Oblique cordons are slightly different, as they need to be planted at an angle. Site them about 10cm (4in) away from the structure that they are going to be trained on. After digging the hole the tree should be set in the ground at an angle of 45 degrees. Backfill the hole mixing compost or well-rotted manure with the spoil from the hole. Any roots sticking above the ground after planting should be removed with secateurs.

Spacing tree forms

Don't be greedy and crowd your trees – it really isn't easy to move them later.
Oblique cordons 70cm (28in) apart but with care and the right rootstock you might get away with half this for upright cordons
Stepover 1.5m (5ft)
Pyramid 1.8m (6ft)
Spindle tree 1.8m (6ft)
Espalier 4m (13ft) – about two standard fence panels will do
Fan 4m (13ft) – about two standard fence panels will do
Bush on M27 1.5m (5ft)
Bush on M9/M26 1.8m (6ft)

Growing and pruning

Apply a general fertiliser around the root area at 50g (2oz) for each tree in early spring. Mulch with well-rotted manure to a depth of 5cm (2in) afterwards, keeping the mulch slightly away from the trunk. Keep the area around the trunk free from weeds. Water the trees during any dry spells.

Pruning an apple tree is simple once a few basic rules are learnt. Free-standing trees, such as bush forms and standards, should be pruned in winter when the leaves have fallen. Check to see if your variety is mainly a tip bearer or spur bearer. If it produces most of its fruit on the tips, then thin the branches out to open up the centre, ensuring that the tips of the remaining branches are uncut.

Spur-bearing varieties need to have some of their shoots cut back to about four buds to encourage new spurs to develop. Thin out existing spurs and remove dead or diseased wood and any branches growing towards the centre.

Trained trees, such as espaliers, stepovers, and cordons, should be pruned in late summer, when the new growth is cut back to two buds. They also benefit from a second prune in winter, when some of the older spurs will need to be thinned out.

Thinning fruitlets

Apples tend to have a habit of thinning themselves slightly by dropping some of their fruit in early summer, known as the 'June drop'. However, if you still have a huge, bumper crop in midsummer then you will need to thin. Reduce dessert apples down to one or two apples every hand's width apart. Cookers need a bit more space, about two hands' widths apart.

Check over the fruitlets carefully before thinning, to make sure that the ones you will be leaving on the tree aren't damaged. The centre of each cluster has an apple called the king fruit, and it's best to remove this one as it usually develops into a misshapen fruit.

Heavy crops of apples should be thinned out in June to avoid branches snapping.

Harvesting

Timings for apple harvest are relatively complicated. Earlies, such as 'Discovery' or 'James Grieve', should be eaten straight off the tree and will only keep for a few days. Mid-season apples should be eaten within a few weeks, and late season apples are often inedible when harvested so need to be kept in storage for weeks or even months before being ready for eating. Some varieties such as 'Bramley's Seedling' are cookers when picked, but if stored for a few months can be eaten as dessert apples.

Apples lying on the ground under a tree are the first indicator that they are ready for picking. Gently cup a fruit with your hand, lift, and twist. It should come off in your hand with the stalk attached.

Keep apples that can be stored in a dark cool place with good ventilation. Sheds are alright, but a garage is usually better. Place them in a well-ventilated or slatted box, spaced out so air can circulate between the fruit. Regularly check over and remove any rots.

Yield: At least 2.5kg (5lb) from a cordon, many times more from espaliers.

AT A GLANCE

Apples are easy to grow and there are over 2000 varieties to choose from, which in the United Kingdom are divided into dessert, cooking, and cider apples. Some are dual-purpose, meaning they can be used for both eating and cooking. Many other countries, including America, do not make the distinction between cookers and eaters. Grow them on dwarf rootstocks to fit lots into your garden.

ALLOTMENT ADVICE:
what I wish I'd known

Pests and diseases can quickly arrive on an allotment and once established are very hard to eradicate, particularly when growing fruit organically. Always pick windfalls off the ground as soon as they fall from the tree. If you allow them to rot on the ground, they will harbour fungus and pests that can then quickly transfer to the remaining fruit on the tree. If picked up promptly, they can easily be cooked or pressed to make cider.

TRIED AND TESTED
RHS VARIETIES

Cookers: 'Blenheim Orange' (AGM, dual-purpose), 'Bountiful', 'Bramley's Seedling' (AGM), 'Edward VII' (AGM), 'Golden Noble' (AGM), 'Grenadier' (AGM), 'Howgate Wonder', 'Reverend W. Wilks'
Desserts: 'Cox's Orange Pippin', 'Discovery' (AGM), 'Egremont Russet' (AGM), 'Fiesta' (AGM), 'James Grieve' (AGM), 'Jonagold' (AGM), 'Kidd's Orange Red' (AGM), 'Lord Lambourne' (AGM), 'Sunset' (AGM), 'Worcester Pearmain' (AGM)
Cider: 'Brown Snout', 'Dabinett', 'Kingston Black', 'Michelin'

Apples make attractive features on the allotment when grown as a free-standing tree.

Pears

Their beautiful gnarled trunks and branches densely covered with spurs make pears as impressive a feature in winter as they are when covered in white blossom in spring. However, it is their succulent fruit with its soft, melting flesh and buttery-rich flavours that make this such a popular fruit tree.

Pollination groups

Pears usually need a 'friend' to help with pollination. Take a look at the pollination groups for pears (*see* page 163), and when purchasing your trees, check the label carefully to find out if they are compatible.

Rootstocks

Surprisingly, pears are grafted not only on to other pear rootstocks, but on to quince. This helps to slow down the vigour of these naturally large trees.

There are usually just two types available. Quince A is ideal for espaliers, fans, or a pyramid, but is too vigorous for training as a cordon. Quince C is slightly less vigorous than Quince A, making it suitable for cordons, as well as espaliers, fans, and pyramids.

Where to grow

Pears are slightly trickier to grow than apples, as they require more warmth. They are extremely susceptible to frost damage because of their early flowering habit – they are usually in blossom two or three weeks before apples.

Select a sunny site that is sheltered from prevailing winds, which can wreak havoc with their blossom and fruit. If you cannot offer them a sheltered, frost-free area, be prepared to cover them with fleece when cold weather is predicted. If you live in a frost-prone area, you can make a bit less work for yourself by choosing to grow later-flowering varieties such as 'Beth', 'Catillac', or 'Doyenne de Comice'.

On an allotment pears are generally suitable for growing as espaliers, fans, and cordons due to their compact, spur-bearing habit (*see* pages 160-1). They can also be grown successfully as bush trees or pyramids. There are some pears, such as 'Jargonelle', that are mainly tip bearers, so do check before purchasing a tree. Unfortunately, even on dwarfing rootstocks pears are too vigorous to be grown as stepovers.

Pears also make an attractive feature trained over an arch. This adds height to the design of the allotment and creates a focal point. (It is also a great way of holding your fruit up high as if showing off your produce to your neighbouring allotment holders, but make sure you net the fruit before the birds spot them.) Plant one tree on each side of the arch and train the leader (or highest branch) up the arch each year. All other new shoots should be pruned back to two buds in late summer.

Planting and growing

Pears can be planted at any time of the year, although autumn is best because of their early flowering habit. They can start into growth as early as late winter, so young trees need to be in the ground well before this.

Feed with a general fertiliser around the root area at 50g (2oz) in early spring. Mulch with well-rotted manure to a depth of 5cm (2in) afterwards.

Water trees frequently in dry weather. Pears require plenty of moisture during spring and early summer.

A juicy, succulent pear is delicious and yet much easier to grow than you may think.

Pruning

Trees trained as cordons and espaliers need new growth pruned back to two buds in late summer. Thin out the spurs in winter. Prune bush trees in winter, removing diseased or dead wood and branches growing into the centre. Older branches may need support from stakes.

Thinning fruitlets

Pears require thinning to prevent over-stressing the tree and to allow the remaining fruit to reach their full size and attain high enough sugar levels to taste sweet. It also prevents the branches becoming over-laden with fruit and snapping.

Thin in midsummer – the earlier the thinning, the larger the fruit will be. Thin out each cluster to leave two fruitlets on a bush or standard, and one on cordons, espaliers, and pyramids.

Harvesting

Harvesting and storing pears is a tricky business, as they quickly deteriorate. They should be picked when slightly under-ripe, although early pears will

Pears flower early in the year, so avoid planting in frost pockets.

still taste sweet. The fruit should have turned to the expected colour and should feel firm but yield slightly when pressed with a thumb. Cup the base of the pear with your hand, lift, and gently twist. The pear should part from the tree without you having to pull or tear.

Early maturing pears should be eaten within a couple of weeks, but some of the later varieties should be stored for eating over the next few months. Place them in slatted wooden or plastic boxes in a cool, dark place that is rodent free. Extra vigilance is required when checking over this crop, as pears can quickly change from being slightly under-ripe to rotting in a matter of days. Speed up their ripening by bringing a few pears into the warmth occasionally as required.

Yield: 2kg (4lb) of fruit from a cordon and 6kg (12lb) from an espalier.

Pears should be harvested when slightly under-ripe and allowed to ripen at home before eating.

AT A GLANCE

Perhaps more suited to the warmer climates of mid- and southern Europe, pears are trickier to grow than apples as they require a warmer site. They are suitable for growing as cordons, espaliers, fans, pyramids, and bushes.

ALLOTMENT ADVICE:
what I wish I'd known

Pear midge can cause young fruitlets to fall prematurely off the tree before they develop. Placing carpet under the pear tree prevents the pest from developing in the soil and therefore helps to eradicate the problem.

TRIED AND TESTED
RHS VARIETIES

'Beth' (AGM), 'Beurre Hardy' (AGM), 'Concorde' (AGM), 'Conference', 'Doyenné du Comice' (AGM), 'Glou Morceau', 'Williams' Bon Chrétien' (AGM)

Plums

With succulent flesh and translucent skin, plums are the quintessential English fruit. Keep some dried in your pocket as you work on your allotment for a delicious re-fuelling snack.

Pollination and rootstocks

Most widely grown plums are self-fertile, but for damsons and gages do check pollination groups (*see* page 163). Trees should be grafted on to dwarfing rootstocks such as 'St Julien A' or the slightly more dwarfing 'Pixy', otherwise they become large trees.

Where to grow

Plums require a position sheltered from winds on medium to heavy soil with good drainage. If you are stuck in a frost pocket, select late-flowering varieties such as 'Czar' and 'Marjorie's Seedling'. Grow as a fan (*see* page 161) on a sheltered, sunny fence panel or shed wall, or as a free-standing pyramid.

Growing and pruning

Apply a general fertiliser around the root area at 110g (4oz) in early spring. Afterwards apply a mulch of well-rotted manure around the base of the tree, ensuring that it is kept clear of the trunk. Prune plums in spring or summer to avoid silver leaf disease.

Pinch shoots not required for the framework of a fan back to three or four leaves in late summer. This will encourage fruiting spurs and fruit buds to develop towards the base of the shoots. Pull out any suckers from the base of the tree. Net the fan as the fruit ripens to avoid bird damage to the crop.

Plums are easy to grow but require a sheltered, warm aspect to ripen fully.

Thinning and harvesting

Thin fruitlets to 5–8cm (2–3in) apart: a glut in one year can mean nothing the next. Pick with the stalk attached. Use slightly under-ripe plums for cooking.

Yield: About 14kg (30lb) of fruit from an established fan tree. Plums can be fickle, and vary from famine to feast from year to year.

AT A GLANCE

There are culinary and dessert plums, but both make excellent jams and fillings for pies. Most, like 'Victoria', are self-fertile. Check the label when purchasing. They are closely related to gages, bullaces, damsons, and Mirabelle cherries, and the same general growing principles apply for all these fruits.

ALLOTMENT ADVICE:
what I wish I'd known

Plums are prone to both silver leaf and bacterial canker. These problems are easily transmitted on secateurs when moving from one tree to another. One way to avoid this is to disinfect your secateurs between pruning each tree by keeping a spray dispenser full of household disinfectant at the allotment to be sprayed over the blades. Wipe it off with a dry tissue, as the disinfectant can cause the blades to rust.

TRIED AND TESTED
RHS VARIETIES

(sf – denotes self fertile)
Desert plums: (all sf) 'Blue Tit' (AGM), 'Herman', 'Opal' (AGM), 'Victoria' (AGM)
Culinary: 'Czar' (AGM, sf), 'Marjorie's Seedling' (AGM, dual purpose), 'Purple Pershore' (sf)
Gage: 'Cambridge Gage' (AGM, partial sf), 'Oullin's Gage' (AGM, sf)
Damsons: 'Farleigh Damson' (sf), 'Merryweather' (sf)

Cherries

There are two types of cherries: sour, which are used for cooking and jam, and sweet, which are for eating.

Pollination and rootstocks

Until recently, cherry trees were more suited to orchards than allotments due to their huge size. Dwarfing rootstocks now make it possible for anybody to grow these red beauties. Buy trees on 'Colt' or even better 'Gisela 5' as this will form a tree only about 2m (6ft) high.

Many cherries are self-fertile, so you only need one tree (*see* page 163).

Where to grow

Cherries like a fertile, well-drained soil and sheltered spot. Sweet cherries ripen best in full sun, but sour cherries will happily grow in shade on a north-facing wall of a shed. Grow them as fans or pyramids (*see* page 161).

Growing and pruning

Cherries are vigorous growers and need a high amount of a general compound fertiliser at 110g/sq m (4oz/sq yd).

Water during dry periods, but avoid watering just prior to harvest as this can cause the skins to split. Birds love the fruit, so make sure nets are in place over them well before they ripen.

Like plums, cherries should only be pruned in spring or summer to avoid silver leaf disease. Sweet cherries fruit on wood produced the previous year and their training should be like that of a peach (*see* page 173). Sour cherries fruit on a system of older spurs and should be pruned like a plum.

Harvesting

Use snips or scissors to cut the stalks. Make two or three pickings over a few days to get the fruit at optimal ripeness.

Yield: 10kg (22lb) from a fan.

Cherries are a 'must have' on the allotment for jams and pies.

AT A GLANCE

Acid (or sour) cherries have a different growing system from sweet cherries, meaning that they require different pruning, but both types are best grown as fans or pyramids on dwarfing rootstocks. Sweet cherries can vary in colour from yellow through red and black. Most cherries are self-fertile meaning they only require one tree to produce fruit.

ALLOTMENT ADVICE:
what I wish I'd known

A common problem with cherries is the skin splitting just before harvest time. This usually happens after rainfall or watering, as once cherries have reached a certain size, their skin isn't able to stretch anymore. Commercial orchards resort to 'blow-drying' their trees with helicopters; this is beyond most of our budgets, so rig up a polythene roof over the cherry fan a week or two prior to harvesting to prevent it happening.

TRIED AND TESTED
RHS VARIETIES

(sf – denotes self fertile)
Sweet: 'Celeste' (sf), 'Early Rivers', 'Lapins' (sf), 'Merton Glory', 'Stella' (AGM, sf), 'Sunburst' (sf)
Sour: 'Morello' (AGM, sf), 'Nabella' (sf)

Figs

Although they conjure up images of balmy, Mediterranean living, figs are surprisingly easy to grow in cooler climes. The variety 'Brown Turkey' is the hardiest and happily grows outdoors, producing an abundance of figs year after year.

Where to grow
Figs like a warm, sunny site sheltered from prevailing winds. They are slightly tender, so avoid frost pockets. The best way to grow them is as a fan against a sunny wall or side of a shed where it will absorb all the sun's rays during the hottest part of the day.

Planting
Young trees are best planted in spring after the risk of frosts is over. Figs will crop best if their roots are restricted, which will also restrict the vigour of the plant. Dig a pit about 50cm (20in) deep and wide and line it with patio slabs or bricks. Backfill with the spoil from the hole and some well-rotted manure, and then plant the fig.

Growing
Prune a fig fan in a similar way to a peach, removing some of the older wood and replacing it with younger shoots. Ideally prune in late summer or spring.

Because a fig has its roots restricted, ensure that it is frequently watered.

Feed in spring with a balanced fertiliser at a rate of 50g/sq m (2oz/sq yd) over the planting pit. If a harsh frost is predicted, cover the fig with fleece. This will prevent the small, embryonic fruit being damaged.

The fruit forms in the tips of the new shoots in summer and will go through the winter as a pea-sized fruitlet. Remove any green, unripe figs larger than a pea in late summer, as they won't survive the winter.

Figs should have their roots restricted in order to increase yields of fruit.

Harvesting
Grown outdoors, figs only bear one crop a year. Small figs that have overwintered continue to ripen during the spring and will be ready for harvest by summer.

Figs are ready when they soften and start to droop downwards.

Yield: Expect anything; yields vary.

AT A GLANCE

Figs require a warm, sheltered spot. They are always supplied on their own roots, and the only way to keep them in bounds is to constrict them. If the plant does outgrow its space, just remember that figs can take the hardest of pruning, almost right down to ground level. They are very forgiving plants and will tolerate this harsh treatment. The benefit of doing this is that although you will inevitably forgo a crop the following year, it will encourage lots of new, healthy young wood to fruit the year after. 'Brown Turkey' is the most reliable outdoors variety, but even

this probably benefits from being covered over winter with fleece if possible. It's also a good idea to move figs grown in containers into a sheltered position, such as the porch, during winter. Unless growing permanently under cover, only expect one crop each year.

ALLOTMENT ADVICE:
what I wish I'd known

When pruning a fig be aware of where the sap is going, because it's a major irritant when it comes into contact with skin and particularly if it gets in the eyes. Always start your pruning at the bottom of the fan or

bush and work upwards. If you start at the top, the sap will drip on you as you move lower down the plant.

TRIED AND TESTED
RHS VARIETIES

Brown- or purple-fruited: 'Brown Turkey' (AGM), 'Brunswick', 'Rouge de Bordeaux'
White-fruited: 'White Ischia', 'White Marseilles'

Peaches

Peaches like it hot, making them one of the more challenging fruits to ripen on an allotment. However, the effort is well worth it as it has one of the most exquisite flavours imaginable. Never again will you settle for a supermarket peach flown around the globe and labelled 'fresh'. The same goes for nectarines, which are simply peaches that have lost their fuzz.

Where to grow

Peaches need fertile, well-drained soil in a sheltered position. They can only be grown as fans in very warm, sunny situations such as on a fence panel or shed wall where they will bask in the sun all day, particularly over a long afternoon. An alternative structure worth trying is a specially constructed trellis with frosted plastic sheeting sandwiched in the middle to maximise the sun's rays.

Growing and pruning

Apply 110g/sq m (4oz/sq yd) of a general fertiliser in early spring around the root area. Trees may need additional liquid feeding throughout the year. Mulch around the tree afterwards with a thick layer of well-rotted manure.

Peaches should be thinned out twice in the season. When they reach the size of hazelnuts thin to single fruits about 10cm (4in) apart; when they're the size of walnuts thin them again to their final spacing of 20cm (8in) apart. Protect the fruit with nets to ensure they don't get eaten by birds.

Peaches fruit on wood produced the previous year. Prune your fan in spring or summer, removing a portion of the old wood and replacing it with new

Peaches should be grown as a fan in a warm sheltered position in full sun.

shoots that will bear the crop next year. Pinch out some shoots to about six leaves to encourage new growth.

Harvesting

Ripe fruit is soft to the touch and easily parts from the tree. Fruit should be eaten immediately after picking, although slightly under-ripe peaches will ripen in the fruit bowl a couple of days later.

If you want to be really clever, you can grow fans that have a peach on one half of the plant and a nectarine on the other half. Contact a specialist grower to see if they can graft one for you.

Yield: About 9kg (20lb) of fruit from a fan.

AT A GLANCE

Peaches require lots of warmth, and are really only grown as fans in our climate. For this reason, the tree needs to be grafted on to the rootstock 'St Julien A'.

Peaches are self-fertile, but they need hand pollinating because they flower early in the year, when there is a lack of pollinating insects around. Use a small, soft brush to gently stroke the inside of the flower, transferring the pollen from one to another.

ALLOTMENT ADVICE:
what I wish I'd known

To prevent peach leaf-curl, cover trees with polythene sheets during winter and early spring to keep out damp and fungal spores. Lift the sheets back on warm days during flowering to allow pollinating insects to get to the blossoms.

TRIED AND TESTED
RHS VARIETIES

Peaches: 'Duke of York' (AGM), 'Early Rivers', 'Peregrine', 'Rochester' (AGM)
Nectarines: 'Lord Napier', Early Rivers' (AGM)

Soft fruit

Basic techniques

Every allotment should have an area set aside for soft fruit. Most of the plants are compact enough to squeeze into the smallest of spaces: strawberries can even be used to edge vegetable beds.

Preparing a soft fruit bed
Dig over the area, breaking up large clods of soil with the back of a fork and removing any perennial weeds and their roots. Add plenty of well-rotted organic matter, such as manure or garden compost, rake it level and leave it to settle for a few weeks.

The method is slightly different for preparing a bed for blueberries, as they prefer acidic conditions. Grow them in a raised bed or in pots in ericaceous compost. (*See* page 181.)

Maintenance pruning
Pruning is essential to control the size of the plant and keep it in good shape. All woody soft fruit plants should be pruned at least once a year, usually in winter. They also benefit from a second pruning in summer. This usually entails cutting back some of the new growth to about five buds, allowing sunlight to penetrate the canopy and air to circulate around the fruit, reducing the chances of botrytis and grey mould.

BUSH FORMS
Fruit like redcurrants and gooseberries can be grown as bushes or trained into attractive ornamental shapes such as fans (*see* page 161) and cordons.

Bush
The most common method of growing soft fruit is as a bush, which needs no staking or wires. However, it is important to understand how the plants produce fruit, as this dictates the details.

Gooseberries and redcurrants should be grown as bushes with an open centre, meaning branches growing into the centre should be removed to leave four or five main branches on a small

trunk about 20cm (8in) high. Because they fruit on old wood and the base of young wood, new growth should be pruned back to two buds when the plant is dormant. The leading shoot on each branch should be cut back by a third.

Gooseberries and redcurrants can also be grown as standards. The training is the same as for a bush, but the central stem is much longer – about 1m (3ft) high – so it does need a stake.

Blackcurrants have a different growth habit and fruit on young wood produced the previous year. Because of this,

blackcurrants are planted deeply into the ground to encourage lots of new growth from the base each spring – known as a stool bush. This takes a lot of energy each year, so be heavy handed when mulching and feeding. (*See* page 178 for more detail.)

Cordons
Gooseberries, redcurrants, and whitecurrants also lend themselves to being trained on upright single stems known as cordons. This is a great way of squeezing lots of varieties into a

5

6

7

1) *Blackcurrants should be planted deeply as a stool bush.*
2) *Gooseberry laterals should be pruned back to two buds in winter.*
3) *Autumn raspberries should be cut back to ground level in late winter.*
4) *Gooseberries should be thinned to allow the remaining fruit to ripen.*
5) *Tie in the new canes of summer fruiting raspberries after harvesting fruit from the old canes.*
6) *Blackberries make attractive features when trained on a trellis.*
7) *Remember to cover fruit plants with a net to protect them from birds.*

small space. These are usually grown as vertical cordons, rather than the oblique cordons seen in apple and pear training, because these plants are less vigorous. Stretch two or three wires between two stout posts and attach a vertical bamboo cane to each place where a cordon is going to be grown – they can be as close together as 20cm (8in). This method of training doesn't work well for blackcurrants or blueberries.

Double cordons make an impressive feature in the garden, particularly when spectacular coloured fruit, such as redcurrants, are hanging from them. Train them as for a single cordon, but with two stems rather than just one.

Other fruits

Strawberries are herbaceous plants, so none of these training methods apply to them. However, they do make beautiful features in pots, containers, and planters, especially if they are stacked up into a pyramid-shaped cascade.

Cane fruits are basically raspberries and blackberries (including hybrids such as loganberries, tayberries, and many more in a growing tribe). Some plants fruit on canes produced the previous year and should have their new shoots tied on to wires stretched between posts after they have fruited. Others, such as the autumn raspberries, fruit on the growth made in the current year and just need a simple cut down to ground level in late winter.

Climbing fruits such as vines and kiwis are perfect for trailing over a shed, or across a pergola. Vines are adaptable and can be grown as standards, bushes, or single-stem cordons.

Netting soft fruit

When growing soft fruit, never forget that the birds will also be eyeing up the fruits of your labours. The most effective way of keeping them off your crop is to throw a net over it as soon as the fruit starts to ripen. Nets may also be needed at other times of the year to prevent birds from pecking out the fruit buds, usually in the middle of winter.

It is possible to buy frame kits to construct around your plants. Much cheaper, though, is building your own using bamboo canes with elastic bands to hold the structure in place. Place upturned pots or plastic bottles over the tops of the upright stakes to support the netting, and secure the edge to the ground using plenty of pegs or a long bar to weight it down, to prevent birds from sneaking under.

Blackcurrants

Easy to grow, hard to pick, blackcurrants have an intensity of flavour that might not be to everybody's taste. However, it's certainly worth finding space for two or three of these bushes. They are packed full of vitamin C, giving fantastic health benefits. They can be eaten raw, but taste best cooked in pies, made into jam or squeezed to make a cordial. In fact, their qualities as a drink have made their botanical name of *Ribes* into a household name. A curious child of the blackcurrant is the jostaberry, a hybrid with the gooseberry (*see* page 180). Grown like a blackcurrant, it is vigorous and disease-resistant, with bigger fruit.

Where to grow

Blackcurrants are tolerant plants in many ways. The 'Ben' varieties are Scottish and correspondingly hardy, and bushes will crop in partial shade. A wide range of soil types is tolerated, including slightly alkaline ones: the only absolute requirements are that the soil is moisture retentive and highly fertile.

Planting and growing

Although closely related to redcurrants and gooseberries, blackcurrants can't be trained. In fact, there's really just one way to grow blackcurrants: as a stool bush. This involves planting the bush about 6cm (2.5in) deeper than it was in the pot, so that it sends up lots of shoots each year to fruit the following year. The soil should be dug over and enriched with well-rotted manure, plus slow-release fertiliser if planting on poor soils. Plant stool bushes about 1.8m (6ft) apart. Cut back all growth to ground level after planting; if the plant is still in leaf, wait until late autumn.

Pruning should be done each year when the plant is dormant, from late autumn to late winter. To encourage fresh, young shoots, cut back one in three of the thicker older stems to ground level, removing old branches and shoots that are lying close to the ground.

Blackcurrants produce heavy crops that can be converted into a delicious cordial.

In early spring, mulch around the base with well-rotted manure and add balanced fertiliser at 110g/sq m (4oz/sq yd). Push four evenly spaced bamboo canes into the ground around the plant and tie string around them as a support to prevent branches from flopping. Net against birds before the fruit ripens.

Harvesting

Remove whole 'strigs' from the bush once they have turned black using snips or scissors. Eat blackcurrants fresh, or refrigerate or freeze them.

Yield: About 5kg (11lb) of fruit from a mature bush.

AT A GLANCE

The fruit of modern blackcurrants ripen together on the bush making them easier to pick. Older varieties sometimes ripen at different times, meaning berries have to be picked individually when ready. The only other thing that might put you off is that the smell of the foliage isn't to everybody's liking: to some people it has a distinctly feline aroma.

ALLOTMENT ADVICE:
what I wish I'd known

You may choose to make blackcurrant cordial from the fruit on your allotment. The alcoholic equivalent, *crème de cassis*, is also superb, and it's easy to make: just crush blackcurrants into a refined alcohol, store for two months in a dark place, shaking every now and then, strain, add sugar then set aside for another two weeks until the sugar has dissolved. Add *crème de cassis* to white wine for a Kir, or to a bit of sparkle for a Kir Royale.

TRIED AND TESTED
RHS VARIETIES

'Ben Connan' (AGM), 'Ben Gairn', 'Ben Hope', 'Ben Lomond' (AGM), 'Ben Sarek' (AGM), 'Jostaberry'

Redcurrants

Redcurrants are expensive to buy in the shop, so grow your own for a free supply.

Redcurrants knock the spots off the ornamental flowering currants (*Ribes sanguineum*) when it comes to making an impression. Not only do they have wonderfully lobed and bold-shaped leaves and delicate white flowers, but the fruit drip from the bush when the harvest appears each year. Colours range from deep red to bright scarlet; some varieties have white or pink fruit. The ruby glow and expensive price tag of redcurrants in the shops make them the jewels of the soft fruit kingdom and an essential plant to grow on the allotment.

Where to grow
Like gooseberries (*see* page 180), redcurrants are quite at home when grown in shade. They can be grown as under-planting to larger fruit trees, or trained on the shadier side of a shed. However, they will also tolerate sun and will obviously ripen faster.

Redcurrants are very amenable to training, so they fit in just about anywhere. Grow them as bushes for large crops, or vertical cordons if you have no space (*see* pages 176–7). They can be trained as a fan against a fence or shed, and as stepovers (*see* page 161) to edge an area of the plot. You can try them as a two-tiered espalier (*see* page 161) for really ornamental value, but they probably won't have the vigour for any more tiers than that.

Planting and growing
Plant bushes spaced 1.5m (5ft) apart and cordons 40cm (15in) apart. Add plenty of well-rotted manure to the soil prior to planting, and a small handful of slow-release fertiliser.

The growth habit of the redcurrant is similar to that of the gooseberry. Most people grow them as an open-centred bush on the allotment. Redcurrants have the same fruiting habit as their gooseberry cousins, fruiting on older wood and the base of young wood, so should be pruned in the same way. Any time from late autumn to early spring, prune new growth on cordons and bushes back to two buds, and cut the leaders on bushes back by a third. In summer, prune by cutting new growth back to five leaves.

Fertilise in late winter, giving a balanced feed at a rate of 110g/sq m (4oz/sq yd), and mulch with well-rotted manure. Use a net to protect the fruit from birds.

Harvesting
Redcurrants are one of the fiddliest currants to pick, due to their tiny size. Use scissors to cut individual strigs when the berries are red. Often associated with savoury dishes and redcurrant jelly, they can also be used in desserts such as summer puddings. They freeze well to use at a later date.

Yield: About 6kg (13lb) from a mature bush and 1kg (2.5lb) from a vertical cordon.

Currants can also be pink or white and make a great alternative garnish on a plate.

AT A GLANCE

Redcurrants are more like gooseberries than blackcurrants and should be grown as such. They make a beautiful garnish, and for something a bit more unusual try growing whitecurrants such as 'White Grape' or 'Pink Champagne'.

ALLOTMENT ADVICE:
what I wish I'd known

If your leaves look as if they have been attacked by a plague in midsummer, don't panic. It's the work of the redcurrant blister aphid, and although it looks dreadful it doesn't usually have a detrimental effect on the plant or crop. If you don't like the look of the blistered leaves, you can pull them off and burn them.

TRIED AND TESTED
RHS VARIETIES

Redcurrants: 'Jonkheer van Tets' (AGM), 'Junifer', 'Red Lake' (AGM), 'Red Start', 'Stanza' (AGM)
Whitecurrants: 'Pink Champagne', 'Versailles Blanche', 'White Grape'

Gooseberries

You either love them or loathe them. Many who fall into the latter camp are probably thinking of the sharp, hairy, green bullets sold in supermarkets. Once you have tried the rich, sweet, and juicy flavours of a dessert gooseberry, you quickly change your mind, but you can't get these beauties in the shops - the only way to taste them is to grow them.

Where to grow
Gooseberries are quite at home in those awkward shady corners near a hedge or shed where nothing else will grow. They need a moist but free-draining soil and will tolerate a more exposed site than most other soft fruits. Add plenty of well-rotted manure prior to planting and a small handful of slow-release fertiliser to ensure they get the best start in life.

Planting and growing
Gooseberry bushes should be planted about 1.5m apart (5ft) and cordons about 30cm (12 inches) apart. They fruit on older wood and on the base of young wood, so they can be trained into all sorts of shapes, such as cordons (*see* page 176), and fans, and stepovers (*see* page 161). Prune between late autumn and late winter, cutting new growth back to two buds and leaders on bushes back by one third; pruning new growth to five leaves in summer will also encourage a bigger crop for the following year.

Apply a balanced fertiliser around the root area in late winter at a rate of 110g/sq m (4oz/sq yd) and mulch with well-rotted manure, ensuring it doesn't touch the stem and cause it to rot. Keep the plant well watered - if it's put under stress it will become more susceptible to mildew. Cover bushes with a net as they ripen to prevent birds from stripping the fruit; they will find green and yellow ones too.

Gooseberries from the allotment taste so much better than the under-ripe fruits sold in shops.

Harvesting
A few weeks before they are ripe, remove alternate fruits for cooking. When ripe, the crop will taste delicious straight from the bush, but can also be frozen.

Yield: About 5kg (11lb) from a bush and 1.5kg (3lb) from a vertical cordon.

AT A GLANCE

There are over 150 varieties to choose from. Gooseberries have two categories, cookers or dessert. In fact, most are dual purpose and taste sweeter when left to fully ripen. They also come in five different colours: white, green, yellow, red, and pink.

There is a long history of gooseberry growing in the United Kingdom, especially in Lancashire. In the 19th century members of gooseberry clubs would compete to grow the largest gooseberry. Some clubs still exist.

ALLOTMENT ADVICE:
what I wish I'd known

Always wear gloves when harvesting gooseberries, because those thorns are sharp. If you don't like the thought of picking them because of all the thorns, choose a thornless variety such as 'Pax'.

Mildew can be a real problem so if you don't want to spray, choose 'Invicta' and 'Rokula' which have some resistance. Worcesterberry, a small purple gooseberry relation, has good resistance.

TRIED AND TESTED
RHS VARIETIES

Green-fruited: 'Careless' (AGM), 'Invicta' (AGM)
Red-fruited: 'London', 'Pax', 'Rokula', 'Whinham's Industry' (AGM),
Yellow-fruited: 'Bedford Yellow', 'Golden Drop', 'Leveller' (AGM), 'Yellow Champagne',
White-fruited: 'Langley Gage'

Blueberries

Rewarding the gardener not just with delicious berries but also with a spectacular foliage display of fiery reds and purples in autumn, blueberries are a superb addition to the plot. The fruit also have lots of health benefits as they are packed full of antioxidants.

Where to grow

Blueberries need a sheltered, sunny site with moist, well-drained soil. Much more importantly, they require acidic soil conditions, so if your allotment has a pH higher than 5.5 (*see* page 27) you will need to consider growing them either in containers or in a raised or sunken bed. It is possible to change the existing soil using acidifying materials such as sulphur chips or pine needles, but pH levels can fluctuate and the results are really not reliable.

The advantage of building a sunken or raised bed is that you have full control over what materials go in to

make up the type of soil required. Sunken beds are useful if your allotment is on the dry side, as they retain water (ideal for moisture-loving blueberries), raised beds on the other hand increase drainage and so are ideal for soils that are just too heavy and wet.

Raised or sunken beds should be 60cm (2ft) deep and edged with polythene that has been pierced in a few places with a garden fork to allow drainage. The bed should be filled with neutral or acidic topsoil mixed with ericaceous compost and composted bark in equal quantities. Plant bushes at least 1m (3ft) apart.

Blueberry bushes can be grown in containers using a loam-based ericaceous potting compost. They will need watering most days in summer, so unless you spend every day at the allotment, this is not the option for you.

Growing

Check the soil pH every year. If it has risen, then add acidifying materials such as pine needles or conifer clippings. Avoid well-rotted manure, as this can be too rich for the plants. Apply an annual top-dressing of ericaceous fertiliser.

Prune as for a blackcurrant bush (*see* page 178), removing about a third of the older wood each year. The birds find blueberries irresistible, so drape a net over bushes as soon as they ripen.

Harvesting

Berries are ready for picking when they change colour from green to blue. Most blueberries also develop an attractive bloom when ripe. They must be picked individually, a painstaking task, but well worth the effort – the taste of freshly picked blueberries is sensational.

Yield: About 3kg (7lb) from a mature bush.

Blueberries require an acidic soil but can be grown in containers with ericaceous compost.

AT A GLANCE

Regarded by many as a 'superfood' due to their antioxidant levels, most blueberries are derived from several American species including the northern highbush *Vaccinium corymbosum*. Cranberries are closely related and also prefer acidic conditions: try creating a bog area on the allotment with a pierced pond liner and plant them into it. Use pine needles to mulch around the base each year to maintain acidic conditions.

Blueberries are grown on their own roots so you don't need to worry about rootstocks. They don't need a pollinating partner but tend to fruit better if other varieties are planted nearby.

They are unsuitable for growing as any kind of trained form: just grow them as a bush and prune them like a blackcurrant. They are suitable for growing in pots in loam-based ericaceous compost or in raised or sunken beds.

ALLOTMENT ADVICE: what I wish I'd known

After you've gone to all the effort of planting in the right compost and finding pine needles to mulch your bushes, don't undo your good work by watering with tap water. Remember that tap water can alter the acidity of your soil, and try to use nothing but rainwater on your blueberry bushes. Not only is this more environmentally sound, your plants will appreciate the water quality. Make sure that you have lots of water butts on your allotment, and use all your shed space to attach gutters and downpipes to collect as much as possible. You will need plenty, because these are thirsty plants.

TRIED AND TESTED RHS VARIETIES

'Berkeley', 'Duke' (AGM), 'Earliblue', 'Jersey', 'Nelson', 'Spartan' (AGM), 'Top Hat'

Raspberries

Nothing beats the taste of freshly picked raspberries. North of Hadrian's Wall these are favoured due to their suitability for a cool, moist climate: they should thrive on any allotment.

Where to grow

Raspberries require a sheltered spot in full sun or partial shade. They prefer a light, slightly acidic, well-drained but moisture-retentive soil.

Summer varieties should ideally be trained on two parallel wires, equally stretched between 1.8m (6ft) posts. Autumn raspberries don't need support but can be contained as a thicket between two sets of parallel wires and posts about an arm's length wide.

Plant canes in rows about 6cm (2.5in) below the soil surface. Don't plant them too deeply, or they will never grow up through the ground. Use your feet to measure out the spacing of canes: it will be about one foot length from cane to cane (more if you have dainty little feet).

Raspberries live for about ten years before they lose their vigour and need replanting. Bear this in mind if you take over an allotment with an existing row.

Plant both summer and autumn raspberries to ensure bumper crops throughout the year.

Freshly picked raspberries are the perfect addition to smoothies, fruit pies, and muesli.

Growing

Mulch the crop each year with well-rotted manure, being careful not to apply it too deeply and smother the plant. Keep the mulch off the base of the canes or it will cause them to rot. Don't use mushroom manure; it's too alkaline. Keep the plants weed free but avoid hoeing, because this risks disturbing the shallow roots.

There are two types of raspberries. Summer-fruiting types produce fruit on canes grown the previous year; cut the canes that have just produced fruit down to ground level just after picking. Autumn-fruiting raspberries produce fruit on canes grown in the current year; cut to ground level in late winter. Pull up any suckers growing between rows.

Harvesting

Raspberries won't all ripen together, so keep an eye on your crop and pick as and when they are ready. Eat fresh with cream, make jam, or freeze them.

Yield: About 5kg (11lb) from a 3m (10ft) row of mature canes. Autumn raspberries will produce about half that.

AT A GLANCE

Bountiful summer- and more moderate autumn-fruiting raspberries are pruned and supported slightly differently, but both types prefer slightly acidic soils and are grown on their own roots.

ALLOTMENT ADVICE:
what I wish I'd known

If you can never grow enough to put on the table, make jam or raspberry wine. If your allotment plot is full, you could instead fit in the small, prostrate Arctic raspberries. They are low plants that produce delicious but smaller raspberries. They like a sunny, sheltered spot in well drained soil. The downside of growing these compact plants is that children can reach all the fruit on them and will devour a whole bush's worth while your back is turned.

TRIED AND TESTED
RHS VARIETIES

Summer: 'Glen Ample' (AGM), 'Glen Moy' (AGM), 'Glen Prosen' (AGM)
Autumn: 'Autumn Bliss' (AGM), 'Joan J'

Blackberries

These are regarded by many as a weed, but do consider making some room for their late-summer fruit. They are easy to grow and many of the named varieties provide far better fruits that are double the size of the wild ones.

Where to grow

Blackberries are vigorous plants that grow just as well in partial shade as in the sun. They flower late so can even be

Blackberries on the allotment taste so much better than the wild ones in hedgerows.

planted in frost pockets. However, they need lots of space, so bear this in mind when buying one. They like moisture-retentive but well-drained soil and will benefit from the addition of well-rotted manure before planting. They fruit on canes produced the previous year, which can be trained on to a fence or shed.

They can also be planted as a dense hedge, which may be useful for creating a screen or even providing protection from wildlife that might enjoy munching on your veggies. It will need constant checking and pruning if you don't want it to take over the allotment. Allow at least 3.5m (11ft) between plants.

Growing

Treat them in a similar way to summer fruiting raspberries and loganberries, by cutting the canes that have cropped this year down to ground level. Do this soon after harvesting, and tie in new canes that will produce fruit next year. Mulch the plants with well-rotted manure in late winter and top-dress with a general-purpose fertiliser.

Harvesting

Watch out for those thorns and wear gloves when picking. The fruit is usually ready for harvesting from midsummer onwards although fruit growing in the shade will ripen later. Eat them fresh with cream, or use them to make bramble jelly, an easy set because they are rich in pectin. Apple and blackberry crumble is another classic favourite.

Yield: About 5kg (11lb) from a mature bush, although this can vary enormously from variety to variety and with how large you let the bush grow.

AT A GLANCE

Blackberries are self-fertile so only one plant is required, but they sucker and layer very readily making the production of new plants very easy. They are vigorous, so make sure you have lots of space for them. They grow on their own roots, so there's no need to worry about selection of rootstocks.

Consider other related berries, such as loganberries, tayberries, and boysenberries. The European dewberry produces small, purple fruits that taste great, and the cloudberry has delicious golden fruit. The

Japanese wineberry is also worth trying, as it produces attractive red stems that make a great feature in winter.

ALLOTMENT ADVICE:
what I wish I'd known

If you don't like the thought of contending with sharp thorns when pruning and picking, there are thornless varieties such as 'Oregon Thornless' which also have decorative, deeply cut leaves that turn a beautiful rich red colour in autumn. Because they have no thorns, you can grow them up and over an

archway over a path. 'Fantasia' is another delicious variety and a particularly apt plant for an allotment plot because it was first discovered growing on an allotment.

TRIED AND TESTED
RHS VARIETIES

'Ashton Cross', 'Fantasia' (AGM), 'Loch Ness' (AGM), 'Oregon Thornless', 'Silvan' (AGM), 'Waldo'

Strawberries

Strawberries aren't just a pleasure to be enjoyed during the two weeks of Wimbledon. By choosing varieties carefully it is possible to have your allotment dripping with delicious, succulent fruit from mid-spring until late autumn. Whereas many shops have elected to sell strawberries that travel and store well (or fairly well), gardeners can ignore this criteria and choose varieties purely for their taste.

Where to grow

Strawberries like to be grown in full sun in fertile, well-drained soil. If growing them directly into the soil, they can be included as part of a crop rotation programme (*see* page 44).

They also thrive in growing bags, planters, or even hanging baskets. They will need watering every day during dry periods, so make sure you can get down to the allotment frequently.

Dig over the plot prior to planting, ensuring that plenty of organic matter is added to the soil. Strawberries should be 45cm (18in) apart in a row with 1m (3ft) between rows. The best time for planting is late summer. Buy virus-free stock and plan to keep the plants in the ground for two to three years before rotating them to another area of the allotment. Avoid planting into soil that has previously had potatoes, tomatoes, or chrysanthemums in it as these can all suffer from verticillium wilt and can transmit it via the soil.

Growing

As strawberries ripen they will need straw or some other dry material tucked under them to prevent the fruit coming into contact with the ground and rotting. After harvesting, the straw should be removed and composted. Chop back the old leaves after harvesting to expose some of the crown of the plant to sunlight for the rest of the summer; this will encourage more

fruit next year. If the plants have been in the ground for more than three years they should be dug up, composted, and the ground prepared for a different crop for the following year.

Make sure that the beds are kept free from weeds, and water the plants during dry periods. Botrytis can be a problem, particularly in wet years. This can be exacerbated by overhead watering splashing on to leaves and fruit. Water at the base of the plant and be prepared to spray with a fungicide every couple of weeks from when the flowers open until fruit ripens.

Avoid extortionate shop prices by creating your own strawberry patch on the allotment.

Regularly use a liquid feed, providing something high in potash, such as a tomato feed, during their growing and fruiting season.

If you want an extra-early crop, then place a cloche over an early fruiting variety as it starts to flower, remembering to ventilate on hot days. This can give you a crop about a week earlier than you'd usually pick it.

Net the crop against birds and resign yourself to losing some of

Dining al fresco

There's something special about food picked from the plot and eaten straight away. What could be better than to sit back and enjoy the freshest of fresh cooking in the open air? Imagine you've just lifted the first of your early potatoes, there's mint nearby, the asparagus is still in season, or maybe the mangetout are perfect for picking, and the garlic is ready to lift. A few fresh salad leaves and some peppery, mouth-cleansing radishes will add colour to the plate, and the strawberries are juicy, red and ripe for afters. Later in the season, sample the sweetest sweetcorn of your life, taking it from the stem to the steam of a bubbling pan of water for a few minutes. By now the tomatoes are ready, and wonderful served with basil, and for dessert there could be strawberries, plums, autumn raspberries and blackberries. You need little more than your camping stove, a pan, and butter to make a gastronomic delight: the ingredients are all there and this is produce at its peak. Forget food miles: take your chair or rug, invite family and friends or call over your fellow allotment holders, and enjoy your food metres.

Pack straw under the plants as the fruits start to ripen to prevent them rotting on the ground.

these low-growing crops to slugs before you have a chance to pick them.

Propagating

Strawberries propagate by producing runners, which anchor themselves into the ground and set down roots. These should be removed from plants that are going to be cropping that year, as they pinch nutrients that you want the plants to use for fruit production. If you want to propagate extra plants, create a separate area on the allotment where plants can freely produce runners. Nip out flowers on the mother plant to ensure that all the energy goes into runner production. Remove runners in late summer and plant out in strawberry beds. Alpine strawberries tend not to send out runners, so must be propagated from seed.

Harvesting

Strawberries ripen individually, so pick and eat as ready. Eat as soon as possible and chill as little as possible. They tend not to freeze well and will just

defrost into a mush. However, this is fine for ice cream or jam, and everybody knows that strawberries make the best jam, although it is tricky to get to the setting point due to lack of pectin.

Yield: About 450g (1lb) of fruit per plant. Early varieties tend to be lighter croppers. Perpetual croppers generally have two flushes of growth.

An alternative to straw is a weed-suppressing membrane. It also saves on weeding.

AT A GLANCE

Strawberries that we know today are a cross between the Chilean strawberry and the Virginian strawberry. They are herbaceous perennials that will crop well for about two to three years before they should be disregarded, and unlike most fruit crops you can incorporate them into a crop rotation program.

There are three types of strawberries. The summer-fruiting varieties (the type we associate with Wimbledon) are divided into early, mid-, and late-season types. The perpetual types have two flushes of growth during summer. The alpine strawberries have much smaller fruits, usually red but also white or yellow, that appear in small flushes through summer. They tend to tolerate shade better, and make attractive edges to paths and beds.

ALLOTMENT ADVICE:
what I wish I'd known

Not only do strawberries taste great, they also have masses of ornamental value. Plant them in a hanging basket: their habit lends itself perfectly to showing off flowers and fruit each year, and a perpetual will put on a constant show of either flowers or red fruits throughout summer and into early autumn. A basket can even be placed in the greenhouse in early spring to bring the flowers on.

For a spectacular display that slugs will struggle to ruin, pack a whole growing bag with plants and suspend it from an arch or trellis – but keep it well watered.

TRIED AND TESTED
RHS VARIETIES

Early: 'Emily', 'Honeoye' (AGM),
Mid: 'Hapil' (AGM), 'Pegasus' (AGM), 'Cambridge Favourite' (AGM)
Late: 'Rhapsody' (AGM), 'Symphony' (AGM)
Perpetual: 'Aromel' (AGM), 'Bolero'
Alpine: 'Viva Rosa', 'Mara des Bois'

Vine fruit and stems

Grapes

There is nothing more rewarding than drinking chilled white wine made from vines grown on your own allotment – unless you have a greenhouse, you're more or less limited to wine grapes. Climate change with hotter summers makes a mini-vineyard on the allotment a realistic possibility in most of the country: English and Welsh vineyards are now winning international wine awards. Not only does home-made wine have unique flavours that can only be created from your unique allotment plot, but it will save you money compared to stocking up at the supermarket.

Where to grow

Grapes don't need as fertile a soil as some of the other fruits; they tend to make excessive and luxuriant foliage growth at the expense of fruit in such conditions. However, the soil should be improved with well-rotted manure if it is very shallow and poor. Vines will grow in a wide range of soils, including chalky ground, sand, and gravel.

What grapes do need is as much warmth and sun as they can get to ripen and develop the highest possible sugar levels. High sugar levels are important, not just to make dessert grapes taste better, but also to become the alcohol in wine. Avoid frost pockets, as a single frost in late spring will destroy emerging shoots and flowers.

Grapevines are naturally climbing plants, using their tendrils to clamber upwards towards the sun. Use this to your advantage by training them over arches, pergolas, or the sunny side of a shed. Alternatively grow them 1.5m (5ft) apart within rows and with 1.5m (5ft) between rows. The simplest training method is to grow vertical cordons. This involves training a single trunk upwards on a post with a system of short fruiting spurs off either side of it.

Most vineyards are planted on south-facing slopes, which angles them like solar panels towards the sun and

maximises the amount of warmth. If your allotment is on a south-facing slope, face the plants into the sun to get as much as possible on all the spurs.

Growing

There is no need to annually feed and mulch vines unless low nutrient levels are noted. Magnesium deficiency can be treated with a foliar spray of Epsom salts.

In the winter, prune back new growth to two buds. Winter is also a great time for fixing and tightening any wires or support systems. If vines are small enough, throw fleece over them when frost is predicted. Alternatively light a chiminea or a barbecue near them.

In summer, cut fresh new growth back to five leaves. Prune sublaterals (the sideshoots off sideshoots) back to one leaf. Continue cutting back growth

Create your own mini-vineyard on the allotment. Each grapevine produces two bottles.

during the summer to keep the vine tidy and to allow the sunlight to penetrate the canopy. Thin the grapes out on cordons in summer, allowing just one bunch to form per spur.

Keep the area around the vines weed free. A mulch between rows will help to suppress weeds and retain moisture. Place broken slates around the base of the trunks, if liked, to absorb the heat from the sun and warm up the soil.

Throw a net over the fruit bunches as they start to ripen to prevent birds from destroying your vintage.

Harvesting

Grapes are ready when they are soft to the touch and the skin loses its coarse texture and takes on soft, translucent hues. They should taste sweet, although wine grapes will still have a slight sharpness. Cut them off in whole bunches with the stem attached.

Yield: How long is a piece of string? You should get one or two bottles of wine per vine, although this varies with how large the vine is. Huge sprawling vines trained over pergolas will produce lots more, but the quality will not be so good. Limiting the number of grapes improves their sugar content and your wine.

Making wine

Pick wine grapes in dry weather, as rain will dilute the grape juice. You can try pressing the grapes yourself, but it's easier to find a winery who may be willing to crush, ferment, and bottle your wine for you. It will be cheaper if you get together with others who want to do the same. There is nothing like an autumn harvest celebration with bottles of your own wine on the allotment.

White grapes ripen better than the reds in the UK, producing crisp, aromatic, herbaceous flavours. German

Grapevines make attractive features when trained on pergolas or up arches.

hybrids are the most popular, with higher yields and good acidity, but some of the classic French varieties such as 'Chardonnay' and 'Sauvignon Blanc' are still worth trying despite lower yields in warmer regions. Reds are harder to produce because the colour depends on the skins, which rarely develop enough in cool climates.

German Allotments

Germany's 'gardens for the poor' began in the 19th century. Rural migration to the cities led to poor living conditions, and land was supplied for growing food to help alleviate malnutrition. The Schreber movement encouraged children to learn self-sufficiency and interact with nature. These were the first organised allotments, and the term *Schrebergarten* still exists to describe allotment gardens in Germany.

Later, the allotment became vital for securing a source of food, especially during the wartime and interwar periods when there was widespread poverty. In 1919 the first legislation about allotment gardens was passed, fixing rents and providing security of tenure. In 1946, Berlin had more than 200,000 allotments.

These days they are very much social, recreational, and back-to-nature green havens, with around 1.4 million of them in the country. Their role in conservation in city environments is key, and in urban settings where much of the population lives in apartments, access to a garden is enjoyed by all sorts of people. In fact, in Berlin, thousands of allotments even have small, habitable constructions that plot holders are allowed to spend the night in.

AT A GLANCE

Grapevines are rampant, vigorous plants that use their tendrils to climb upwards. They can be used to create screens or scramble over trellises. They must be grown in a sunny, sheltered aspect for the grapes to fully ripen. Don't overfeed them as they will produce too much vegetative growth and little fruit.

Outdoor grapes are usually wine grapes: dessert grapes are bigger but should be grown in a greenhouse. If you plant a mini-vineyard of three rows with four vines in each row, you should get around 24 to 36 bottles of wine.

Grapevines are usually sold grafted on to rootstocks. This isn't to control the vigour but to provide resistance against a root-eating insect called phylloxera. Don't expect a harvest until three years after planting. Fruit produced in previous years shouldn't be allowed to ripen, but removed early on in the season.

ALLOTMENT ADVICE:
what I wish I'd known

The prunings from grape vines make excellent kindling when dried out for a few months. Tie together into bundles in late autumn and leave them in a shed or other dry place to overwinter. In spring you can use them to light a chiminea or barbecue when putting it out next to the rows of vines for frost protection.

If netting a vine to protect it from bird damage is too awkward, such as when you have one growing over an arch, wrap the individual bunches of grapes in muslin bags or old nylon tights.

TRIED AND TESTED
RHS VARIETIES

White wine grapes for outdoors: 'Bacchus', 'Chardonnay', 'Madeleine Angevine', 'Orion', 'Phoenix', 'Riesling', 'Seyval Blanc'
Black wine grapes for outdoors: 'Dornfelder', 'Pinot Noir', 'Regent', 'Rondo'
Dessert grapes for a greenhouse: 'Black Hamburgh', 'Foster's Seedling', 'Muscat of Alexandria'

Kiwi fruit

This is a fruit usually associated with New Zealand, but the cool climate of Northern Europe is not so different from this antipodean island country. Allotments are prime settings for this large, sprawling plant, which produces delicious, ripe kiwis with a searing freshness and unique zingy contrast of sweetness and sharpness.

Where to grow

Kiwis need a fertile, well-drained soil enriched with well-rotted manure. These deciduous shrubs have two other main requirements: lots of sun and lots of space. They can be used to crawl over trellises, arches, pergolas, and sheds but will crop best if trained on a system of posts and wires.

Some varieties are self-fertile, so don't require a pollinating 'friend', and these are better for an allotment, as they take up less space. Otherwise, grow male and female plants close to each other to ensure good pollination. Self-fertile varieties can be trained as espaliers on posts and wires.

Growing

The main pruning should be carried out in winter. Flowers and fruit will be produced on the base of new shoots and along the length of one-year-old wood. Some new shoots can be tied on to wires (or trellis, arch etc) while other shoots can be shortened back to 12–15cm (5–6in) to create fruiting spurs. Remove older wood and tie in the replacement shoots. In summer, prune new shoots back to a few leaves from the nearest fruit to the tips.

Kiwi plants are very greedy, so mulch around the base of each plant in late winter with well-rotted manure. Apply a general-purpose fertiliser at a rate of 110g/sq m (4oz/sq yd). Keep the area weed free so that the plant doesn't have any competition for nutrients and moisture. Water at the base of the plant in dry, hot periods.

Choose a self-fertile type of kiwi fruit such as 'Jenny' to save on space.

Harvesting

Fruits ripen late in the season and must be harvested before the first frosts. After picking, store them indoors in a fruit bowl for a few weeks before they are ready for eating. They will keep for about three months if stored carefully in a pierced plastic bag in a refrigerator.

Yield: 9kg (20lb) from a mature kiwi vine.

AT A GLANCE

Despite associations with New Zealand, this is really the national fruit of southern China, hence one of its common names, Chinese gooseberry. The fruit are packed full of vitamin C: one fruit will supply you with far more than the minimum daily dose. Choose a self-fertile variety, because one plant takes up much less space than two.

ALLOTMENT ADVICE:
what I wish I'd known

If you inherit a kiwi plant on your plot you will need to check if it is a self-fertile variety or a single-sex plant. If it is purely male or female it will require a pollinating partner.

Only a plant producing female flowers will produce fruit, but it requires the male flowers to pollinate it.

Study the centre of the flower. Female flowers have only a pure white central stigma, while male flowers have lots of yellow-tipped anthers and no stigma. A self-fertile variety will have both types of flower and can pollinate itself.

TRIED AND TESTED
RHS VARIETIES

'Hayward' (female), 'Tomuri' (male, plant with Hayward), 'Jenny' (self fertile)

Rhubarb

The succulent leaf stalks or 'sticks' of rhubarb produce a delicious crop from late winter (if forced) to midsummer.

Planting

Rhubarb prefers a sunny spot, but will make do with any situation. Before planting, prepare the soil well to ensure good crops for several years. Dig it over to a good depth, adding plenty of well-rotted manure or compost. Drainage is important, as is removing stray bits of perennial weeds, because plants will remain for a number of years. Plant the crown with the growing point at or just below the soil surface; on wetter soils plant with the buds just above the soil to prevent rotting. Space plants 1m (3ft) apart, with 1-1.8m (3-6ft) between rows.

Growing

Rhubarb will appreciate a generous mulch around the crowns with organic matter in late winter or early spring. Also in late winter or early spring apply

Rhubarb plants spread over a wide area, so give them plenty of room to develop in.

The young sticks of forced rhubarb have a fantastic flavour.

a granular general fertiliser at a rate of 110g/sq m (4oz/sq yd).

Keep the plants well watered during dry weather and feed again with a general fertiliser after cropping. Mulching helps reduce drought stress during summer and ensures a longer picking season. Remove any flowering shoots.

Poor crops and thin, weak sticks can mean that the crowns have become overcrowded and need dividing; divide them every five or six years. Lift the crowns when dormant, from late autumn to late winter, using a fork to avoid damage. Split into sections with a spade, ensuring each has a healthy portion of thick root and at least one strong bud.

Harvesting

Rhubarb is pulled, not cut: hold the sticks close to the ground and then pull upwards with a twisting motion. Don't strip a whole plant in one go; always leave at least four sticks.

For a very early harvest, try forcing. Lift a whole crown in early winter and leave it on the soil surface to be chilled, preferably frozen solid, for two weeks. Then either replant it or pot up with compost and bring into a cool room or greenhouse at 7-16°C (45-61°F). Totally exclude light using forcing pots, buckets or black polythene. Stack rotting organic matter over the covers of outdoor crowns to insulate, or just put the roots in a black bin and replace the lid. Keep damp and uncover at night to ventilate, and harvest the pink stems when they're tall enough. Forced crowns grown in the ground need a season to recover; discard those in pots.

Yield: Around 2-2.5kg (4-5lb) from each plant.

AT A GLANCE

This is a reliable and low-input crop, quietly producing sticks in a wide range of conditions. These are not always red: green ones can be just as good. Don't make the mistake of thinking that rhubarb needs no attention; badly fed clumps and hot, dry summers combine to slow down growth and produce a poor and bitter-tasting crop.

ALLOTMENT ADVICE:
what I wish I'd known

Rhubarb plants need to establish well before you can start cropping, so don't be tempted to pull a crop in the first year.

In the second year, start pulling in late spring and finish before midsummer; pulling any later will weaken the crowns and reduce yields next year.

TRIED AND TESTED
RHS VARIETIES

'Champagne Early', 'Glaskins Perpetual', 'Prince Albert', 'Stockbridge Arrow', 'Timperley Early' (AGM), 'Victoria'

Allotment flowers

Basic techniques

Some traditionalists argue that there's no room for flowers on an allotment, as the plot should be for growing food, and anyway, many herbs, vegetables and fruit trees produce attractive flowers. But ornamentals increase biodiversity, extend flowering periods, give larger blooms and beautify your plot with an abundance of colours and scents.

Where to grow them

There's a wide palette of plants available to create a floral paradise on the plot. Flowers can be incorporated in the vegetable garden as companion plants, used as edging or as under-planting for fruit trees. If you just want to grow flowers to add colour to the veg plot and attract insects, your only restriction is your imagination. Plant between rows, in hanging baskets and containers, around the shed, along pathways. Go mad.

If you want a bed for cut flowers, choose a specific area, ideally in full sun, dig it over, enrich it with well-rotted organic matter, and rake. Plants in rows are easier to manage.

Annuals

Annuals are ideal for a quick splash of colour and cost just the price of a few packs of seed. Most hardy annuals can be sown directly into the soil in early spring as soon as temperatures reach 7°C (45°F). Others do better with a longer growing season and can be sown in autumn in a greenhouse before being hardened off and planted out in spring.

Prepare the ground thoroughly before sowing, removing all perennial weeds and adding well-rotted manure. Rake over the ground, tread it down and then rake it lightly again. Sow annuals in straight rows so that it is easy to tell them from the weeds when they emerge. Sow rows about 30cm (12in) apart, but check the information on the seed packets. Thin out seedlings as they emerge to ensure they don't overcrowd and compete with each other.

Biennials

As the name suggests, these plants live for two years: they grow in the first, flower in the second, then die. Popular examples include foxgloves (*Digitalis*) and hollyhocks (*Alcea*). Wallflowers (*Erysium*) are perennials treated as biennials, sold in their first year and ditched after flowering in their second.

Herbaceous perennials

Herbaceous perennials are the bedrock of the cutting garden. There are hundreds of plants to choose from and

many of them are suitable for cut flowers. These plants put on a flowering display each year, emerging in spring and fading back below the ground from autumn to winter before appearing again in spring.

Shrubs

Realistically there just isn't room on allotments for many ornamental woody plants, but if you want the ultimate in cut flowers then roses are essential. Climbing or rambling roses trained over arches make a beautiful feature and

1) *Many annuals can be sown individually in modules and planted out later in the year.*
2) *Some plants can be sown in shallow drills before being thinned out and transplanted.*
3) *Many plants need staking to prevent them flopping over.*
4) *Ensure bulbs are the right way up when planting them.*
5) *Cut dahlia flowers with snips in either the morning or evening, retaining a long stem.*
6) *Deadhead flowers frequently to extend the flowering season.*
7) *Anemones are a popular cut flower.*

Deadheading

Keep the flowering display of annuals and herbaceous plants going for longer by removing flowerheads as they fade. This will prevent the plant directing its energy into seed production instead of flower production. It will also keep the allotment looking fresh and tidy and prolong the flowering display. Most flowers should be snapped off just behind the head, but some, such as delphinium, need the whole flowering stem to be cut back.

Don't deadhead flowers that you intend to collect seed from for propagating next year, and hold back on plants that produce attractive seedheads such as honesty (*Lunaria*).

Staking

Taller plants will need staking to prevent blooms from flopping. Tie heavy stems individually to bamboo canes with soft twine. Pea netting stretched between stout wooden stakes is a popular support on an allotment: plants can weave themselves through the gaps.

If using bamboo canes for staking, put plastic cane toppers or empty bottles over them to protect eyes.

Dividing

Divide herbaceous perennials in autumn or early spring; it's an easy way to make more plants and reduces congestion in the middle. Slice cleanly through the plants with a spade, replant some of the clumps and give others away.

add height to an otherwise flat plot. Sprigs of holly, perhaps grown in a hedge, can be cut for Christmas, while sarcococca provides scented winter flowers and dogwood's colourful stems make colourful displays in the house.

Bulbs

Bulbous plants, including tubers, corms and rhizomes, are some of our most familiar flowers including most of our spring flowers (*see* pages 196-7). Many of them can be grown as cut flowers, others make a useful splash of colour.

Planting

On an allotment, straight rows are the easiest to manage, particularly for larger plants such as dahlias and lilies. A more natural effect can be created with smaller bulbous plants such as crocus and daffodils if space allows – perhaps near your shed – by randomly scattering a few bulbs on the surface and planting them where they fall. They should usually be planted about two to three times their own depth with the growing tip pointing upwards. Tuck smaller plants, including bulbs, in at plot edges.

Spring flowers

DAFFODILS *Narcissus*
Everybody's favourite springtime flower, daffs from the allotment are wonderful for spring bouquets. The sight of these nodding flowers in white and shades of gold really does make it feel like spring.

Growing
Most hybrid daffodils tolerate a wide range of conditions, but prefer slightly moist but well-drained soil in full sun or dappled shade. Plant in autumn and add grit to heavy soils. Bulbs should be planted three times their depth. Plant larger varieties 10–13cm (4–5in) apart and smaller types 5–10cm (2–4in) apart.

There's not much else to do: remove the flowerheads as they fade, but leave the foliage for another six weeks, as allowing it to die back naturally enables nutrients to go back down into the bulb. Otherwise they won't flower next year. Most types are fully hardy and bulbs can be left in the ground over winter.

Cutting
Cut as their buds are about to open, but before they are fully in flower. Narcissus flowers like to sit in cold water in a vase.

HYACINTHS *Hyacinthus*
Easy to grow and often filling the crisp spring air with an intoxicating scent, hyacinths give a bright, vivid display on the allotment. Their dense spikes of tubular flowers also provide an amazing natural air freshener for the house.

Growing
Make an attractive feature of them by planting them along pathways or near a seat where you can catch their heady scent when pausing for a cuppa from your flask. Hyacinths aren't too fussy about their conditions. They prefer well-drained, fertile soil in full sun but they will tolerate partial shade. Plant in autumn, 8–10cm (3¼–4in) deep.

There's little to do after that, really. Let the flowers and leaves die down to allow the energy into the bulbs. Bulbs can be left in the soil from year to year, but for a better display of flowers lift them after flowering when the foliage has died down and store them in the shed in dry compost.

Cutting
Cut flower spikes as they start to bloom and place them into water immediately. They should provide a good, scented display for about ten days.

LILY OF THE VALLEY
Convallaria majalis

The beauty of this plant is that the sweetly scented, bell-shaped flowers will thrive in the shady corners where all other crops struggle. They make a beautiful display in their own right, and your neighbours will thank you for providing a heavenly scent during those crisp fresh mornings in spring.

Growing

Lily of the valley prefers partial shade but will also grow in deep shade and full sun. Try them at the foot of a shed. They like moisture-retentive soil, but will grow in most conditions. Plant the bulbs from mid-autumn to early spring 2.5cm (1in) deep and 10cm (4in) apart.

After the leaves have died down in autumn, top-dress with manure or compost. Clumps can be divided in late summer, but they are hardy and there's no need to lift them. Keep the area well watered during dry periods, as they will particularly struggle in dry shade.

Cutting

Flower spikes should be picked as they come into bud and arranged in a vase, adding some of their lance-shaped leaves to make a pretty and beautifully scented arrangement which will last four or five days.

AT A GLANCE

Lily of the valley flowers are produced from rhizomes, which spread under the soil by means of small shoots known as pips. Variegated forms have attractive patterned foliage and tend to prefer more sunny conditions.

ALLOTMENT ADVICE:
what I wish I'd known

The plant is quite invasive and will quickly colonise an area, so you need to keep a check on it to prevent it taking over other parts of the allotment. To extend the growing season, plant some in the shade and some in the sun.

TRIED AND TESTED RHS VARIETIES

'Geant de Fortin', 'Hardwick Hall', *C. majalis* var. *rosea*, 'Variegata'

TULIPS *Tulipa*

A riot of colour on the allotment or in vases, tulips are a cheerful sign that winter is over.

Growing

Tulips like a well-draining, fertile soil in full sun. Plant in autumn, 10cm (4in) deep and 10m (4in) apart. Keep bulbs well watered in spring. Depending on where you are, you may have to use pots and store them in a frost-free place over winter. In warmer areas leave in the ground. Split every three to four years.

Cutting

Cut when the bud has coloured up but is still closed. Tulips have a relatively short cut-flower life, so ensure you have plenty to cut on the allotment.

AT A GLANCE

Despite the association with Holland, the tulip is from Turkey and the surrounding area. It is Turkey's national flower and the name tulip is from *tulband*, the Dutch word for turban. In the 16th century 'tulipomania' gripped Holland – bulbs were sold for the price of a house.

ALLOTMENT ADVICE:
what I wish I'd known

Lift the bulbs after the foliage has died down in midsummer. This frees up space on the allotment to sow a quick-growing crop such as lettuce or radishes.

TRIED AND TESTED RHS VARIETIES

'Aladdin', 'Ballerina' (AGM), 'Humming Bird', 'Maureen' (AGM), 'Queen of Night', 'Queen of Sheba', 'West Point' (AGM)

Summer flowers

COSMOS

Cosmos are popular cut-flower annuals for the allotment, due to their large, colourful flowers and their attractive, feathery foliage. They are easy to grow and come in a range of colours including pink, white, and red, with single, double, and quilled flowers.

Growing

These plants thrive in a sunny aspect with moist but well-drained soil. In mild areas they can be sown directly into the soil in late spring. For early flowering they need to be sown indoors on a bright windowsill at home in mid-spring, and planted out after the risk of frosts has passed.

Keep them well watered and the surrounding area weed free. Frequent deadheading of flowers that have gone over will extend the period. Dig up the plants after the flowers have finished and add them to the compost heap.

Cutting

Cut the flowers as soon as the buds open. Try to cut as much of their long stems as possible when cutting, as their delicate, feathery foliage sets off and balances the large, bright flowerheads perfectly. The flowers will last for about ten days in a vase.

AT A GLANCE

Cosmos are half-hardy annuals with attractive ferny foliage and large flowerheads. *Cosmos bipinnatus* is the most common annual species grown on allotments for cut flowers. *Cosmos sulphureus* generally have brighter flowers, but they are not easily found.

ALLOTMENT ADVICE:
what I wish I'd known

The flowers are quite large and it's a good idea to stake the stems with twiggy sticks early in the season to prevent them flopping over later.

TRIED AND TESTED RHS VARIETIES

Cosmos bipinnatus: 'Candy Stripe', 'Purity', 'Sea Shells', Sonata series
Cosmos sulphureus: 'Sunset'

GLADIOLI

If you like hot colours then this is the cut flower for you, with strap-like leaves and showy, bright flowers in shades of pink, red, and orange. Excuse the pun, but you will be 'glad' you tried these.

Growing

Gladioli prefer free-draining soil in a sheltered, sunny spot. Add grit if the soil is heavy. Check the type of gladioli you are buying: some, but not all, are hardy. Flowering times run from spring to late summer. Plant in spring 10-15cm (4-6in) deep and 15cm (6in) apart.

Feed with tomato fertiliser every 14 days as soon as they start flowering. Remove the flower stem after flowering leaving the foliage to grow into autumn. Lift the more tender gladioli in autumn. Dig the corms out of the ground and store them in a dry, frost-free, but cold place such as a shed. Bury them in dry compost for the winter before planting out again in spring. Hardier types are fine outdoors with a mulch.

Cutting

Cut stems as they start to flower and remove some of the lower foliage. Flowers last 10-14 days.

AT A GLANCE

Most gladioli are native to Southern Africa. Modern hybrids make growing easier, with larger and more abundant flowers. *Gladius* is Latin for sword, and describes their thin, narrow leaves.

ALLOTMENT ADVICE:
what I wish I'd known

Mulch around your plant in spring with gravel. Gladioli like the free-draining conditions created by gravel as it washes through the soil, and it keeps slugs and snails off the young shoots.

TRIED AND TESTED RHS VARIETIES

'Columbine', *G.* x *colvillii* 'The Bride' (AGM), *G. communis* subsp. *byzantinus* (AGM), 'Flowersong', 'Green Woodpecker', 'Prins Claus', 'Stromboli', 'White City'

LILIES *Lilium*

Add a touch of class to the allotment with exotic-looking lilies. They may not bloom the first year, but in subsequent years you will be rewarded with exquisite flowers and delicious scent. These plants might be trickier to grow than some, but they are addictive.

Growing

Generally lilies prefer to have the bulbs in light shade and the rest of the plant in the sun. Some of the older species are fussy about their soil conditions, but most of the hybrids are easy to please and thrive in a wide range of soil types, as long as they are fertile and well-drained. Bulbs should be planted as soon as they are bought in early spring; don't let them dry out. Plant 10-15cm (4-6in) deep, smaller ones closer to the surface.

Some of the large-flowering lilies will need staking. Remove red lily beetles by hand when you see them. Don't let the plants dry out, and use a liquid feed during the growing season. Deadhead to prolong the display.

Cutting

If cutting blooms, take them with two-thirds of the stem when the buds have just begun to open. Leaving one third will feed the bulb. Stand in tepid water.

LOVE IN A MIST *Nigella*

Love in a mist is a traditional cottage garden favourite, but is also ideal for the cut flower border on the allotment. It's easy to grow and provides a mass of flowers with feathery foliage and attractive seedheads.

Growing

These hardy annuals thrive in fertile soil conditions in full sun. Sow the seeds in shallow drills in a cultivated bed in early spring. Thin to the required spacing on the label – usually about 20cm (8in) – when the seedlings start to appear.

On exposed, windy allotments the tall stems may need support from twiggy pea sticks. Deadhead as the flowers fade to extend the flowering season, but allow a few to develop seedheads, as they also make an attractive feature. Nigella is an annual, so remove the plants after flowering and add them to the compost heap.

Cutting

Cut the flower stems frequently as their buds open. It you get them into water immediately, they should provide a beautiful display for about ten days. Later in the season, the seed heads are attractive for dry use, or the seeds can be collected, placed in an envelope and sown next year.

ROSES *Rosa*

The nation's favourite flower comes in almost every colour and a range of shapes and sizes. They make great cut flowers, attract pollinators, and many repeat flower all summer long. Perhaps best of all is their heady fragrance.

Growing

The key to successful rose-growing is deep, fertile soil. Dig the ground over and enrich it with well-rotted manure or garden compost. Most roses prefer full sun, but some will tolerate light shade. For cut flowers, choose compact varieties with large blooms and plant them in rows. Train climbers and ramblers over arches and pergolas, and plant species as wildlife hedges and screens. Deadhead flowers as they fade. Mulch around the plant in late winter and feed in spring with a balanced feed. Shorten branches in late autumn to reduce wind-rock; prune in late winter.

Cutting

Cut just above a leaf when buds are showing colour. Remove lower leaves and thorns and cut a 2cm (¾in) groove in the base of the stem. Plunge in tepid water with a dessert spoon of sugar, and leave overnight before arranging.

AT A GLANCE

Buy bare-root in late autumn or in pots all year round. Prune modern types hard each year, old-fashioned shrubs more lightly. Avoid planting in soil where roses or fruit trees have previously been grown.

ALLOTMENT ADVICE:
what I wish I'd known

If you want to create a wildlife haven then avoid fat double roses: bees find it hard to get through the petals to the nectar.

TRIED AND TESTED RHS VARIETIES

Bush: 'Charles de Mills' (AGM), 'Evelyn' (AGM), 'Gertrude Jekyll' (AGM), 'Golden Celebration' (AGM), 'Graham Thomas' (AGM), 'L.D. Braithwaite' (AGM)
Climbing: *Rosa filipes* 'Kiftsgate', 'Golden Showers' (AGM), 'Rambling Rector' (AGM)

SUNFLOWERS
Helianthus annuus

If you want a splash of colour on the plot try these. They are easy to grow, and children love competing to see who can grow the tallest. Wildlife love them too: they produce pollen and nectar for bees and seeds for birds. Look out for compact varieties with colours including chocolate brown and fiery red.

Growing

As the name suggests, sunflowers like warm, sunny positions. Avoid windy areas, as the taller varieties will get flattened. They like fertile, well-drained soil. Grow them in a cut-flower area to make life easier. Sow in pots in early to mid-spring and plant out when 10cm (4in) tall, or sow outdoors in mid-spring, 5cm (2in) deep and 45cm (18in) apart. Give a liquid feed weekly. Stake taller varieties and keep an eye out for slugs and snails when the plants are small.

Cutting

If growing cut flowers to take home, remove the blooms as they emerge. Pick in the morning but after dew has gone. Remove most of the leaves, keeping just a few below the flowerhead. Place stems in water in a vase. They should provide a display for 14 days.

AT A GLANCE

These hardy annuals originated in the Americas and first domesticated in Mexico. They flower from midsummer right through to early autumn. The record to beat for the tallest sunflower is over 8m (25ft). Leave seedheads on the plants or string them up outside a window to provide feed for birds.

ALLOTMENT ADVICE:
what I wish I'd known

For a succession of flowers for cutting, sow a handful of seeds each week during spring and early summer. It takes 60 days from sowing to cutting.

TRIED AND TESTED RHS VARIETIES

'Pastiche', 'Russian Giant', 'Tall Single', 'Teddy Bear', 'Tiffany', 'Velvet Queen'

SWEET PEAS *Lathyrus odoratus*

This classic provides an abundance of blooms throughout summer and fills the whole allotment with its beautiful fragrance. Modern varieties have longer and straighter stems.

Growing

Their climbing habit means they can be trained on bamboo wigwams, arches, or make fragrant tunnels on hazel rods. They can be used to form screens, or interplanted with runner beans. Flowers intended for competitions should be grown as cordons on single stems.

Sow indoors in autumn for a longer flowering period the following summer. Sow individually in pots or root trainers and plant out in early spring into fertile soil with added compost. Alternatively sow directly into the ground. Pinch out the growing tips when the first two leaves are produced. Tie them onto the support system and water in dry spells.

Cutting

Pick flowers frequently to take home, otherwise the plants will go to seed and quickly stop producing fresh blooms. After they have finished, cut them down and dig over the soil, and it's ready for another crop.

HELENIUMS

Fiery-hot reds and oranges mean these stately perennials deserve a spot in any cutting garden on the allotment. Not only do the intense shades of the daisy-like flowers provide a vibrant flash of colour during summer and into autumn but they also make excellent indoor floral displays. There is just one note of caution to sound: one common name for these plants is sneezeweed, and the pollen is a reason for that.

Growing

Heleniums should be grown in full sun in fertile but well-drained soil. Bear in mind that as perennials they will ideally be growing in the same place for a few years, so ensure that they won't be in the way of a crop rotation programme. Plant 50cm (20in) apart in autumn.

Mulch around the base of the plants in early spring and water the plant in dry weather. Deadheading extends the flowering period, and taller varieties will need staking. The foliage should be allowed to die back before removing it and adding it to the compost heap. Divide plants in early spring or autumn every couple of years.

Cutting

Cut the stems as they come into flower and place them into water immediately. They look good in vases with other prairie-type plants such as rudbeckias and echinacea.

Autumn and winter flowers

ASTERS

Star by name and star by nature, these daisy-shaped flowers are eye-catching, bright, and a beacon on the allotment when other colours fade in late summer and early autumn.

Growing

Asters need a good fertile soil and full sun. They can be grown in a late-

summer cutting bed or planted in the rest of the allotment to provide a late-season splash of colour. Dig in lots of well-rotted manure prior to planting in late autumn or early spring. Space large varieties about 40–60cm (16–24in) apart, smaller varieties closer.

Asters are one of the easier flowers to grow and require less maintenance than many. The taller types will need staking as they start to grow. They are prone to mildew, so keep well watered and mulch around the base of the plant to prevent the plants drying out. Deadhead the flowers to improve the appearance, and remove stems that have gone over.

Cutting

Their sturdy stems make them ideal for cut flowers in late summer; cooler evenings mean they are less likely to wilt before they get home. Cut the stem low and remove the lower leaves.

AT A GLANCE

The most popular type of asters are *Aster novi-belgii*, commonly called Michaelmas daisies. There are also annual asters which are sown for late-summer bedding.

ALLOTMENT ADVICE:
what I wish I'd known

Asters will need dividing frequently, about every couple of years. Do it in late winter, using a sharp spade to divide congested clumps. Replant in freshly cultivated soil.

TRIED AND TESTED
RHS VARIETIES

Aster amellus 'King George' (AGM)
Aster novae-angliae 'Harrington's Pink' (AGM)
Aster novi-belgii 'Crimson Brocade', 'Royal Velvet', 'Snowsprite', 'Winston S. Churchill'

HOLLIES *Ilex*

Hollies on the allotment provide a wonderful opportunity to make your own Christmas decorations or wreaths. They provide winter interest with their berries in colours including scarlet-red, orange, and yellow, and foliage that can be variegated with silver or gold, and prickly or smooth. For berries you will need both a female to bear the berries and a male to ensure pollination.

Growing

Hollies will be in the same patch of ground for many years so prepare the area well prior to planting by digging over the soil and adding plenty of organic matter. They can tolerate shade but like a fertile, well-drained soil.

Hollies can become large shrubs but they tolerate any amount of cutting back, and through regular pruning they can be kept compact, perfect for easy picking of sprigs for home decorations.

Trim plants in spring to maintain their shape and keep their vigour. They respond to hard pruning if they have become too big.

Cutting

Harvest sprigs of holly with berries on just before Christmas. Either place them into a display in a vase on the Christmas table or make them into a wreath. Hollies with variegated foliage and different coloured berries make more interesting displays.

AT A GLANCE

Hollies are evergreen shrubs that can become very large if not kept in check. They grow well in the shade but variegated forms require more sun.

ALLOTMENT ADVICE:
what I wish I'd known

If growing holly for berries, don't rely on the name of the variety to tell you if it's male or female: many are misleading.

TRIED AND TESTED
RHS VARIETIES

(f - female, m - male)
Ilex x altaclerensis 'Golden King' (f, AGM)
Ilex aquifolium 'Ferox' (m), 'Handsworth New Silver' (f, AGM), 'J.C. van Tol' (f, AGM), 'Pyramidalis' (f, AGM), 'Silver Queen' (m, AGM)
Ilex opaca

CHRYSANTHEMUMS

Florists and gardeners both love these for their shameless riot of colour in late summer and autumn. They will keep flowering up until a few weeks before Christmas. There is a huge range of sizes to choose from. Affectionately known as mums by the enthusiasts, chrysanthemums should be the number one choice for the cutting garden.

Growing

Grow them in free-draining fertile soil in full sun. Add well-rotted manure or garden compost if the soil is thin.

The large flowering types destined for the show bench will need a stout stake to support the plant as it grows. Small-flowered garden types, such as the Shasta daisy, require less maintenance. Deadhead as blooms fade and cut to ground level after flowering. Keep them watered during dry periods and mulch around the base of the plant each year.

They can be divided every two or three years. Avoid more tender indoor types.

Cutting

Cut stems for displays when the flowers open. Remove the lower leaves and place in water; leave them to stand for a day in water before using them in flower arrangements. The flowers should last for 14 days in a vase.

AT A GLANCE

There are many types including charm, pompon, and spray, flowering right through autumn. Annual types can be sown from seed.

ALLOTMENT ADVICE:
what I wish I'd known

Your plant will require disbudding if you want to enter your blooms in your local flower show. The aim is to produce one flower per stem by removing laterals and all buds on the stem except the chosen one. For general cut flowers, remove just some of the buds in early summer.

TRIED AND TESTED RHS VARIETIES

'Esther', 'George Griffiths' (AGM), 'Green Envy', 'Madeleine' (AGM), 'Pennine Oriel' (AGM), 'Sam Oldham', 'Wendy' (AGM)

DAHLIAS

These are show-stoppers, some bright, garish and in-your-face, others more subtle and refined. There is a dahlia to suit everybody's taste.

Growing

Plant out dahlia tubers 10cm (4in) deep once the soil has started to warm up in late spring. They need a sunny, sheltered bed with fertile, well-drained soil. The taller types and ones with large flowerheads will need individually staking with a cane. Dahlias make an attractive display when interplanted with other cut flowers, but fanatics will want to dedicate whole beds to them.

Keep weed free but don't hoe, due to the shallow rooting of the plant. Water in dry periods. Pinch out the growing tips three weeks after planting if a bushy plant is required, and give tomato feed every 14 days. Enthusiasts get larger flowers by removing some buds. Deadhead to keep the flowering display going, and cut back the foliage to near ground level after flowering.

Cutting

Cut flowers in the morning or evening and place them in warm water as soon as possible. Remove all foliage that will sit in water in the vase as it rots quickly.

AT A GLANCE

There are over 50,000 dahlias available, including bedding types, with a range of different types of flowers from anemone-flowered to pompon. They can range in height from 30cm (1ft) to 1.5m (5ft).

ALLOTMENT ADVICE:
what I wish I'd known

If you live in a cold area, the tubers will need to be dug up before the first frosts. Cut the foliage back to about 10cm (4in). Lift the tubers and hang them in the shed for a few days to dry out, then put them in trays and cover with dry compost.

TRIED AND TESTED RHS VARIETIES

'Bishop of Llandaff' (AGM), 'Chat Noir', 'Doris Day', 'Hillcrest Royal' (AGM), 'Moonfire' (AGM), 'Sam Hopkins'

Keeping livestock

Beekeeping

Beehives make beautiful rustic features on an allotment and are always a good talking point. Keeping bees on your allotment not only provides you with a supply of honey for your toast, it also increases your fruit and vegetable yields, as bees pollinate plants when flying from flower to flower.

Honeybees might be small but they are incredibly important for pollinating flowers when foraging for nectar and pollen. Without bees we would be without many of our food crops, and colour would be lost from the countryside as our wildflowers would disappear. Placing a beehive on your allotment will provide the area with up to 60,000 honeybees in summer. That's a lot of pollinators.

Where to keep them

Firstly, check with the council that they allow bees to be kept on the allotment. If they do, it's only polite to check with the people next to you and discuss any concerns they might have. Often an explanation about the decline in bee numbers and their importance in crop pollination, the prospect of increased yields, and the promise of jars of honey will bring round any doubters.

Although honeybees are naturally woodland creatures and tolerate some shade, they will be far more productive if the hive is placed in the sun. Try to place the beehive so that its entrance is not facing onto a path or a neighbour's allotment. If you have a plot on the boundary, you can face the entrance towards the hedge or fence. If you haven't, then erect a mesh screen – such as shade netting – about 2m (6½ft) high about a 1m (3ft) in front of the hive. This will lift the bees above head height when flying, ensuring that they don't collide with people in their flight path.

Types of beehives

There are a few different types of hives available, but the main two used in the

United Kingdom are the WBC and the National. The WBC is the traditional, pretty, tiered beehive that most people associate with beekeeping. They make a great rustic feature on the allotment, but they can be harder work when inspecting bees as they have an outer skin (called lifts) to remove before getting to the inner boxes. The boxier Nationals are the most popular type of beehive in the UK and are easy to stack and to access the frames.

A hive can contain up to 60,000 bees in the height of summer.

Most beehives are made of wood but there are a few new materials now available. Polystyrene hives are quickly becoming popular due to their cheapness, lightness and the extra warmth and insulation they give bees during winter. They can be painted, making them hard to distinguish from wooden hives. New plastic hives are

A smoker, a simple firebox and bellows, is used to generate smoke to subdue the bees.

also practical and easy to clean, but not so aesthetically pleasing as their shiny exterior can look incongruous among flowers, vegetables, and wooden sheds.

Whatever material they are made from or style they are made in, all hives have the same components.

A floor and stand These are sometimes combined into one. Modern beehives have a tray that catches varroa mites, which allows the beekeeper to count and monitor them.

A brood box Placed onto the floor, this is where the queen lays her eggs and rears her young. The entrance to the hive is usually here.

Super box Usually placed above the larger brood box, this is where the bees store their honey.

Queen excluder This is a piece of mesh with holes too small for the queen but big enough for worker bees. It prevents the queen moving up from the brood box to the super and laying eggs in the honey that you will be extracting.

Crown board This is a piece of wood placed over the super to insulate the colony and keep it dark.

A roof This ensures that the beehive is kept dry. They can be flat or pitched.

Frames These hold the honeycomb in sections suspended inside the brood box and supers.

Other equipment

Some beekeeping equipment is not too costly: a honey extractor is expensive, but many beekeeping associations loan them out to their members.

Smoker This is used to pacify the bees.

Hive tool This is essential for prising open the boxes.

Protective clothing Beginners should wear a bee suit with a veil, gloves, and boots. Old hands may be less cautious.

Harvesting

Expect about 13.5kg (30lb) of honey from one hive in an average year, and as much as 45kg (100lb) in a good year. Remove supers from the hive in late summer and take to a bee-free shed or kitchen. Remove the capping of the honeycomb with a knife and spin frames in a centrifugal honey extractor. The honey should be strained, allowed to settle, and then bottled into jars.

Hive tools are used to prise open the beehive's boxes, which the bees cement with propolis.

AT A GLANCE

British bees need you. Bees are now in trouble as 30 per cent of British honeybee colonies died during the year 2007-8. This is mainly due to varroa mite (*Varroa destructor*), a parasitic mite that sucks bee blood (haemolymph, to give it the technical name) from the larvae, pupae, and bees themselves. This not only debilitates a colony, but also transmits viruses that kill the bees. Other theories about their decline include insecticides, intensive farming, and climate change. Becoming a beekeeper can help keep bees alive, because beekeepers monitor and treat their colonies.

ALLOTMENT ADVICE:
what I wish I'd known

Green woodpeckers can quickly ruin a hive as they peck into the wood to get at the larvae and honey. To keep them out, wrap chicken wire around the beehive as soon as the honey has been extracted, and place mouse guards across the entrances to the beehives at the same time.

If woodpeckers are a real problem in your area, consider using WBC hives instead of Nationals: the double skin of this design is a deterrent to the woodpeckers.

WHO IS WHO?

The queen There is only one queen in a hive. She lays all the eggs – as many as 2,000 to 3,000 a day. She will live for a few years before being replaced by a younger queen.
Worker bees The majority of the bees in a hive are worker bees. They are the daughters of the queen and do everything from foraging for nectar and pollen and cleaning the hive, to defending the colony and feeding the young brood.
Drones The males don't do a lot except eat (you can add your own punchline to that). They occasionally mate with a queen from another colony, but die in the process.

Chickens, hens, and bantams

Chicken keeping is a fascinating hobby and with their friendly, inquisitive nature and love of human company, these birds make wonderful companions for the allotment. Put them on an area that needs weeding and they do the job for you. They will devour slugs and snails and convert them into chicken manure.

As if that isn't enough, they will lay an egg every day, rewarding you with delicious, healthy food full of essential amino acids, vitamins, and minerals.

How many chickens

Three chickens is about the right amount on an allotment where space is a premium. Two is also okay, but never keep a lone chicken, because they are naturally social birds and one will be unhappy. Anything more than three can become hard work: droppings increase, noise increases, and they require a bigger run. Far better to have less chickens with more space.

It is not necessary to have a cockerel if you are keeping chickens for egg production. The hens will still lay eggs without him, and a cockerel can be very noisy first thing in the morning, which will make you unpopular if houses are nearby (remember just how early first thing in the morning can be in summer).

Chicken house

There are many chicken houses available, ranging in size from small arks to large converted sheds. The main criteria are that it should provide a dry, water-tight shelter with a door that can be closed at night to keep out foxes. It must also contain a perch and a nest box.

Chickens prefer to sleep on a perch raised off the floor. They like to feel snug on the perch and will sit closely together when sleeping. Each bird requires a space of at least 15-20cm (6-8in) along the perch – bantams slightly less. Perches should be round, like dowelling, rather than squared timber with sharp right angles, as these hurt their feet.

The nest box and floor of the house should be filled with either straw or wood shavings. Avoid hay and sawdust, as the dust in these can cause respiratory problems. One nest box is needed for every four chickens.

The house should be cleaned out twice a month, and the dirty bedding added to the compost heap. Replace with clean straw and wood shavings.

Chicken run

Chickens need a secure outside run where they can stretch their legs, scratch around in the earth, and give themselves a dust bath.

The run should be as big as possible, because this is where your chickens will spend the majority of the day. Runs should be made fox-proof. This involves digging chicken wire down 30cm (9in) deep into the soil and turning the buried part outwards at the bottom, away from the run. The door on the chicken run should be closed at night and kept bolted. Foxes are very cunning and persistent, and will check a run each night for any openings.

Sussex hybrids are a popular allotment choice.

In addition to this, if you wish to move the chickens around the allotment, a moveable frame covered with chicken wire can be made to place over the chickens to restrain them and prevent them wandering onto other allotments. Obviously this can't be dug into the ground, so make sure your chickens are back in secure quarters when you leave.

Feeding

Chickens should be fed with good quality layer's pellets or layer's mash each morning. These provide all the nutrients and minerals that they need to live a long and healthy life. This should be placed in a feeder which can be kept inside the house or in the run.

Hybrid hens, such as warrens, are good layers, providing an egg each almost every day.

It can be supplemented with corn or wheat as a treat, which the chickens adore. Mix oyster shell and grit into their feed each day. This provides chickens with calcium needed to make good strong egg shells, and the grit also helps grind down the food.

They will also enjoy pecking at freshly pulled weeds, fresh grass clippings, allotment pests (just throw any slugs or snails you find into the run), and any surplus fruit and vegetables and their peelings. Bread and cooked pasta and rice can also be given to them. Avoid feeding them with meat and dairy products, particularly egg and eggshell. At the end of the day, clear away any food that hasn't been eaten as this will attract vermin. Chickens must have fresh water each day.

Harvesting

Check each day for eggs in the nest box. If they are left there for too long, the chickens may get broody and start to sit on them. Eggs can be stored for about three weeks at room temperature, except in hot weather when they can be placed in the fridge. To check if an egg is fresh, place it in a bowl of water. If it floats it's old, if it sinks it's still fresh. Very fresh egg whites won't make meringues, so leave them a few days before trying this.

Crop planner

Use this chart as a quick reference to what to do on your allotment, and when, then check with the main entry for each plant for the detail on sowing, planting out, and harvesting. Remember, the chart is not prescriptive: there will, of course, be variation depending on weather and geographic location.

Consider crop rotation in order to minimise pest and disease problems (*see* page 44) and make the most of the beneficial effects of leguminous plants like peas and beans on the fertility of the soil. Think about successional crops too. For example, once the early potatoes are lifted in midsummer, what might go in their place? And what can you grow early in the year in that area you've earmarked for summer sowings? There are all sorts of short-term crops that could fill the gap with flower or flavour.

CROPS	WEEKS	IN AND OUT	EARLY SPRING	MID-SPRING	LATE SPRING	EARLY SUMMER	MID-SUMMER	LATE SUMMER	EARLY AUTMUN	MID-AUTUMN	LATE AUTUMN	EARLY WINTER	MID-WINTER	LATE WINTER
Asparagus	1-2 yrs (crown)	OUT		H	H	H								P
Aubergines	18-20	CVR	S	T	T		H	H	H	H			S	S
		OUT				T			H	H				
Basil	6-8	CVR	S	S	S/T	T								
		OUT			S	S	S	H	H	H	H			
Bay			P	P	P/H	P/H	P/H	P/H	P/H	P/H	P/H	H	H	H
Beetroots	10-15	CVR	S	S	S	H	H	H						
		OUT		S	S	S	S/H	H	H	H				
Borage	4-8	OUT		S	S	S	S/H	H	H	H	H			
Broad beans	10	CVR	S	S	T	T							S	S
		OUT	S	S	H	H	H	H	H		S			
Broccoli and calabrese	42-45	OUT	H/S	H/S	H/S	S/T	T	T	H	H	H			
	12	OUT	S	S	S	H/S	H/S	H/S	H	H	H			
Brussels sprouts	28-36	OUT	S	S	S	T	T	H	H	H	H	H	H	H/S
Cabbage														
Spring	32-36	OUT		H	H		S	S	T	T	T			
Summer	20-36	OUT	S	S	S/T	T/H	H	H	H	H				
Winter	20-36	OUT	H	S	S	S/T	T			H	H	H	H	
Carrots	10-16	CVR	S		H	H				S			S	S
		OUT		S	S	S/H	S/H	H	H	H	H			
Cauliflowers	18-25/	CVR	T	T									S	S
	50	OUT	H	S/H	S/H	T	H	H	H	H	H	H	H	H
Celeriac	30-35	CVR	S	S/T	T			H	H	H	H			S

Key: **P** = plant   **H** = harvest   **T** = transplant   **D** = divide   **S** = sow   **CVR** = with cover or protection   **OUT** = outside

CROPS	WEEKS	IN AND OUT	EARLY SPRING	MID-SPRING	LATE SPRING	EARLY SUMMER	MID-SUMMER	LATE SUMMER	EARLY AUTUMN	MID-AUTUMN	LATE AUTUMN	EARLY WINTER	MID-WINTER	LATE WINTER
Celery	25-40	CVR	S	S										
		OUT			T	T		H	H	H	H			
Chard	12	OUT		S	S	S	S	H	H	H	H	H	H	H
Chicory														
Heading	8-12	OUT	S	S	S	S	S/H	H	H	H	H			
Forcing	25-26+	OUT			S	S	S				H	H	H	H
Chives	4-9		S/D	S/D	S/T	T	H	H	H	H	H/D			
Coriander	4-8		S	S	S/H	S/H	S/H	S/H	H	H	H			
Courgettes	10-12	CVR		S	S									
		OUT			T	S/T	T	H	H	H				
Cucumber	12-14	CVR	S	S/T	T	T	H	H	H	H				S
		OUT				S/T	T	H	H	H				
Dill		CVR	S	S	S/T									
		OUT			S	S/H	S/H	S/H	H	H	H			
Fennel		CVR	S	S	S/T									
		OUT			S	S/H	S/H	S/H	H	H	H			
French beans	9-14	CVR	S	S	T	T								
		OUT			S	S	S/H	H	H	H				
Garlic	22-32	OUT	P		H	H	H	H		P	P	P	P	P
Jersualem artichokes	40-50	OUT	P	P							H	H	H	H
Kale	30-36	OUT	S/H	S/H	S/H	S					H	H	H	H
Leeks	30-45	OUT	S/H	S			T			H	H	H	H	H
Lettuce	6-12	CVR	H	H					S	S	S	H	H	S/H
		OUT	S	S	S/H	S/H	S/H	S/H	H	H				
Marjoram		CVR	S/D	S/D	T									
		OUT				H	H	H	H/D	H	H			
Marrows, summer squashes	20-24	CVR		S	S	S								
		OUT			T	S/T			H	H	H			
Melons	13-16	CVR	S	S		T		H	H	H				
		OUT				T			H	H				
Mint		OUT		D	D	H	H	H	H	D/H	D/H			

CROPS	WEEKS	IN AND OUT	EARLY SPRING	MID-SPRING	LATE SPRING	EARLY SUMMER	MID-SUMMER	LATE SUMMER	EARLY AUTUMN	MID-AUTUMN	LATE AUTUMN	EARLY WINTER	MID-WINTER	LATE WINTER
Onions	20-35	CVR	S/P	S/P				S/H	P/H					S
		OUT												
Salad leaves, Oriental veg		CVR	S/H	H	H	H				S	S	S/H	H	S/H
		OUT		S	S	S/H	S/H	S/H	H	H	H	H		
Parsley		CVR	S	S/T	S/T							H	H	H/S
		OUT			S	S	S/H	S/H	H	H	H			
Parsnips	32-35	OUT	S/H	S	S					H	H	H	H	H
Peas	11-16	OUT	S	S	S	S/H	H	H	H					
Peppers, Chilli peppers	18-20 (up to 24 for hot chillies)	CVR	S	S/T	T			H	H	H	H			S
		OUT			T	T			H	H	H			
Potatoes Earlies	13+	OUT	P	P		H	H	H						
Maincrop	22	OUT		P	P		H	H	H	H				
Pumpkins, winter squashes	20-24	CVR		S	S	S								
		OUT			T	S/T			H	H	H			
Radishes Summer	3-6		S	S/H	S/H	S/H	S/H	S/H	H					
Winter	up to 12					S	S	S	H	H	H			
Rhubarb			P						P	P	P/D	P/D	P/D	P/D
Forced			H	H										H
Unforced					H	H	H							
Rocket	4-8	CVR	S	H	H			S	S	H	H	H		S
Rosemary		OUT	H	H/C	H/C	H	H	H/C	H/C	H	H	H	H	H
Runner beans	14	CVR		S										
		OUT			S/T	S/T	H	H	H	H				
Sage		CVR	S	S										
		OUT			S/T/C	S/H/C	H	H	H/C	H	H	H	H	H
Shallots	18	OUT	S/P	S	S			H	H					P
Spinach	8-12	OUT	S/H	S/H	S/H	H	H	S/H	S/H	H	H	H	H	H
Swedes	21-25	OUT	S	S	S	S		H	H	H	H	H		

Key: **P** = plant **H** = harvest **T** = transplant **D** = divide **S** = sow **CVR** = with cover or protection **OUT** = outside

CROPS	WEEKS	IN AND OUT	EARLY SPRING	MID-SPRING	LATE SPRING	EARLY SUMMER	MID-SUMMER	LATE SUMMER	EARLY AUTUMN	MID-AUTUMN	LATE AUTUMN	EARLY WINTER	MID-WINTER	LATE WINTER
Sweetcorn	14-18	CVR	S	S	S	S								
		OUT			S/T	S/T	H	H	H	H				
Tarragon		OUT			D	D/H	C/H	H	H	H				
Thyme		OUT			S/D	S/D	C/H	H	H	H				
Tomatoes	16-20	CVR	S	S	T	T	H	H	H	H	H		S	S
Turnips	6-12	CVR												S
		OUT	S	S	S/H	S/H	S/H	S/H	S/H	H	H			

FRUIT

Most fruits are grown as medium- or long term perennials, and can be planted in containers almost the whole year round. There are peak times, though, usually autumn and spring, with most fruit trees dug up to order and sold bare-root in autumn.

You can plant strawberries at different times of year, either as potted plants or as cold-stored runners: put them in place by September to fruit the following year, or in early spring to fruit in the new season, or plant cold-stored runners anytime in the growing season to get a crop after about 60 days. There are different cultivars of some soft fruits that will extend the cropping period, including raspberries and perpetual strawberries.

Have fun, experiment, and use this chart as a basic guide as to when to expect the main harvests.

FRUIT CROPS	EARLY SPRING	MID-SPRING	LATE SPRING	EARLY SUMMER	MID-SUMMER	LATE SUMMER	EARLY AUTUMN	MID-AUTUMN	LATE AUTUMN	EARLY WINTER	MID-WINTER	LATE WINTER
Apples					H	H	H	H	H			
Blackberries					H	H	H					
Blueberries					H	H	H					
Cherries				H	H	H						
Currants					H	H						
Figs				H	H	H						
Gooseberries				H	H	H						
Grapes						H	H	H				
Kiwi							H	H				
Peaches				H	H	H						
Pears						H	H	H	H			
Plums					H	H	H					
Raspberries				H	H	H	H	H	H			
Strawberries			H	H	H	H	H	H				

Weeds

Fat hen

Chickweed

Annual nettle

Weeds thrive in the fertile soils of a well-run allotment. If you spy something unfamiliar, be sure to find out if it's an annual or perennial weed so you deal with it in the most appropriate manner. Your fellow allotment-holders may be able to help identify it. Do not add perennial weeds or weed seedheads to the compost heap, as they are likely to survive and you'll be spreading them around again! (*See also* pages 28–9.)

Control strategies

Annual weeds: Annual weeds complete their life cycle within one year. They produce thousands of tiny seeds that may lie in the soil for years waiting to germinate. Different weeds grow in response to different conditions, but generally germination is sparked by changes in light and temperature, the same growing conditions that your crops will appreciate.

A good proportion of annual weeds can be flushed out in spring before you plant any crops, in a technique known as a 'stale seedbed'. Prepare the soil so that weed seeds germinate in response to the soil disturbance. Once the flush of seedlings is through, hoe them off or apply a contact weedkiller.

Keep empty patches mulched. Most annual weed seeds are tiny and aren't able to push through a thick layer of organic mulch, and it will add to the fertility and structure of the soil too. Aim for at least 5cm (2in) of well-rotted organic matter. Any material that excludes light will suppress weed growth, so an opaque 'sheet mulch' such as black plastic weed-control fabric is a quick and easy option. You can make holes in it and plant through it to control weeds while the crop is growing.

Any weeds that continue to germinate should be relatively easy to control by pulling by hand or hoeing. Hoe weeds off in dry or windy weather, running the flat edge back and forth through the soil surface to lift weeds and cut off their roots.

Finally, there is an old saying that every allotment holder should bear in mind with good reason: 'One year's seeding gives seven years weeding'. The enormous quantity of seed that can be produced by one plant is a great incentive to remove every annual weed before it sets seed.

Perennial weeds: Perennial weeds are those that live from year to year, with the majority able to grow from very small sections of underground stem (rhizome) which can be difficult to eradicate. There are a number of ways to deal with these plants, so don't be disheartened.

Repeatedly cutting down the foliage wins some temporary control, and although the plant will regenerate, it will gradually weaken. This is a long-term solution, requiring patience.

These weeds persist by their underground structures, so you can remove the problem by digging them out. In a weed such as ground elder, the rhizomes are relatively close to the surface, and thorough removal can give you satisfying results. The roots of other weeds, such as bindweed, horsetail, and Japanese knotweed, penetrate very deeply, and digging will provide only a temporary respite.

Smothering weeds is very effective. Weed-suppressing material blocks out light and prevents weeds from reaching the light, which weakens them as they are unable to replenish their reserves. It takes time to eradicate them completely.

When individual perennial weeds appear, such as dandelion or dock, loosen them off with a fork and extract them with the thick tap root intact – don't compost this. Preventing them from setting seed makes the task less of a chore each year.

A systemic weedkiller containing glyphosate is a good way to combat perennial weeds. It is applied to the leaves in full growth, and is moved throughout the plant and into the roots. It is non-selective, so take care to avoid inadvertently applying the weedkiller to plants you want to keep, and do not spray if there is any possibility of it drifting to your neighbour's plot. Always follow the manufacturer's instructions.

Annuals

There are many weeds that you may encounter on an allotment. These are some of the main offenders:

Annual meadow grass *(Poa annua):* Common throughout the United Kingdom, this is a low-growing, tufted grass that is in flower for most of the year and grows rapidly from seed.

Shepherd's purse

Kew weed

Bindweed

Hairy bittercress *(Cardamine hirsuta)***:** Often seen in containerised plants from nurseries, this is a member of the brassica (cabbage) family and produces small white flowers on wiry stems throughout most months of the year. The seed pods often burst explosively, sending the seeds far and wide. They germinate in autumn and the seedlings are often green throughout winter.

Black nightshade *(Solanum nigrum)***:** A native plant common to most of England but less so as you go further north and west. It prefers nitrogen-rich soil and is a quick grower but is susceptible to frost. It produces black berries.

Fat hen *(Chenopodium album)***:** This is a native summer annual with slightly succulent leaves that occurs throughout Britain. It grows best on fertile soils, and was eaten as a vegetable until it was replaced in the diet by spinach and cabbage. It is rich in vitamin C, and is closely related to quinoa.

Groundsel *(Senecio vulgaris)***:** A member of the daisy family with distinctive yellow flowerheads, prolific on good land. It may be an alternate host for cucumber mosaic virus.

Chickweed *(Stellaria media)***:** One of the most common weeds of cultivated land in the United Kingdom. It prefers light, nitrogen-rich soil, is sensitive to drought and grows best in cool, humid conditions. It is a host of several damaging virus diseases of crop plants and may be an alternate host for cucumber mosaic virus.

Common field speedwell *(Veronica persica)***:** Distinctive by its pretty blue flowers, it is one of the most common annual weeds. It has weak stems, a prostrate habit and small, coarsely serrated leaves.

Annual nettle *(Urtica urens)***:** Found particularly on light soils with a high organic matter content, its presence is considered to be an indication of the need for lime.

Shepherd's purse *(Capsella bursa-pastoris)***:** This gets its common name from its triangular, purse-like pods. It is a member of the brassica (cabbage) family and can produce several generations a year.

Kew weed/gallant soldier *(Galinsoga parviflora)***:** This weed loves hot weather; it is mostly found in the south-east and is common on allotments with light soil in the Thames valley. It re-roots quickly if hoed, breaks off easily at ground level if pulled, and sets seeds even in adverse conditions.

Perennial

The selection of perennials that you may encounter is smaller, but they are none the less troublesome for that.

Couch grass *(Elymus repens)***:** A common and invasive weed that rapidly spreads by wiry rhizomes (underground stems). From their tips, new shoots emerge in spring and autumn that quickly produce tufts of leaves and more rhizomes, quickly colonising an area.

Bindweed *(Convolvulus arvensis)* and **bellbind** *(Calystegia sepium)***:** Bindweed refers to two similar trumpet-flowered weeds, both of which twine around other plant stems, smothering them in the process. They spread rapidly through the soil with shallow, fleshy but brittle underground stems from which they can regenerate from small sections. Hedge bindweed or bellbind (*Calystegia sepium*) has pure white trumpet flowers, and the smaller field bindweed (*Convolvulus arvensis*) has white or pink flowers.

Ground elder *(Aegopodium podagraria)***:** A widespread, invasive garden weed. Its whitish, fleshy underground rhizome creeps around and chokes other plants.

Creeping thistle *(Cirsium arvense)***:** An aggressive weed, especially on deep, well-aerated soils. It can tolerate very low temperatures and is less successful in hot, dry conditions.

Field horsetail *(Equisetum arvense)***:** It has creeping rhizomes which may reach 2m (6½ft) below the surface. There are two types of shoots: in late spring asparagus-like light brown, fertile stems 20–50cm (8–20in) appear, ending in cone-like spore-producing structures. Later, the more familiar thin, green, branched stems appear and these sterile shoots develop into 60cm (24in) fir-tree-like plants.

Pests

Blackfly

Currant blister aphid

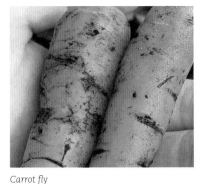

Carrot fly

Healthy plants are better able to recover from insect damage. Keep your crops well fed and watered and use barrier methods to minimise attacks from pests.

Mammals

Mice are renowned for eating pea, bean, and sweetcorn seed; rats like sweetcorn cobs. Rabbits will nibble away on many plants including brassicas, beetroot and tree bark. Squirrels enjoy strawberries, sunflowers, apples, and pears. Moles undermine plants with their tunnels and devour earthworms, and badgers tend to damage plants with their large mass.

Raise beans and peas in pots or modules for transplanting into place. Bar entry to large mammals with fencing: anything below about 50cm (20in) above ground level is at risk from rabbits. They are likely to try anything once, and new plants will arouse interest. Install tree guards around susceptible plants or surround the entire plot, not forgetting the gate, with rabbit-proof fencing such as metal chicken wire. A height of 1.2–1.4m (4–4½ft) is recommended, with 30cm (12in) below ground level, angled out, to prevent them burrowing under.

Find a professional vermin catcher to deal with the problem and advise on how to make the allotment site less hospitable. Animal repellent substances and scaring devices may give short-term protection.

Birds

Wood pigeons adore brassicas, peas, and beans, as do pheasants. Protect your produce with purpose-made vibrating tape or cover the crop with suitable netting, making sure that the birds can't peck through it, or invest in fruit cages. Bird decoys have limited use, but jingly, sparkly items moving in the wind can help too, or try a scarecrow.

Insects and invertebrates

Aphids, including greenfly and blackfly: Small insects, usually green, grey or black, attack many fruit and vegetable crops. They suck sap from the plants and some transmit viruses. Some may distort foliage on crops such as plum or currants (like currant blister aphid). Rub off with your fingers, using soapy water, or spray with a pesticide. Encourage aphid-eating insects such as ladybirds, hoverflies, and lacewings. Winter washes can help control overwintering eggs on fruit trees and bushes.

Asparagus beetle: Pretty black, red, and yellow beetles and their larvae devour precious asparagus spears. Pick off by hand or spray with pyrethrum insecticide. Burn old stems to kill off overwintering beetles.

Carrot fly: Carrots, parsnips, parsley, and celery are at risk when creamy white maggots tunnel into the roots of the crops. Control with fleece or fine netting over the crop, or solid barriers at least 50cm (20in) high around the crop. Some carrot cultivars have a degree of resistance. Carefully chosen sowing dates may help to miss the three generations per year. The fly is attracted by smell when thinning crops, so sow thinly.

Caterpillars: Most caterpillars, such as the cabbage white butterfly larvae, eat leaves, though some attack roots, stems, or fruit. Check leaves, especially the undersides, for eggs and caterpillars and remove by hand. Cover crops with a fine insect mesh to prevent the adults from laying eggs. Spray with an appropriate insecticide.

Cabbage root fly: White maggots eat the roots of brassicas and the stems start to rot. Use root collars, either purpose-made or home-made discs 10cm (4in) diameter of cardboard or carpet, to encircle the neck of the plant and stop the fly from laying its eggs.

Codling moth: Maggoty apples and pears are caused when caterpillars tunnel through from the eye of the fruit into the core and sometimes out near the stalk end. Pheromone traps lure and capture males, which stops the females' eggs being fertilised.

Cutworms: Young brassicas, lettuce or leek plants have roots severed below the soil surface. These creamy- or greenish-brown caterpillars may also eat cavities in root vegetable

Cabbage root fly

Gooseberry saw fly

Slugs

crops, and feed above ground at night. Control is by weed control and searching or sieving the soil near affected plants, working along a row.

Eelworm: Microscopic worm-like parasites carry viruses and diseases and feed in or on the roots of their numerous hosts. Control by good garden hygiene and rotation, as the eggs and dormant larvae can remain in the soil for years, and they and their associated viruses are easily spread on plant debris, or on soil on equipment.

Gooseberry sawfly: Gooseberries and red- and whitecurrants suffer severe defoliation caused by pale green and black-spotted caterpillar-like larvae. Regularly check the plants from mid-spring onwards and pick off the larvae by hand or use a suitable insecticide.

Leek moth: Leaf-mining caterpillars about 1cm (½in) long bore into leeks, onions, and shallots, creating white or brown patches and making them prone to secondary infections. Cover with fleece to prevent the moths from laying.

Onion fly: In early or late summer, maggots up to 8mm (³⁄₈in) eat the roots of onions, shallots, leeks, and garlic, causing young plants to collapse. In late summer they tend to burrow into bulbs, causing secondary infections. Raise onions from sets instead of seed, and keep the adults from laying eggs by using horticultural fleece. Lift and destroy any infected plants before the maggots pupate in the soil.

Pea moth: This moth lays eggs in pea flowers, and the caterpillar hatches inside the pod and eats the peas. Control by sowing in either early or late summer to miss the heaviest infestations, or spray with an appropriate insecticide just after the flowers form.

Raspberry beetle: Ripe fruit show dry patches at the stalk end and creamy-white grubs feed at the base and into the core of the berry of any cane fruit. Control with pyrethrum.

Red spider mite: The two-spotted mites feed on leaves, which lose their colour and develop a silvery sheen. Very fine webbing and a pale mottled effect may be visible. The tiny mites and their eggs reside on the underside of the leaves.

Sometimes the leaves will fall prematurely leaving only the youngest leaves at the tip. The two different species affect tree fruits and glasshouse crops, although both will attack other outdoor crops in hot, dry summers. Control under glass by damping down the floor to keep humidity levels high, or use a predatory mite.

Slugs and snails: Not many crops escape the attention of slugs and snails, especially in warm, wet weather and after dark. They feed at night, mainly on young, tender growth, although some live underground and eat tubers like potatoes. Control by keeping a tidy plot with nowhere for them to shelter by day, by hunting at night with a torch, or enticing them with beer traps or grapefruit skins and disposing of them in the morning. Encourage their predators – toads and frogs, slow-worms, hedgehogs, ground beetles, and thrushes for snails – or use specialist parasitic nematode worms and follow the instructions when the soil is warm enough. Slug pellets, if used as directed, can help and the iron phosphate-based pellets are less likely to cause harm to wildlife than metaldehyde-based ones. Ultimately, slugs and snails can't be eradicated, so protect sturdy transplants with plastic cloches rather than sowing direct, defend susceptible plants with slug-repellent materials and barriers, or try cultivars with some resistance, for example the potatoes 'Charlotte' and 'Estima'.

Vine weevil: Container-grown crops and strawberries are particularly vulnerable to damage caused by the root-eating grub of the vine weevil. The adults eat irregular notches from leaf margins, though this damage is mainly cosmetic. Collect by torchlight, or use pathogenic nematodes.

Whitefly: Tiny sap-sucking white flies on brassicas excrete honey dew which attracts sooty moulds. Tolerate light infestations, but spray heavy ones with an appropriate insecticide. Glasshouse crops such as peppers, tomatoes, and cucumbers may also be attacked by a similar but different species; this problem can be controlled by a parasitic wasp, *Encarsia formosa*.

Diseases

Potato blight

Clubroot

Onion downy mildew

Plants are most susceptible to fungi, bacteria, and viruses when under stress, so the best defence is to keep crops well watered, well fed and well spaced to allow good air circulation, and weed free. No fungicides that will cure fungal problems are available for amateur use on edible crops, but there are some that can be used to prevent them. Here are the most common disorders you may encounter on an allotment:

Blight (potato and tomato): When black or brown patches appear on the tips and margins of potato and tomato leaves, you've got blight. The patches get bigger, the leaflets curl and wither, and it may spread to the stems and fruits or down into potato tubers. Blighted tubers develop dark patches on the skin with firm, reddish-brown rots below, which often succumb to secondary infections that cause them to rot. It is the fungus *Phytophthora infestans* that is responsible for this, spread by wind and rain and preferring warmth and high humidity. Control by applying Bordeaux mixture or copper oxychloride before plants become infected and hope for hot, dry weather. Earthing up can help protect tubers, as can prompt removal of infected foliage, which should be destroyed before lifting the tubers. Good hygiene is also essential, ensuring all diseased tubers are removed. Choose cultivars that show some resistance. First and second earlies are less likely to fall prey to blight than later-maturing maincrops.

Blossom end rot: Tomatoes develop a leathery brown patch at the blossom end. This is a disorder rather than a disease, caused by erratic watering which inhibits calcium uptake by the plant. Pick off affected fruits and water more regularly.

Botrytis (grey mould): Fuzzy grey fungal growth is easily identified on almost any part of a plant above ground. It will usually attack as a secondary infection, gaining entry via an open wound. Control with good hygiene, clearing all infected material quickly.

Canker: Many stone fruits suffer from bacterial canker, seen as flat and sunken bark, from which amber-coloured sap may ooze. Buds and leaves may fail to open, or wither and die. Fungal canker causes bark on apples, pears, and mulberries to become sunken, discoloured and cracked. As the canker gets bigger it may encircle the branch and cause die back. Fruits rot before they ripen. The canker may have white pustules in summer or red fruiting bodies in winter. Control both cankers by pruning out affected areas where possible. On trunks or large branches cut away and dispose of all infected bark. Improve cultural conditions and avoid susceptible cultivars. Some sprays are available. Be aware that most infections enter through wounds.

Chocolate spot: Broad beans may develop chocolate-brown spots on their upper leaf surfaces and brown streaks on pods, stems, and even flowers. Chocolate spot will reduce yields or even kill the plants. Control by giving increased air flow with wider spacings than usual, and be thorough with weeding to reduce the humidity around the plants that this fungus enjoys.

Clubroot: Brassicas may develop swollen and distorted roots and pale leaves as a result of clubroot, reducing yields or killing the plants completely. Control with good garden hygiene as this disease is caused by a soil-borne slime mould. It is most prolific in acid or damp soil conditions, so improve drainage and lime the soil to increase the pH (*see* page 27). Some weeds are a secondary host. Try cultivars known to have some resistance.

Downy mildew: Fuzzy pale grey or purplish fungal growth on undersides and discoloured, sometimes yellow, patches on upper leaf surfaces indicate downy mildew. Brassicas, lettuce, grapes, spinach, and onions are among the most commonly affected crops. This widespread fungal infection is most common on young plants and thrives in damp conditions. Control by improving air circulation including good weed control, and remove infected leaves immediately.

Halo blight: Dwarf French and runner beans may show small angular spots on their leaves which darken and develop a

Onion white rot

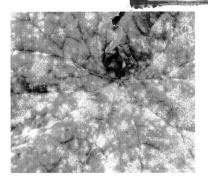

Cucumber powdery mildew

Amercian goosegog mildew

yellow 'halo'. Eventually the leaf will die and yields will fall. Control by avoiding water splash on the plants. Remove and burn infected material and do not store the seed. Try cultivars with some resistance.

Honey fungus: Tree and fruit bushes, globe artichokes, strawberries, rhubarb, and others are susceptible to honey fungus. The plants may wither and die or fail to leaf up. Death can be quick or drawn out depending on the strain. Roots develop a white fungal sheet with a mushroomy smell, or this may be visible under the bark of woody plants. Black bootlace 'rhizomorphs' may be found in the soil. In late summer or autumn clumps of honey-coloured toadstools may appear. Control by keeping the plants healthy and better able to withstand attack. Remove dead woody plants and as much of their root system as possible.

Leek rust: Leeks develop bright orange pustules 1–2mm (1/16in) long on their outer leaves, which later turn yellow and die back. Control by destroying affected leaves, practicing crop rotation to avoid growing other alliums in the same soil, giving wider spacing, and weeding well.

Mosaic virus: Stunted and deformed leaves that show a distinct yellow mosaic pattern indicate the presence of this virus on a wide range of hosts including cucumbers and courgettes. Flowering is reduced and any fruits that are produced are pitted and small, often a darker colour than normal with bright yellow patches. Control by destroying infected plants to minimise the spread of this virus by sap sucking insects, usually aphids, or your own hands. Be vigilant with weeds that can be an alternate host, such as chickweed. Try cultivars that show some resistance.

Onion white rot: Foliage of members of the onion family turns yellow and wilts, and the base of the bulb and roots develop fluffy white growth. In time they produce black fruiting bodies that can fall into the soil and lie dormant for several years. Control by destroying affected plants at once, and avoid planting other onions in the same spot for at least eight years. Try cultivars with some resistance.

Powdery mildews: If you see a dusty, whitish powder coating leaves, shoot tips, and flowers, your crops may be suffering from the fungal disease powdery mildew. Many edible plants are affected including apple, blackcurrant, gooseberry, grapes, brassicas, courgettes, marrows, cucumbers, and peas. It overwinters on dead plants, or in the buds and branches of perennials. Stagnant air, high humidity, and stress from drought all make plants more likely to succumb, so ensure good ventilation, water regularly, and mulch well. Feed plants with a general rather than high-nitrogen fertiliser. Prune out and destroy infected leaves or branches promptly, and prune to improve air circulation. Try cultivars that offer some resistance. Green or yellow sulphur may help.

Wormeries

Many of us compost garden and allotment waste to return organic matter and nutrients to the soil, but we can also recycle kitchen waste to produce liquid feed and rich compost by using a wormery. A wormery is a purpose-built container that, unlike a traditional compost heap, doesn't go through a 'hot' stage, but breaks down waste solely by worm and micro-organism action. These worms are native manure or tiger worms and red worms such as *Eisenia fetida* and *Dendrobaena veneta,* as opposed to earthworms. Your wormery should be started with around 1,000 of these composting worms (available from specialist suppliers). They are temperature sensitive, so need to be moved to a frost-free location for winter.

You can add almost any organic waste to your wormery: raw and cooked vegetables, fruit, teabags, eggshells, coffee grounds, and small amounts of cardboard. Things to avoid include meat, fish, and dairy products, woody material, citrus fruits, pineapple, onions, and leeks. Unlike conventional heaps, only add small amounts at a time and wait until the worms are at the top before adding more.

Once established, nutrient-rich, odour-free compost and liquid feed will be produced in a matter of months. Drain and dilute this liquid with ten parts water to feed garden plants, and use the compost as a general soil conditioner, rich in nutrients, and especially useful for greedy feeders like courgettes or fruit trees.

Useful contacts

Allotment organisations

Allotment sites are usually run by a committee made up of volunteers from the site. They deal with the issues involved in running the allotments, including setting and collecting rent, maintaining the site fencing, path upkeep, and ensuring the plots are in good order, and they deal with the landlord – which is often, but not always, the local authority. If you're lucky they may also run a shop where members of the allotment society can buy seeds and sundries at competitive rates, and they may arrange pest control, delivery of manure, social events, shows, and so on. They will probably be affiliated to an organisation like the Royal Horticultural Society through which they'll also buy public liability insurance. All allotment committees need support, and welcome any help.

The National Society of Allotment and Leisure Gardeners (NSALG)
O'Dell House, Hunters Road, Corby, Northamptonshire, NN17 5JE
Tel: 01536 266576
www.nsalg.org.uk
Offers advice and help to amateur gardeners.

Scottish Allotments and Gardens Society
www.sags.org.uk
For allotment sites and plot-holders throughout Scotland, affiliated to NSALG.

Allotments Regeneration Initiative
The GreenHouse, Hereford Street, Bedminster, Bristol, BS3 4NA
Tel: 01179 631551
www.farmgarden.org.uk/ari/
A collaborative project involving a number of organisations with the aim of increasing the uptake of allotments.

National Allotment Gardens Trust
NAGTrust, PO Box 1448, Marston, Oxford, OX3 3AY
Tel: 01752 363379
www.nagtrust.org
A charitable organisation that aims to promote allotment gardening to improve education and social welfare of the public.

Insuring your allotment

Public liability insurance is one of the things the allotment association will have to fund out of rent revenue in order to keep the site running, usually via affiliation with the NSALG

or RHS. The insurance may impose conditions that cover things such as bonfires, which is why it is vital to check what the rules are that apply to your site. Sometimes the individual plot-holder needs to take out an insurance policy in their own name, for example if they keep bees or livestock on site, but the value of sheds and their contents should normally not be too excessive, and you may decide it is simpler to underwrite it yourself.

Laws and tenancy agreements

If a local authority deems there is a demand, it has a statutory duty to provide a sufficient quantity of plots to lease to its residents. If residents think there is an unmet demand, any six who are registered on the electoral roll are able to come together and present their case to the local authority which must then consider the case.

When you rent a plot you are given a tenancy agreement to sign. This is a legally binding document that sets out your rights and responsibilities as a plot holder, and is usually for a year, renewable until the tenant or landlord gives notice. The rules and content of these agreements will vary from site to site, but by law it needs to cover:

- rent, including the amount, collection, arrears, water charges
- what constitutes a nuisance
- use of barbed wire
- notice to quit
- compensation
- conditions of lease
- prohibition of trade or business
- prohibition of sub-letting
- erection of structures
- livestock/bee-keeping

There are a number of other things that might be covered on a more local level including the use of radios, size, shape, and colour of sheds, use of hosepipes, restrictions on planting trees, restrictions on bonfires, waste disposal, ponds, and sales.

Selling allotment produce

There is often confusion over whether produce grown on an allotment can be sold. The Allotments Acts, 1908-1950 (section 22, subsection 1) clearly state that you are not allowed to use your plot to support a business; the allotment is there for the cultivation of produce to support the allotment-holder and his or her family.

However, genuine surplus may be sold or given away. There is, after all, a limit to how many courgettes any family can eat in a week. The Acts do not distinguish between an individual selling for private profit and an association selling to raise funds. In practice, as many sites already have a shop where the profits go to the association, they are not regarded as a form of 'business'. For more information, see (with or without 'www.'): organiclea.org.uk/sellingallotmentproduce.pdf

Allotments on the internet

These days the internet is a place for many people to find out about local allotments. First port of call is to check your local authority website (check www.direct.gov.uk to confirm your local authority), where allotments are commonly under 'Leisure and Culture' or 'Parks and Gardens', or similar. Here you should find what sites exist in your area and contact details for someone at the council responsible for helping residents apply for a plot. There is usually a site representative at each location too, and it is worthwhile trying to meet them in person at the allotment. Using Google Earth (www.google.co.uk/earth) you can type in your own postcode and see what comes up locally to you – allotment plots are often easy to spot by their regular layout, and especially common near railway lines.

Another way is to join a social networking site such as Facebook, where there are plenty of groups with people who can give help and advice on how to find a plot. A few minutes on a search engine should reveal many different websites full of advice on how to start. Some sites are privately administered, so word of mouth and exploring them online, or via the local library, are good ways to discover more.

Other useful organisations

British Beekeepers' Association
The National Bee Centre, National Agricultural Centre, Stoneleigh Park, Warwickshire, CV8 2LG
Tel: 02476 696679
www.britishbee.org.uk

Garden Organic
Ryton, Coventry, Warwickshire, CV8 3LG
Tel: 02476 303517
www.gardenorganic.co.uk
Formerly HDRA, the leading organic gardening charity with a wealth of knowledge.

Happy Chicks
Thornton House Farm, 227 Pilling Lane,
Preesall, Poulton Le Fylde, Lancashire,
FY6 0HH
Tel: 01253 813178
www.happychicks.co.uk
Everything you need to know for keeping
chickens.

National Vegetable Society
www.nvsuk.org.uk
Concentrating on growing show-standard
vegetables.

The Royal Horticultural Society
80 Vincent Square, London, SW1P 2PE
Tel: 08452 605000
www.rhs.org.uk
Advice on all aspects of gardening, including
excellent resources online.

Thrive
The Geoffrey Udall Centre, Beech Hill,
Reading, RG7 2AT
Tel: 01189 885688
www.thrive.org.uk
A charity that aims to improve people's lives
through gardening.

Seeds and plants

Delfland Nurseries Limited
Benwick Road, Doddington, March,
Cambridgeshire, PE15 0TU
Tel: 01354 740553
www.organicplants.co.uk
Soil Association approved

Kings Seeds
Monks Farm, Kelvedon, Colchester, Essex,
CO5 9PG
Tel: 01376 570000
www.kingsseeds.com

Moles Seeds (UK) Ltd
Turkey Cock Lane, Stanway, Colchester, Essex,
CO3 8PD
Tel: 01206 213213
www.molesseeds.co.uk
Good for bulk buying seed.

Nickys Nursery Ltd.
Fairfield Road, Broadstairs, Kent, CT10 2JU
Tel: 01843 600972
www.nickys-nursery.co.uk

Thompson & Morgan
Poplar Lane, Ipswich, Suffolk, IP8 3BU
Tel: 01473 695200
www.thompson-morgan.com

Tozer Seeds Direct
PO Box 11, Louth, LN11 0WA
Tel: 08454 301615
www.tozerseedsdirect.com
Good for bulk buying seed.

Edwin Tucker and Sons Ltd
Brewery Meadow, Stonepark, Ashburton,
Devon, TQ13 7DG
Tel: 01364 652403
www.edwintucker.com

Fruit specialists

Blackmoor Nurseries
Blackmoor, Nr Liss, Hampshire, GU33 6BS
Tel: 01420 477978
www.blackmoor.co.uk

Keepers Nursery
Gallants Court, East Farleigh, Maidstone, Kent,
ME15 0LE
Tel: 01622 726465
www.keepers-nursery.co.uk

Ken Muir
Rectory Road, Weeley Heath, Clacton on Sea,
Essex, CO16 9BJ
Tel: 01255 830181
www.kenmuiur.co.uk

Sundries

Garden Warehouse
Standroyd Mill, Cottontree, Colne, Lancashire,
BB8 7BW
Tel: 01282 873370
www.lbsgardenwarehouse.co.uk

Harrod Horticultural
Pinbush Road, Lowestoft, Suffolk, NR33 7NL
Tel: 08454 025300
www.harrodhorticultural.com

N A Kays Horticultural Products
Unit 10, Sneckyeat Industrial Estate,
Hensingham, Whitehaven, Cumbria,
CA28 8PF
Tel: 01946 692134

Gardening books

**Pests, Diseases and Disorders of Garden
Plants** Stefan T. Buczacki and Keith M. Harris,
Collins Photo Guides, 1997

Vegetable and Herb Expert Dr D.G.
Hessayon, Expert Books, 1997

RHS Grow Your Own Veg Carol Klein,
Mitchell Beazley, 2007

RHS Grow Your Own Fruit Carol Klein,
Mitchell Beazley, 2009

RHS Grow Your Own Veg Journal Carol
Klein, Mitchell Beazley, 2008

RHS The Half-Hour Allotment Lia Leendertz,
Frances Lincoln, 2006

Grow Your Own Cut Flowers Sarah Raven,
BBC Books, 2002

RHS Grow Your Own Kitchen Garden Year
RHS Experts, Mitchell Beazley, 2009

**RHS New Encyclopedia of Gardening
Techniques: The Essential Practical Guide**
RHS Experts, Mitchell Beazley, 2008

Livestock books

Chicken Runs and Vegetable Plots Charlotte
Popescu, Cavalier Paperbacks, 2009

Teach Yourself Beekeeping Adrian Waring,
Hodder Education, 2006

Keeping Bees Paul Peacock, Gaia, 2006

Cookery books

RHS Cook Your Own Veg Carol Klein, Mitchell
Beazley, 2007

Allotment Gardeners Cookbook Readers
Digest, David & Charles, 2007

**Tender (volume I): A Cook and His
Vegetable Patch** Nigel Slater, HarperCollins,
2009

Index

allotments 10
  allotment organisations 220
  applying for a plot 22-3
  check-list 23
  community spirit 14
  design 43
  dining al fresco 184
  etiquette 25
  history 16
  maximising the benefits 14
  neighbours 24
  plot assessment 24
  plot size 23
  practical constraints 43
  sharing produce 14-15
  taking on 47
apples 33, 161
  choosing a tree 164
  growing 165, 166
  harvesting 166
  planting 165-6
  pollination 162-3, 164
  pruning 166
  rootstocks 164-5
  spacing tree forms 166
  thinning 166
asparagus 14, 30, 33
  growing 98
  planting 98
  sowing 98
asparagus peas 105
asters (*Aster*) 202
aubergines 72
  growing 82
  harvesting 82
  sowing 82

basil 142
bay 143
beans *see* broad beans; French
  beans; runner beans;
  soya beans
beekeeping 206-7
beetroots 13, 56, 57
  growing 62
  harvesting 62
  leaf beets 101
  sowing 62
biodynamic theories 37
birds 38, 168, 170, 173
  bird scarers 47
  soft fruit 177, 178, 179, 180,
    181, 184
blackberries 13, 18
  growing 183
  harvesting 183
blackcurrants 176, 177
  growing 178
  harvesting 178
  planting 178
blueberries 176, 177
  growing 181
  harvesting 181
bonfires 39
borage 144

boundaries 43-4
brassicas 30, 44, 56, 57
  growing 116
  pests and diseases 117
  raising from seed 116-17
Britain 16
broad beans 30, 44, 104, 105
  growing 108
  harvesting 108
  sowing 108
broccoli 116
  growing 121
  harvesting 121
  sowing 121
Brussels sprouts 44, 116
  growing 122
  harvesting 122
  sowing 122
buckler-leaved sorrel 135
burglar alarms 52

cabbages 13, 30, 116
  growing 118
  harvesting 118
  sowing 118
calabrese 13, 116
carrots 13, 14, 30, 51, 56, 57
  growing 60
  harvesting 60
  sowing 60
cauliflowers 30, 116
  growing 120
  harvesting 120
  sowing 120
celeriac 56
  growing 100
  harvesting 100
  sowing 100
celery 99
Ceylon spinach 135
chard 101
chemicals 36
cherries
  growing 171
  harvesting 171
  pollination 163, 171
  pruning 171
  rootstocks 171
chickens 208-9
chicory 131
children 18-19, 30
chilli peppers 85
Chinese cabbage 127
  growing 134, 138
Chinese mustard greens 136, 138
chives 145
chopsuey greens 136, 138
chrysanthemums 30, 203
cloches 47, 50, 57, 72, 73, 126
comfrey 147
companion planting 34, 44
compost 43, 47
coriander 146
corn salad 127
  growing 134, 138

cosmos (*Cosmos*) 33, 198
costs 50
courgettes 13, 18, 72, 73
  growing 78-9
  harvesting 79
  sowing 78
crop planner 210-13
crops 13-14
  choosing 30-3
  mixing 44-7
  monoculture crops 37
  protecting 47
cucumbers 30, 72, 73
  growing 76
  harvesting 76
  indoors 76
  outdoors 76
  sowing 76
currants 13
  see blackcurrants;
    redcurrants; whitecurrants

daffodils (*Narcissus*) 33, 196
dahlias (*Dahlia*) 30, 203
damsons 163
deer 38
digging
  double digging 35
  no-dig alternatives 35
dill 147
disabilities 10
diseases 30-3, 36, 44, 218-19

eccentrics 33
edible flowers 132-3
endive 127
  growing 134, 138

families 18-19
fennel
  Florence fennel 57
  growing 148
  harvesting 148
  sowing 148
figs 172
fleece 23, 33, 34, 47, 50, 52, 57,
  116, 117
flowers 18, 30, 33, 39
  annuals 194
  autumn and winter 202-3
  biennials 194
  bulbs 195
  deadheading 195
  dividing 195
  edible flowers 132-3
  growing 194
  herbaceous perennials 194
  planting 195
  shrubs 194-5
  spring 196-7
  staking 195
  summer 198-201
food provenance 10
frames 50, 72, 126
France 16, 131

French beans 13, 30, 33, 44, 105
  growing 112-13
  harvesting 113
  sowing 112
fruit 13, 18, 30, 33, 38
  fruit cages 38
  see soft fruit; tree fruit
furniture 48

gages 163
garlic 88, 89
  growing 92
  harvesting 92
  planting 92
  sowing 92
Germany 16, 189
gladioli (*Gladiolus*) 198
gluts 14
  coping with 78
Good King Henry 135
gooseberries 13, 18, 176
  growing 180
  harvesting 180
  planting 180
grapes
  growing 188
  harvesting 188-9
  making wine 189
greenhouses 39, 50, 72, 126
ground clearing 26
growing under cover 39

hardening off 72
health 10
heleniums (*Helenium*) 201
herbs 18, 30, 39
Holland 16
hollies (*Ilex*) 202
hyacinths (*Hyacinthus*) 196

insects, beneficial 163
intercropping 44, 89

Japanese mustard spinach
  136, 138
Japanese turnip 136
Jerusalem artichokes 30, 57
  growing 67
  harvesting 67
  planting 67

kale 116
  growing 123
  harvesting 123
  sowing 123
kiwi fruit 177
  growing 190
  harvesting 190
kohlrabi 57, 116
komatsuna *see* Japanese
  mustard spinach

land cress 127
  growing 134
leaf beets 101

leaves *see* salad leaves
leeks 13, 30, 88, 89
 growing 94-5
 harvesting 95
 sowing 94
legumes 30, 116
 crops to grow 105
 feeding needs 105
 sowing 104-5
lettuces 30, 44, 126, 127
 growing 128-9
 harvesting 129
 sowing 128
lilies (*Lilium*) 199
lily of the valley (*Convallaria
 majalis*) 197
lime 27
loganberries 177
love in a mist (*Nigella*) 199

marjoram 149
marrows 73
 growing 78-9
 harvesting 79
 sowing 78
melons 77
mesh 34, 36, 50, 117
mibuna and mizuma 136-7
mint 150
mulching 28, 35

netting 50, 117, 177
North America 81

onion family
 diseases 89
 growing 88-9
 planting 88
 soil preparation 88
 sowing 88
onions 14, 30, 33, 44, 50, 88, 89
 growing 90-1
 harvesting 91
 planting 90
 sowing 90
 storage 91
organic gardening 34, 36, 37
organisations 220-1
Oriental vegetables 127, 135-7

pak choi 137, 138
parsley 151
parsnips 13, 30, 56
 growing 64
 harvesting 64
 sowing 64
paths 43-4
peaches
 growing 173
 harvesting 173
 pruning 173
pears 33, 161
 growing 168
 harvesting 169
 planting 168

pollination 163, 168
 pruning 169
 rootstocks 168
 thinning 169
peas 18, 30, 44, 51, 104, 105
 growing 106-7
 harvesting 107
 sowing 106
 types of pea 106
peppers 30, 72
 growing 84
 harvesting 84
 sowing 84
pests 30-3, 34, 44, 36, 216-17
plots 22-3, 24, 42-3
 stocking 50
plums
 growing 170
 harvesting 170
 pollination 163, 170
 pruning 170
 rootstocks 170
 thinning 170
polytunnels 39, 50, 72, 126
potatoes 13, 14, 18, 30, 33, 36, 44,
 51, 57
 growing 58-9
 harvesting 59
 planting 56, 58
pumpkins 18, 30, 44, 73
 growing 80-1
 harvesting 81
 sowing 80
purslane 127
 growing 134-5, 138

radishes 18
 growing 68
 harvesting 68
 sowing 68
raised beds 35, 36
raspberries 13, 33, 177
 growing 182
 harvesting 182
red orach 135
redcurrants 176, 177
 growing 179
 harvesting 179
 planting 179
rhubarb 18
 growing 191
 harvesting 191
 planting 191
rocket 18, 127
 growing 139
 harvesting 139
 sowing 139
root crops 30, 44
 crops to grow 57
 growing 56
 raising from seed 56-7
 soil preparation 56
rosemary 152
roses (*Rosa*) 200
rotation schemes 44, 56, 116

runner beans 13, 44, 105
 flower set 110-11
 growing 110
 harvesting 111
 sowing 110
Russia 16

safety considerations 18
sage 153
salad leaves 13, 30, 134-5
 growing 126-7
 micro leaves 127
 watering and care 127
scarecrows 47
scorzonera 30
security 52
shallots 88, 89
 growing 93
 harvesting 93
 planting 93
 sowing 93
sheds 13, 48-9
Smallholdings and Allotment
 Act 1908 16
soft fruit 14, 33
 bushes 176
 cordons 176-7
 maintenance pruning 176
 netting 177
 preparing bed 176
 types of soft fruit 177
soil 26-7, 30
 dry conditions 51-2
 testing 27
 wet conditions 50-1
soya beans 105
spinach
 growing 130
 harvesting 130
 sowing 130
spring onions 30, 88
squashes 13, 30, 33, 44, 73
 see summer squashes;
 winter squashes
strawberries 13, 18, 33, 177
 growing 184-5
 harvesting 185
 propagating 185
successional sowing 47
summer squashes
 growing 78-9
 harvesting 79
 sowing 78
sunflowers (*Helianthus annuus*)
 18, 30, 33, 200
swedes 13, 56, 57, 116
 growing 65
 harvesting 65
 sowing 65
sweet peas (*Lathyrus odoratus*)
 18, 33, 201
sweet potatoes 33, 44
sweetcorn 13, 18, 30, 33, 44, 72, 89
 growing 83
 harvesting 83

 sowing 83

tarragon 154
tayberries 177
texel greens 137
thyme 155
tomatoes 33, 44, 72, 73
 blight 36, 74
 growing 74-5
 harvesting 75
 sowing 74
tools 17, 159
tree fruit
 double cordons 160
 espaliers 160-1
 fans 161
 goblets 161
 half-standards 161
 open-centre bushes 161
 planting 158
 pollination 162-3
 pruning 158-9
 pruning tools 159
 pruning with a saw 159
 pruning with secateurs 159
 pyramids 161
 single cordons 160
 standards 161
 stepovers 161
 thinning 160
tulips (*Tulipa*) 197
turnips 44, 56, 57, 116
 growing 66
 harvesting 66
 sowing 66

value for money 15
varieties 12
vegetable fruits
 feeding and watering 73
 growing outdoors 72-3
 planting pockets 73
 raising from seed 72
vegetables 13, 18, 30, 37, 38
vines 177

watercress 126
watering 44, 73, 51-2, 127
weather 50-2
Weed Act 1959 29
weeding 35, 50
 annual weeds 28, 214-15
 invasive and reportable
 weeds 29
 perennial weeds 28, 214, 215
whitecurrants 176
wildlife 144
winter radish 30
winter squashes
 growing 80-1
 harvesting 81
 sowing 80
woodpigeons 38, 117

zinnias 33

Acknowledgements

Picture credits in source order

All photographs are by Jo Whitworth with the following exceptions:

Key: a above, b below, c centre, l left, r right

Alamy Arco Images GmbH 70; C J Wheeler 123 a; Jon Stokes 122 a; Nigel Cattlin 59, 218 c; Tony Morris/Wildscape 44.

Corbis Amiard/photocuisine 109 br; Image Source 65 b, 95 a.

Fotolia Jeff Gynane 47 a; Norman Chan 203 a; studiogriffon.com 191 a; adisa 214 c; Adrian Sumner 200 a; Adso 190; Agatha Brown 66 b; Aleksandr Lobanov 194 br; Alison Bowden 199 b; Andi Taranczuk 217 r; Andrzej Włodarczyk 173; ason 74 b; audaxi 119 bl; auris 107; Bluestock 32 br, 63 br; Claudia Schiffer 202 b; Clivia 27 al; David Whitfield 63 bl; DLeonis 135 b; DramaSan 68 a; DX 66 a; Elena Moiseeva 98 b; ExQuisine 147; Guilu 120; Hazel Proudlove 93 a, 121 a, 148, 151 b, 163 r; Heinrich 119 ar; Inspir8tion 80 br; Joann Hansen 84 a; Kadmy 75 a; Karin Lau 149; Kerioak 95 b; Kica Henk 201 b; L Shat 109 ar; Iftewart 152 b; Lulu 133 ar; mahey 81 b; Margo Harrison 196 a; Marilyn Barbone 179 r; Martina Berg 133 br; Michael Ireland 162 c; mickael di cataldo 132; N Siemsen 146; naffarts 63 ar; ndan 144; nsphotography 60 b; Outdoor Photos 77 bl; Petra Louise 110 ac; PhotoAR 145; Pixelwolf2 98 a; posh 119 br; SGCP 199 a; Sharpshot 110; Silvana Comugnero 57 b; swisshippo 81 a; Wouter Tolenaars 196 b; Xetra 69 a; zee 123 b; Zina Seletskaya 197 a.

GAP Photos Dave Bevan 160 a; FhF Greenmedia 11 br, 109 al, 139 b, 218 r; Fiona McLeod 135 a; Geoff Kidd 161 a; Heather Edwards/design Nick Williams-Ellis 174; Howard Rice 99 a; Jo Whitworth 136 b, 156; John Glover 35 r, 160 b; Jonathan Buckley 131 a, 136 a; Lee Avison 109 bl; Mark Bolton 197 b; Maxine Adcock 108.

Garden World Images Dave Bevan 219 l; Flowerphotos/Carol Sharp 65 a; John Swithinbank 99 b, 116 bl; Martin Hughes-Jones 134 b; Nicholas Appleby 216 r; Sine Chesterman 216 c, 218 l; Trevor Sims 219 r.

Marianne Majerus Garden Images Marianne Majerus/Wyken Hall, Suffolk 161 b.

Octopus Publishing Group Jane Sebire 27 b, 92 b; Mark Winwood 38 r, 77 br, 172; Sarah Heneghan 195 al, 198 a; Torie Chugg 35 l, 38 l, 77 al and ar, 158 al, ar and bl, 159, 162 l and r, 163 ac and al, 167 a and b, 169 a, 176 all, 177 a and bl, 180, 183, 185 a, 189, 194 ar, 194 al and bl, 195 ar and b, 202 a.

Photolibrary DEA/E Martini 215 l; Garden Picture Library/Andrea Jones 134 a; Garden Picture Library/Francois de Heel 116 ar, 217 l; Garden Picture Library/Jo Whitworth 131 b; Garden Picture Library/ John Swithinbank 217 c; Garden Picture Library/Juliette Wade 75 b; Garden Picture Library/Paul Hart 219 c; Garden Picture Library/ Rex Butcher 216 l; Garden Picture Library/Mark Bolton 198 b.

RHS Herbarium Graham Titchmarsh 184.

Thanks

We would like to thank the following people for modelling in this book: Guy Akeroyd, Hugh Akeroyd, Lissie Akeroyd, Rebecca Bevan, Ruth Bishop, Leanne Bryan, Alfie Clark, Eva Clark, Alan Coy, Joanna Draycott, Shaun Froud, Yuki Fujimori, Helen Griffin, Suzanne Moss, Juliette Clark, Melissa Robens, and Richard White.

We would like to thank the following individuals and organisations for their help and advice: Annabel Akeroyd, Jim Arbury, Stan Cooper, Will Denne, Jack Marks, Sheila and Albert Pruden, and all the plot holders at Boshers Allotment and Gardeners Association (Egham, Surrey), Maybury Allotment Association (Maybury, Surrey), West Byfleet Allotments and Gardens Association (West Byfleet, Surrey) and the Wisley student allotments (Wisley village, Surrey).